EYES
FOR LEARNING

Preventing and Curing Vision-Related Learning Problems

Antonia Orfield

Rowman & Littlefield Education
Lanham, Maryland • Toronto • Plymouth, UK
2007

Published in the United States of America
by Rowman & Littlefield Education
A Division of Rowman & Littlefield Publishers, Inc.
A wholly owned subsidiary of The Rowman & Littlefield Publishing Group, Inc.
4501 Forbes Boulevard, Suite 200, Lanham, Maryland 20706
www.rowmaneducation.com

Estover Road
Plymouth PL6 7PY
United Kingdom

British Library Cataloguing in Publication Information Available

Library of Congress Cataloging-in-Publication Data
Orfield, Antonia, 1941–
    Eyes for learning : preventing and curing vision-related learning problems /
Antonia Orfield.
        p. cm.
    Includes bibliographical references and index.
    ISBN-13: 978-1-57886-595-6 (hardcover : alk. paper)
    ISBN-10: 1-57886-595-6 (hardcover : alk. paper)
    ISBN-13: 978-1-57886-596-3 (pbk. : alk. paper)
    ISBN-10: 1-57886-596-4 (pbk. : alk. paper)
    1. Vision disorders in children. 2. Visual perception in children. 3.
Vision–Testing.   4. Learning ability. I. Title.
    RE48.2.C5.O74 2007
    618.92'0977–dc22   2006039508

∞™ The paper used in this publication meets the minimum requirements of
American National Standard for Information Sciences—Permanence of
Paper for Printed Library Materials, ANSI/NISO Z39.48-1992.
Manufactured in the United States of America.

For Amy, Sonia, Rosanna, and Jill
For Adam and Joe
And for all the children they will have someday

CONTENTS

FOREWORD

We have too many children in our schools who are not learning because they cannot see well, and they, their parents, and the schools haven't recognized or solved their problem. It is time we did something about it. This important book brings together research on vision problems, wisdom for parents on how to raise children in ways that will minimize visual difficulties in school, guidelines for teachers on how to spot a child who is floundering visually, and advice for both parents and teachers on where to find appropriate help. A student's whole future can hinge on discovering vision difficulties early, treating the problems, and teaching with an eye to helping students see and learn more effectively.

Years ago, Dr. Orfield told me about one of her patients in an inner-city Boston school who was so farsighted that she could not see to read but had lost her glasses at age five. When she examined the child's vision at age seven, it was the spring of this little girl's second year in first grade. The child had already missed the first two years of reading because she could not see clearly up close. We can stop such needless losses.

Parents and teachers often take a child's vision for granted. They assume that because he can see far away, he is equally well equipped to read books. A great deal of educational damage can be done before anyone notices that he can't. Children often cannot recognize a problem of focusing, double vision, or tracking on their own. They assume everyone sees as they do. For underprivileged families or those without health coverage, private treatment costs too much. The schools do not assess vision well and parents cannot afford or find good vision care.

The educational damage from a poor start in school can be very deep simply because a child cannot sustain focus for reading. But this problem is not one of our deep-rooted, intractable educational problems that decades of programs have left largely untouched. With appropriate diagnosis and treatment—sometimes treatment as simple as getting a child the kind of magnifying readers that most older people have to wear to read—that child can catch up. What could be more unfair than to flunk a young person because of something that he has no control over? Clearly it is the responsibility of the adults in the school and community to be certain that we do not punish a child who hasn't received the vision diagnosis and treatment he or she needs to learn and take tests.

Educational failure is more serious than ever as jobs and income are more tightly linked to educational attainment. If a talented student does not go to college, her potential future is drastically limited. Those who do not make it through high school face a disaster. About one-fourth of our students are not even finishing high school—almost half of black, Latino, and American Indian students—and there is no viable future for such young people in a postindustrial economy. They fill in the ranks of the working poor.

Aside from the economic consequences, think of the stress of not seeing clearly, the psychological harm of ongoing underachievement, and the impact on the development of the student's interest in school and learning through reading.

The idea that students must see to learn in our schools seems to have largely escaped education. Yet vision is the most important pathway by which information is received. When vision does not work, it is like trying to enter data into a computer when the cable is not adequately connected. Yet we bring millions of kids into our schools without even checking to see if they are physically capable of receiving the knowledge. We have huge numbers of kids we define as poor learners who may not even know they have vision problems, whose parents assume the teachers and school would catch such problems, or who just cannot afford even the simplest treatment. They may internalize the idea that they are stupid.

In the research world there has been very little contact between those who study vision and those who study learning. Research is done by people in separate professions. Educators typically focus their work on the impact of various educational methods and curricula and school strategies. With vision, much of the research focus is on disease or surgical treatments, not on developing processes for mass assessment and treatment of huge numbers of children.

Dr. Antonia Orfield has been working on vision development for many years, starting with the remarkable change in her own vision (described in chapter four) that grew out of therapy twenty-five years ago. That experience led her to study optometry. She has devoted her career and her research to treating problems in the way children's eyes work together for reading and other near work and creating knowledge and treatment methods that cross the borders between vision and learning (Orfield 2001). As a mother, she successfully applied these techniques to reverse her own children's developing vision problems, so she knows the possibilities and difficulties of therapy both at home and at the clinic. She has experience as a teacher and a good understanding of the pressures teachers confront. Years of work treating and studying hundreds of children in a pioneering clinic in a Boston public school and then spearheading a national conference on the issue at Harvard gave rise to this important book.

As a researcher, I am a trained skeptic about claims of simple answers to anything, but I am fascinated with the development of new findings that can make a difference for educational opportunity. Decades of research have shown too few things that actually improve educational attainment. It was my great privilege to moderate the first national conference on the vision and learning issue in 2001 at the Harvard Graduate School of Education, appropriately titled "An Educational Barrier We Can Actually Eliminate." There, researchers and clinicians from across the United States gathered to present chilling data on the high incidence of readily treatable vision problems and their relationship to educational failure. It was remarkable to see how researchers working in a variety of communities—with African-American, white,

American Indian, Asian, and Latino children—were finding similar patterns.

This research was conducted by optometrists, who tend to focus more on functional vision than ophthalmologists—MDs who focus more on eye disease and methods of effective surgery. Behavioral optometrists view vision as something that can be trained with therapy or therapeutic glasses. Much of the research discussed here was produced as a byproduct of efforts to treat children in schools and other settings. This research has not had major funding, and most of it does not have the kind of control groups and rich longitudinal data that we should have on such important issues, although there has been a large and sophisticated study in Baltimore. Obviously we need major studies combining experts in vision and visual systems with experts on education and evaluation research.

In the meantime, we cannot write off another generation of students. We have to take the best available information about the incidence and treatment of these problems and apply it as widely as possible as soon as we can. The costs of lost opportunity to treat vision-related learning problems are very high (more than a quarter-million dollars in lost lifetime income for each high school dropout, for example). The cost of treatments that seem likely to work, in contrast, is modest. Many of our school districts and states now give students tests at different ages that they must pass or be forced to repeat a grade and tests that they must pass if they are to receive a diploma. It is very costly as well—$10,000 or more in many districts—to have another year of education. If the underlying problem is that the numbers in a student's math test jump around when he looks at them, flunking will not solve it, and the failure to treat an easily curable problem—like farsightedness with convergence problems—is inexcusable.

Many readers are probably thinking, "Don't the schools check this?" I remember looking at that vision chart when I was in school. The sad reality is that schools who do test often use obsolete methods that miss the most common problems shown by recent research. The old vision chart can tell you something important about reading blackboards but nothing really about reading a book or filling in an answer sheet. It turns out that those are the more common problems, some of which can be solved by testing and distributing inexpensive reading glasses. If we are ruining children's futures over such trivial expenditures, we are doing something educationally inexcusable. We need good tests of the type Dr. Orfield describes for all children, particularly as they begin to read.

Medicaid, which is theoretically the medical system that protects disadvantaged children, cannot assure a supply of doctors and clinics that offer necessary tests and preventative care for vision development. Vision care in stores that sell glasses is likely to be done without the extra testing for functional vision problems that affect learning. In addition, if the need is for glasses, coverage is normally for a single pair and, as all parents know, children can easily lose or break their glasses. If glasses cannot be replaced, these incidents can ruin a year of learning. Dr. Orfield knows the realities from working with hundreds of parents and children. Her book offers readers a clear description of what is known about solutions and a good deal of wisdom for parents, teachers, and policy makers on how to raise visually competent children; how to identify those needing help; and how to fix their problems with glasses, vision exercises, and appropriate referrals for health issues that impact vision. Dr. Orfield collected statistics and carried out research on hundreds of cases in her school clinic and worked with Dr. Frank Basa, MD (who also holds a PhD) and Professor John Yun, now of the University of California, Santa Barbara, to systematically evaluate the evidence.

The work of behavioral optometrists addresses a very serious problem that can often be solved with minimal cost; it is a problem that affects a large percentage of today's children in schools serving low-income and minority students. This is a fascinating and important story, but I urge readers to do more than read this book. I urge them to think about where they would be in life if they grew up with serious, untreated vision problems and then take action in their families and communities to remove barriers that waste the talent and damage the lives of too many children.

Gary Orfield
Professor of Education and Social Policy at the Harvard Graduate School of Education

ACKNOWLEDGMENTS

It would have been impossible to write this book without the doctors and authors I have known and read in the fields of behavioral and developmental optometry. They are the creative giants who have been my mentors and teachers in person and in print. They are my inspiration from postdoctoral seminars, from learning in their offices, and from their books and tapes. They are my references. They are the wisdom I am telling, the shoulders I stand on to view the world of vision.

I thank all of them as individuals and as members of the College of Optometrists in Vision Development and the Optometric Extension Program, both trailblazing professional organizations. Dr. Amiel Francke, a retired behavioral optometrist from Washington, D.C., changed my own vision radically with his therapy back in 1981, which brought me out of my nearsightedness and allowed me to see that I wanted to help others in the same way. Without that hands-on, eyes-on experience, I would never have grasped the truth: that vision is very flexible and can be improved at any age with vision therapy and a toolbox of training lenses. Dr. Jim Blumenthal and Dr. Jeffrey Getzell in Illinois helped me complete that learning process.

Dottie Engler, when she was head of the Askwith Education Forums at the Harvard Graduate School of Education, helped me organize the 2001 research conference, "An Educational Barrier We Can Actually Eliminate: Vision Problems of Children in Poverty and Their Interference with Learning." It has had more impact than I ever imagined.

Dr. Larry Clausen and Dr. Maurice Applebaum, then president and dean of the New England College of Optometry, respectively, encouraged me to set up the Mather in-school vision clinic in the early 1990s, apply for the grants, and do the research that led to the Harvard conference. Michael K. Marshall, when he was principal of the Mather School, with his staff and teachers made it possible for me and my optometry interns to work with the children in need and access available test scores and grades for the pilot research that we did in that school.

Optometry is not the only field that has changed my vision. Dr. Marilyn Holbeck in Virginia and Dr. David Newton in Massachusetts, two superbly talented chiropractors, put me on my feet, giving me the underpinnings of good vision. I would not have the highly useful information from other health fields that helps me in my work with children's vision without seeing with my own eyes how vision and body balance are connected and what this connection can do for the children I serve.

For chapter five, I gratefully acknowledge the careful, excellent reports of three great healers: Eliza Bergeson, Brain Gym and primitive reflex integration specialist; Dr. Lydia Knutson, chiropractor; and Begabati Lennihan, homeopath. Retired teacher and educational consultant Dr. Betty Ward, PhD, taught me the late Ed Snapp's wonderful methods for visual reading readiness that have never been published and helped me describe them accurately in chapter six. Also for chapter six, school nurse Kathy Majzoub writes the description of the Framingham schools' vision clinic and tells how she and her colleagues were able to establish it. The highly talented elementary resource teacher, Kathryn Powers, produced her study about reading versus TV in children's exposure to vocabulary and expressive thought just in time to include her findings in chapter seven.

The late Mary B. Allen, PhD in biochemical genetics, long ago saved me from pain and chronic fatigue and my daughter, Sonia, from vision problems and chronic chest congestion with her nutrition treatments.

She has informed much of my thinking regarding the ability of nutrition to impact vision and health.

Readers of the manuscript were hugely important to my ability to push through the writing process. Amy Kohler, Sonia Orfield, and Rosanna and Joe Cavanagh helped more than they can ever imagine with their suggestions and even typing in the first edits to save my back. Amy Kohler helped with not only the first edits, but also the last ones and the index, giving me priceless encouragement. Dr. Jeff Getzell, Jim Caunt, Kim Marshall, and Patricia Lemer each read sections of the manuscript and provided helpful suggestions that I tried to incorporate into the book.

Gary Orfield, as professor of Education and Social Policy at the Harvard Graduate School of Education, moderated the Harvard conference and wrote a thoughtful preface that clarifies the problem of our failure as a society to make sure that all of our children have adequate vision for classroom work.

Suchesta Flynn, my office assistant, found some crucial items buried deep on my office computer that made a huge difference, retyped a section of a chapter that was lost in cyberspace, and kept my office running while the writing process went on and on.

Dear friends provided vital support for my health and well-being as I finished the book: Hilah, Elizabeth, Darin, Mark, Lara, Dorothy, Wynn, Mary, Patty, Linda, W.C., and Primrose.

Thank you, thank you, thank you, to all of these good people and friends.

Thank you to Tom Koerner of Rowman and Littlefield Education, for asking that this book be written and trusting me with the job. And thank you to production editor Andrew Yoder for making my manuscript available for educators and parents, so that more and more children can have eyes for learning.

INTRODUCTION

Imagine you are a bright preschool child who has thrived in a good home setting with two devoted parents to talk to, much computer game time, and a lot of TV. You are curious, intelligent, and verbal. You know your letters. You love to tell stories. You love to be read to. You are eager to go to school. You haven't worked much with your hands at home, though. You haven't played outside much. Suddenly you have to look at small print to learn to read words and sentences and copy print with your small hands. Often this happens in kindergarten, because schools are worried that you might not learn in time for the third- and fourth grade high-stakes tests.

You are exhorted by everyone to take seriously the importance of reading. The sentences are simple and often seem silly to you after hearing Harry Potter books already at home. You are used to the fast pace of TV commercials and the short bits of TV shows. It is hard to sustain interest in the teacher talking about phonemes. You find that reading is not only uninteresting, but also hard because the words are moving around on the page. They are sometimes clear and sometimes blurry, once in a while they even go double, and they are too small to see well, it seems. They definitely don't make sense when you skip a line.

You have a learning-related vision problem, but no one has identified it. The pediatrician checked your eyes and you could easily read the bottom row of his eye chart at 20 feet away. He did not check to see if you could see up close. You start to get headaches after school, but not on the weekends. You get a lot of homework because the teachers are afraid you won't learn enough to pass the high-stakes tests if you just work during the school day. You feel very nervous about reading, and somehow that makes it even harder to see the small print. You have no idea that the kids who are already reading don't have the same problems, and neither do your parents, who are trying to help you at home.

You have a learning-related vision problem. Very likely you don't have a true learning problem. You will be lucky if someone examines your eyes and suggests either vision therapy or reading glasses, or both. It is more likely, though, that they will send you to a neurologist instead, and you will be told you have a right-brain learning deficiency; you will be tested to see in which skills you are deficient and given a special education plan that includes learning those skills in a smaller group setting.

Imagine now that you are a bright child who does not have a middle-class home situation. You have the TV on all day in your apartment. You have not been able to go outside at all because there is no safe place to play in your neighborhood. You are bored and you don't have many toys, but someone gave you a little pocket electronic game. You play that or watch TV.

You don't have healthy food, especially at the end of the month, when the budget is tight. Your mother did not have healthy food when she was pregnant, so you had a low birth weight and have been struggling with asthma and other health issues since. You are in a home without any children's books, and no one reads to you. You could not get into a Headstart program because they were overbooked and had cutbacks. Nevertheless, your eyes shine with intelligence and you are eager to go to school. You go to kindergarten at age five, and you cannot figure out what this reading stuff is all about. No one is pushing you to read at home or helping you with your homework. You also hear that this reading is really important and you must know it before third grade.

You have the same problems the other child has. You saw clearly at a distance at the health clinic. You don't have crossed eyes. However, things are unclear up close; they move around on the page, and sometimes they go double. They don't make sense when you skip a line, and they are boring compared to the fast-paced excitement of TV. You really don't like being in school because the teacher expects that you won't do well, no matter how hard you try. In fact, she tells you to try harder, saying to you that you are really not trying. What does *trying* mean, you wonder? When words are not clear, how do you make them clear? The harder you try and the more you worry, the blurrier they get.

You, too, have a learning-related vision problem, but it is even less likely that it will be identified. You will be lucky if you are in a school with special education programs, Title I Reading Recovery classes—which use big books with big print, or occupational therapy programs to help you write these words and track across whole pages of them.

These two children represent millions of others with the same visual problems. None of them know that they have a vision problem. They think everyone sees the way they do and that other children who take to reading are smarter. By the end of first grade, these children believe they are dumb. The schools believe other things about them. Thousands of children each year in this country are labeled "high verbal IQ, low performance IQ," "right-brain learning disabled," "reading disabled," "hyperactive with attention deficit," "bright but slow learning," "poor at organizing work on a paper (but he knows it in his head)," "deficient in handwriting skills," "behaviorally challenged," and so on.

Many of them might be suited by some of those labels. A great many of them are not. They have a learning-related vision problem. Even the children who actually have one or more of those labeled problems may *also* have a learning-related vision problem. One fall semester in a Boston public school, 34 of the 37 children who were scheduled to have an IEP (individual education plan) had learning-related vision problems, identified by eye exams given in their school eye clinic.

A small group of practitioners know how to diagnose and fix these problems. Most are behavioral optometrists, sometimes also called developmental or functional optometrists. They have OD degrees (doctor of optometry) and specialize in the management of functional vision problems and vision therapy. They can unravel the reasons for the symptoms these children suffer and then treat the problems identified. That child will be different forever after, because visual skills can be learned and reading glasses can help them focus up close.

Behavioral optometrists are usually associates or fellows in the College of Optometrists in Vision Development or members of the Optometric Extension Program. Many are fellows in the American Academy of Optometry as well. All optometry schools teach a course in vision therapy, but these doctors have done hundreds of hours of postdoctoral work in the field. Many have done research studies on learning-related visual disabilities, and many have taught or continue to teach in schools of optometry or binocular vision clinics. They work with not only children, but also adults with similar issues, athletes, head injury patients, and patients who have amblyopia and strabismus. The message is starting to come out through newspaper articles and the Internet that these doctors exist. The message that vision affects learning and that good visual skills can be learned is also beginning to be heard in the schools.

This message is why more and more school systems are requesting comprehensive, functional eye exams for their students before they enter school. This is why the National Parent Teacher Association has supported the concept that every child not succeeding in school must have a comprehensive vision evaluation, whatever his grade. This is why PAVE (Parents Active in Vision Education) is teaching the educators and the parents that such problems exist and correcting them can make a big difference for how children perform in school.

This message that vision affects learning is also why the state of Kansas paid optometrists to do a study of vision training for children with eye teaming problems, which have been shown to interfere with reading. The study did show success in reading as a result of the vision therapy. This is why optometrists in various parts of the country are teaming up with educators to do studies in schools of how poor vision skills affect a child's potential to learn.

That vision affects learning is why a number of optometric associations are convening something called, "The Infants' and Childrens' Vision Coalition," with regular national meetings. This is why the Harvard Graduate School of Education supported a conference in April of 2001 called, "An Educational Barrier We Can Actually Eliminate: The Visual Problems of Children in Poverty and Their Interference with Learning," in which optometry researchers throughout the country presented papers on their shocking findings relating to the high levels of learning-related visual problems among children, especially among disadvantaged children, and those in special education (SPED) classes.

The kind of vision function problems identified interfere with success in school, whether children are just learning to read or falling behind in high school, whether they are in the learning disabilities (LD) track, or whether they are not receiving help because they are considered to be average. They occur in 45 to 55 percent of children tested in Boston and teens studied in New York inner-city environments. Previous estimates report that about 25% of U.S. elementary school children have undiagnosed vision problems significant enough to interfere with their school work and lives. Studies have shown an even higher degree of learning-related vision problems among students who have been incarcerated for juvenile delinquency, Title I children, foster children, and illiterate adults. That range is 80% or higher. It seems that "the eyes have it" when it comes to learning.

The *Phi Delta Kappan*, a premier journal of education, ran a seven-page article in December 2003 called "A Clear Vision for Equity and Opportunity."

"Educators work very hard to help students solve the cognitive problems that impede their learning," the article said, but "sometimes it's the problems we can't 'see' that need to be fixed." Those are the rampant undetected visual problems. The authors did a study in Arizona. They found that 45% of students failed testing with an autorefractor because of unacceptable amounts of nearsightedness, farsightedness, or astigmatism. They did not even test functional vision problems like tracking, eye teaming, and focusing up close. A grant was given by Pearle Vision to help provide these poverty-level children with follow-up eye exams and glasses. Only half the children actually signed up for the exams and glasses.

This problem of inaction is seen in all the areas where children living in poverty have been offered help with glasses. Parents simply do not realize that their children's whole future, their immediate success in school, their comfort and freedom from headaches, and their sense of confidence and well-being can be compromised by not getting appropriate treatment for vision problems, including glasses, to do sustained near school work and reading.

Sometimes an observant teacher or an occupational therapist will know that a child has a vision problem. It will be obvious from the fact that he or she leans very close to the page, covers one eye, has trouble writing on a straight line, skips words and sentences, or cannot organize numbers on the page so that the columns are straight for doing arithmetic.

However, if the student is sent to the local optometrist or ophthalmologist, that doctor may not even do the tests that would identify the underlying vision problems. The child will have clear sight at a twenty foot test distance, and show small amounts of farsightedness (ordinarily considered normal), but which can cause some children trouble when they try to focus on small print. Tests for that will not be done, however. The child will evidence no strabismus (crossed or wandering eyes) or lazy eye, and have good eyeball health. His parents will be told that he doesn't have a vision problem. Nothing more will be tested in this quick, fifteen-minute eye exam.

Sometimes more time will be taken to dilate the eyes and explore the retina for ocular disease. No disease will be found, but that is only the beginning of a proper eye exam for a child. Perhaps the child will receive glasses for a tiny bit of beginning nearsightedness, but those will not relax the eyes to read. Nearsighted glasses for distance sight will take away the adaptation that the child's underdeveloped visual system is trying to make to see clearly up close without too much effort. It will likely be harder to read through the glasses than without them.

The functional problems will not be identified because the assessment is basically covering three areas: distance sight, retinoscopy (assessment of whether eye is nearsighted or farsighted or has astigmatism), and ophthalmoscopy (a check for eye health). Sometimes a cover test to check for strabismus or a stereopsis test for three-dimensional vision will be added. That still leaves eighteen specific visual tests not done that a behavioral optometrist would do that relate to focusing, eye teaming, tracking, peripheral awareness, fixation, and eye–hand coordination.

The testing also leaves out a minimum of three additional tests often done by behavioral optometrists: the Developmental Eye Movement Test for tracking, the Visual/Motor Integration Test, and the Copy

Forms Test or the Wold Sentence Copy Test, depending on the age of the child. The last two relate to eye/hand skills. Several extra tests of visual perception that are sometimes also done by behavioral optometrists, depending on the age of the patient, are the Gardner Reversals Frequency Test, The Piaget Left/Right Awareness Test, and The Gardner Motor Free Visual Perception battery, unless the schools have already done those, prior to the referral.

The purpose of this book is to give parents and teachers some knowledge of how to spot learning-related visual problems in their children and students. Then once they suspect a problem, where to refer the child, what kind of tests to request, how to help the older child after he or she is already suffering with poor visual skills, and how to plan the development of the babies, preschool children, and early grades' children to avoid these problems. The visual development process is crucial because good visual skills are learned through a variety of activities that are less and less a part of our culture of childrearing in the age of TV, video games, automobiles, and stress.

There are a few principles for growing visually competent kids that parents and teachers may want to understand, because it matters to the children. These principles are listed without explanation below. They will be explained in detail in the book:

1) Good vision is a learned motor skill.
2) Two visual systems comprise the eye/brain vision complex: the central visual system and the peripheral system.
3) Many learning problems are the result of a child's difficulty with using his eyes at near.
4) Vision problems left unresolved do not go away but handicap a child for life.
5) Vision therapy is the best learning program for many of the children who struggle with reading and writing.
6) The setup of the school, the desks, the size of print in books and on the board, and the test and time pressures on children all matter for vision and efficient learning.
7) The home setup, opportunities to be in nature, and stress-free lifestyles can foster good vision.
8) Nutrition matters.

9) Kids often need reading glasses and sometimes vision exercises just to develop normal vision.

10) Vision skills are integral to so-called "brain skills."

11) Poor distance sight (usually nearsightedness) is often an adaptation to a child's struggles to focus up close.

12) The eyes and the body are one; musculoskeletal injury, specific head trauma, or other health issues need to be treated adequately for a child to have a healthy infrastructure that will support vision.

Most children are born normal with the potential for good vision development, that will support learning with ease. Based on both my experience examining well over a thousand children and the literature of children's vision development, I would say that if the child is born normal and if many of the activities suggested in this book are programmed into his life, he will be able to develop good functional vision, which is a learned skill. If he does, he will be a good student and live a life that allows him to use his talents to contribute to his community.

When children are not born normal in every way, amazing things can still be done for them if such activities are adapted to their needs. This book focuses on the whole range of kids, from the normal children to those needing vision activities to enhance vision development to the children with problems, such as those on the autism spectrum, and those who have had injuries at birth or after. These are children for whom vision therapy and special training lenses can make a huge difference.

Many of these points are not part of our educators' and parents' wisdom yet. They should be, and they will be eventually, because they will make life easier for parents and teachers and more engaging to good purpose for the kids. My hope is that when my readers finish this book, these ideas will make total sense to them and may inform a lifestyle shift that will help them raise their children with eyes for learning.

Dr. Antonia Orfield
Developmental Behavioral Optometrist
September 2006

I

VISION IS MORE THAN SEEING THE BLACKBOARD: PARENTS AND TEACHERS NEED TO KEEP WATCHFUL EYES ON A CHILD'S NEAR VISION STRUGGLES

Research into children's vision practically shouts at us that the kids of today are not visually competent beings; it is no wonder, therefore, that schools and parents are having so many problems teaching them to read and write. School activities are approximately 85 percent visual, yet many children are coming to school without good vision as their primary mode of exploring the universe. Some are still touching everything, not able to focus at near, not able to use symbols, not able to inspect with their eyes. As a society, we have blamed the teachers when it really is not their fault.

There are social costs to our failure to correct children's vision problems. Not surprisingly, for example, in the testing populations of children who have become juvenile delinquents, the incidence of failure on visual development measures is over 80 percent (Johnson and Zaba 1999). At least partially from vision problems, those children did not do well in school, so they had no stake in the regular process of growing up.

VISION DEVELOPS WITH MOVEMENT AND EYE/HAND ACTIVITIES IN STAGES

There is a developmental sequence that is not complete yet in the children suffering from attention deficit and hyperactivity or those having trouble seeing whole words and remembering them. The developmental process starts with tactile (touching) dominance, moves to tactile with some visual, then visual with some tactile, and finally, visual dominance (Gesell 1949).

Think about how the visually developed and visually dominant child can cruise through a room with his eyes and take in everything down to the littlest expression on someone's face and the location of every object in the room. These children are sponges for information and they will notice things in the room that you never imagined were there; they can describe details of objects from memory that you would have a hard time recalling as vague shapes of color. They are little Sherlock Holmes juniors if they are well developed visually. Most of us adults lost that freshness of vision a long time ago or never had it.

Optometric research demonstrates that there are ways to test vision in children and fix visual problems so that more of them can have Sherlock Holmes eyes. The behavioral optometrists (eye doctors who specialize in analyzing and improving visual function) use these tests in various studies in schools, in screenings, and on all their eye exams. They have found that between 25 percent and 45 percent of school children, depending on how extensive the measures, do not measure up to the good vision standard (Harris 2002; Orfield, Basa, and Yun 2001; Fischbach et al. 1993). More extensive tests might reveal that more than 45 percent of children do not.

What is amazing to those of us who work with children's vision is that so many with such pervasive visual problems still manage to get through childhood. I ran a clinic in the Mather K–5 public school for seven years where only 33 percent of the students were at the national norm in reading and 85 percent were on free breakfasts and lunches. Only 47 percent of the children passed all parts of our extensive screenings. There was a high correlation on our testing between horizontal eye tracking ability and reading skills (Orfield, Basa, and Yun 2001).

Every day there, working at that clinic, I was in awe of the human spirit that kept these children, who faced so many challenges, trying so hard to learn when their visual skills were so compromised. Of 37 children evaluated for an IEP (individual education plan), 34 of them (92 percent!) had vision problems that were interfering with their ability to do close visual work, which is what school is all about.

In my private practice, also, I am astounded at the adaptations many of the children, who are my patients, have made to keep succeeding in school. I am also amazed that so many middle-class children with devoted parents are not developed visually. Given their visual deficits, their efforts are using up much more energy than they would in a child who has a good visual system.

Good visual systems are not inborn; they develop. Our culture of childhood is not fostering their development and has not for decades. On faith we may assume that some children do have good vision in all the ways that our testing could show. Every child could have better vision if we decided that was important to us. I have seen a handful of children with good vision in my practice over 16 years. This chapter describes what these kids look like (and see like), and what is missing when children cannot see that way.

EXAMINING THE VISUALLY DEVELOPED CHILD

When visually developed school-age children walk into the office I notice the good posture, the normal weight, the healthy skin. They confidently climb into the exam chair. Their eyes sweep the room with interest. Then they look me right in the eyes and smile. They expect to be interested in the process of having their vision checked. They can sit for the testing in a calm and confident manner and it does not fatigue them. They ask questions when they are curious or do not understand one of the directions. They use their eyes, not their hands to inspect the equipment.

These children can respond to my questions with a visual description, not by touching the spot on the testing device where they see the answer. When requested to put the occluder over the right or left eye, there is no mistake or hesitancy about left and right. If asked to hold a near vision test card, it is held at a distance that is no closer than the length between their middle knuckle and their elbow. However, when asked to move it further out for the calibrated test distance of 16 inches, they can do that and still read the card easily.

Distance vision and their near vision would be what we call 20/30 for sure, and possibly even 20/20, though younger children are not expected to see the tiny, 20/20 print at distance or up close yet. Incidentally, it is the 20/40 letters on the chart that are required for a driver's license in most states. These numbers mean that what a "normal" person can see from as far away as 30 or 40 feet is only seen by the child or the driver at 20 feet. If the eyes see the 20/20 row, that patient's vision is seeing what the normal person sees at 20 feet. This test is only a tiny part of how vision should be measured.

The numbers at near mean that the sizes of letters have been adjusted for the near distance of 16 inches (sometimes 14) for tests of close-up vision. All children should be tested at near. The visually well-developed students will see the 20/20 row without a lot of brow furrowing or struggling, and they will also see the 20/30 row with great ease and comfort. Children who can barely see the 20/40 row at near will likely be fatigued focusing for a long time and may need reading glasses. Newspapers are generally 20/50 size letters, but to sustain looking at that size print is very hard for children learning to read, unless they have a great deal of extra focusing ability.

The visually successful children will follow a penlight accurately and move their eyes, without moving their heads, from a red pen to a blue pen, because they can use peripheral vision to see where the second target is while they are looking at the first. They can also look at a letter on a popsicle stick without seeing double (or having one eye move outward) as it is moved all the way to their noses.

These fortunate children can also adjust their eyes to a series of prisms both at far and near and keep the target clear and single by converging or diverging the eyes as needed. They can adjust their focus through a series of lenses up to +2.50 or down to −2.50 diopters of power and still read target letters that are very small. They do not need to struggle or furrow their brows to do this. They see all the targets on a stereo test and all the 14 plates on a color vision test without glasses, and they can read a small-sized sentence or letter at 13 inches through at least a −2.50 lens.

When the doctor shines a light in their eyes to estimate any need for eyeglasses, they will show only a mild hyperopia (farsightedness) of about +0.50 or +0.75, which is considered a normal amount of far-sightedness for a child. There will be no nearsightedness, significant astigmatism, or high hyperopia. When asked to copy a sentence or some line figures, they will hold the pen with a proper grip using three fingers and succeed in quick and neat copying that is organized well on the paper and parallel to the top of the paper. The size will be consistent with the size of the target they are copying. All of this will be done with ease.

These children can also cross their midline easily with their eyes and their hands when tracking a penlight or drawing a large lazy eight (infinity sign) on a chalkboard. When asked to take bouncing steps on a minitrampoline (rebounder) while tapping each knee with the opposite hand as they raise the knee, they can do it. They do not become confused and tap knees with hands on the same side. In other words, they are comfortable and skilled with contralateral activity, which means both sides of their brains can work together to use both sides of the body at the same time. If old enough, they can also read letters off a chart while doing this.

Another observation that behavioral optometrists make when assessing the development of a child is something called "motor overflow" from one muscle group to another. Visually developed children do not exhibit any need to move their heads side-to-side along with eyes going side-to-side, or move jaws side-to-side with their eyes. For example, when told to keep their heads still while moving their eyes around they can do this easily and there is no motor overflow of the jaw moving also.

When they are asked to walk "pigeon style"—toes in—across the room, their hands remain straight with palms facing hips at their sides. There are no palms twisting backwards to parallel the feet. The same is true for "duck walking"—toes out. The palms do not turn to face forward and outward to match the toes. It is important that children can separate the actions of the top from the bottom of their bodies. This is necessary for sports and efficient use of everyday powers of movement and vision.

"The eyes and the body are one," a famous optometrist, Dr. Amiel Francke once said to me. He was a very astute observer of how a high shoulder, a hip torque forward, a belt slanting down to one side, or a slightly tilted neck affected visual stamina as well as balance and physical coordination. The fortunate children with excellent visual systems also have bodies in good balance. There is one case of a patient I know who did have excellent functional vision but who had a major weakness from a birth injury on one side of the body. The stress of maintaining excellent vision, though, with the body out of balance might have been one cause for a number of major health and eye health problems that occurred later in the patient's life.

When asked about school, these children with excellent vision are very relaxed. They are reading at the normal level or better for their age, and they can recognize all the words on the Gray oral reading cards for their grade or higher without sounding them out. They are able to sound out new words that they do not know how to read yet. They are engaged enough in the reading process to recognize the words from their spoken vocabulary and read on, uninterrupted by that effort. They can circle letters in a text neatly or color in all the o's with a pen in a paragraph of text without going over the lines.

If they are six or older, there are no reversals when they read from a list of letters; when they have learned to print, they can copy a sentence and it is neat and on the line. If they are five or older, they can balance on a two-by-four, walking easily from one end to the other, heel-to-toe, forwards and backwards. They can hop on each leg. They can draw a man in six parts. By six they can catch beanbags and pitch them into a bucket and see colored shapes held up two feet from the sides of their eyes as they look straight ahead. There is no tendency for them to sneak their eyes over sideways to take a peek, because they already know what is there from their peripheral vision.

When asked about nutrition, the parent reports the child is a good eater and does not crave sweets or refuse vegetables. The child sleeps well and gets a good high-protein breakfast. The parent may report that either he has very little interest in TV or their family has limited TV for all the children to a few hours a week. The child is not a computer geek—yet.

The visually competent child has a life filled with hands-on activities, such as artwork, building hobbies, puzzles and games, and sports. Often the family engages in sports together, like tennis, swimming, skiing, or skating on the weekends, or just shooting baskets regularly and throwing a softball around. It doesn't matter what the sport, but it does matter a lot that the family is engaged in physical, outdoor activity.

This sketch of the children I have seen with excellent visual skills on all testing describes children who are more unusual than any of us would like to think. Naturally, my sense of how rare excellent vision is may be affected by the fact that few people come to me or any other behavioral optometrist if their child is totally without problems. I see these well-developed children when parents are very conscientious or when I have seen other members of the family who did have problems.

The reader may note that perhaps the average child is not in this category either, and neither are their own very special and interesting children. We do not all fit the prototype of what could be, but is not. The good news is that vision can be learned, worked on, improved, transformed, and perfected throughout life, no matter what problems are manifesting.

Two grown-up children come to mind who both did a great deal of vision therapy with me to compensate for uneven function of their two eyes when they were young boys, and I have followed them since. One had a large refractive error (a need for a strong prescription) in just one eye, making good binocular vision difficult. The other had a wandering eye that went out to the side, along with a tiny intractable vertical misalignment from birth (his two eyes' images were not exactly fused, and there was a little overlap visible vertically). Both have excellent functional vision now. The first, from a highly educated family, is now an MD/PhD student at a top medical school; the other, from an inner-city family at the poverty level, was named one of the top-25 highest-scoring students taking the Massachusetts MCAS test required for graduation in the state and won a full scholarship to any Massachusetts state college or university. They both had good binocular vision with glasses when I saw them recently.

As we begin to look at what poor vision is and how it tests, let us keep in mind these positive and encouraging examples of the human capacity for change and healing. But first, we need to define some well-known but not well-understood terms about glasses, lenses, and major visual diagnoses.

TERMS THAT DOCTORS USE AND PARENTS SHOULD KNOW TO TAKE CONTROL OF THEIR OWN AND THEIR CHILDREN'S VISION HEALTH

Nearsighted (myopic) patients (called myopes because they have myopia) wear **minus** lenses to see distance. If the myopia is bad enough, they also need them to see up close. These are concave-shaped lenses that produce virtual images, which bring things closer and make things smaller. They also compress the space between objects in front of the eyes of the beholder. Chapter four helps parents understand how to stop their children from going myopic (nearsighted.)

Myopic patients cannot focus in order to clear up the view at distance. The more they focus, the blurrier it will become. If a nearsighted person can learn to "look softly" and relax her vision, she can often see better in weaker lenses. Myopes in strong minus lenses for distance can often be stabilized by wearing weaker minus lenses for all near work, sometimes with prisms in them.

Farsighted (hyperopic) people sometimes do not need glasses at all because they can focus their eyes in order to see far and focus harder to see near. Seriously farsighted children and adults may need a distance prescription of **plus** lenses to see clearly for driving, the blackboard, television, movies, and so on. To reduce visual stress, they should definitely have reading glasses that will be slightly stronger plus than any distance glasses.

Plus lenses are convex in shape and make things larger. If very small powers of plus lenses are given to children who are holding their books too close for reading, it often helps them to hold things farther away. These lenses relax the eyes. Too much plus will require a patient to hold things closer, because it will make things blurry at arm's length, and it can cause headaches as surely as not having enough plus can cause headaches in people with focusing problems.

Astigmatism, if severe, can also cause headaches without glasses that compensate for it. Think of the eyeball as a globe with one side visible between the lids. Astigmatism is the condition in which one meridian of that globe needs a different prescription from the meridian that is 90 degrees away from it. A special lens called a **cylinder** lens is used to clear both meridians with the same lens. It is not the same prescription all over like a simple plus or minus lens. It gradually variegates the power between the two separate meridians. Small amounts of astigmatism do not always need prescriptions of cylinder lenses. Large amounts do if the child is to have clear vision. Some astigmatism is functionally developed to help a child see up close. Another kind interferes with near vision.

There are different kinds of **strabismus** (misaligned eyes). Children with **esotropia-type strabismus** (crossed eyes) who are also very farsighted (hyperopic) can often be given straight eyes without surgery by wearing plus glasses or contact lenses. Bifocals are often prescribed to give more plus at near than at distance. I recommend vision therapy also in such cases, and would try to start with less than the full amount of plus discovered on the eye exam with drops, in order to give the child room for improvement of his hyperopia. Improvement is called **emmetropization** (normalization) by optometrists, and there is controversy over how much can be improved. Minus lenses, on the other hand, tend to aggravate the tendency to cross eyes.

Children with **exotropia-type strabismus** (eyes that wander out) are sometimes given minus lenses that they do not need to see. This is to force them to focus hard in order to see through the glasses, an action that, theoretically, will pull those eyes in. I find that this does not usually work well, because it makes near work so stressful for children, and they cannot manage school well. Vision therapy, prisms, and very weak plus near glasses often do help.

Strabismus can be cosmetically improved by a surgeon, and sometimes some binocular vision can be obtained with visual training before and after the surgery. However, if the size of the angle of the eye turn is relatively small, the surgeon is not needed for a cosmetic improvement, because statistically surgery will not make the angle any smaller.

Sometimes cranial osteopathic or nonforce chiropractic assessment and treatment of tightened muscles in the neck and pelvis, and poor circulation to the head, will help get rid of imbalances in the whole body that are affecting the eyes. Vision therapy is often the best solution, but if that is not available, the child simply uses one eye, **suppressing** the central view with the other, and he can do a good job in school without interference between eyes, or double vision. Sometimes his eyes constantly **alternate**, so he uses one eye for reading and one for the blackboard, like the middle-aged patients who get contacts set for **monovision**.

Usually, sports skills that require coordination are hampered in children with **amblyopia** or strabismus. However, there seems to be no limit to what some people can accomplish with significant handicaps. I know one man who had cosmetic strabismus surgery as a child and still had one amblyopic, suppressed eye so that he had no depth perception. But he learned to fence in college. I would think sword clashing would require precise stereopsis (three-dimensional binocular vision) that one cannot get with a functional one-eyed system. However, this young man fenced for his college team. That was quite an achievement of a very bright boy. He must have utilized some peripheral vision in the weak eye and lots of awareness of monocular cues to depth. He figured this all out on his own without any vision therapy. Children less brilliant and less lucky can have their whole lives diminished by poor vision.

People who have always had perfect sight often start to need plus glasses to read and sometimes even for distance after they are in their forties. This is called **presbyopia**. Bifocals are often prescribed. People who are seriously nearsighted will need less power to see up close when they reach middle age. Some get contacts with one eye set for near and one eye for far (called monovision), but behavioral optometrists do not like to do this. They feel that it reduces safety for driving and reduces the ability of the two eyes to work together.

When a person has never had his two eyes working together, as in severe **anisometropia** (uneven prescriptions) he may have never seen real depth, and can do okay with monovision (one lens for near, one for far), but he should have a third lens for the near vision eye that is set for distance driving.

The ability to keep both eyes straight and use one for near and one for far has saved that person from strabismus or amblyopia (lazy eye), and also from wearing glasses, but this has not been true binocular vision because it cheats the person out of good depth perception. Amblyopia is the condition in which an eye cannot see 20/20 at near and far with any kind of prescription. The amblyopic child will also have trouble making spatial judgments with that lazy eye, because it has not been used normally, so it will not have learned even monocular cues for depth.

Presbyopia probably will not be avoided by his parents when they reach their midforties and their arms get too short to hold their books out to a place where the print is clear. Even that, though, can be much less of a problem if the visual system has developed well throughout youth and childhood, and exercise outdoors is continued.

LESS OBVIOUS FUNCTIONAL VISION PROBLEMS THAT GREATLY AFFECT SCHOOL SUCCESS

Behavioral optometrists evaluate many other things, too, such as how the eyes **team** and **focus** and **track** together for efficient learning. Their tests identify **perception** problems, poor **eye/hand coordination**, and difficulty with **visualization**. These last three problems are hugely affected by the first three. Such functional vision problems are unheard of by many parents and teachers, but they affect learning very significantly. They are discussed extensively in this chapter and chapter three and four. Most of these conditions may be avoided if the child is born with normal vision and he is developing well visually or receives help early.

WHAT IS POOR VISION FOR SCHOOL AND WHAT KIND OF LEARNING PROBLEMS DOES IT CREATE?

The children with excellent vision tend to fit the description of the visually competent child, but there are numerous patterns of poor vision that we see in our practices of behavioral optometry. All of these patterns interfere with a child performing his best at everything he or she does. However, a few patterns are less problematic for school than others because they can be identified by the pediatric clinic or the school screening even though they do not use the extensive testing of the behavioral optometrist. These occur in about 3–5 percent of children in the early grades.

We will look at those first. They are **high refractive error** (a need for a strong plus, minus, or cylinder lens to see near or far on eye charts with one or both eyes) and strabismus. Both of these conditions can lead to amblyopia, often called "lazy eye."

High refractive error can be corrected with significant prescriptions for distance and near and perhaps bifocals for use in the classroom or contact lenses. Vision therapy helps vision development in these children also.

A college student from Europe, who happened to be a good skier, had constant **diplopia** (double vision), which he had experienced his entire life. He did not know that people were supposed to "see single." He thought that with two eyes, one ought to see two views. He was a good student and a good skier because, as he said, he just picked an eye and stuck with it throughout a particular activity.

This young man came to see me, not for vision therapy, but for a glasses prescription so that both eyes would see equally because one was becoming nearsighted. The angle of his eye turn was very small, so no one had ever noticed it and he had never thought about it. He, too, was a bright kid who had adapted to a visual system that was clearly not optimal.

The visually related learning problems with strabismus come when the child is *intermittently* using one eye and *intermittently* seeing with both. This is a major stress on the child's energy if he does not get the proper glasses and therapy to help him consistently align those eyes. These intermittent strabismics are not always picked up on screenings, but would be on a thorough behavioral optometry exam.

Just yesterday I had an extremely bright six-year-old in my office who had some **stereopsis** (three-dimensional vision) with effort and could intermittently fuse her eyes' images, but most of the time she looked off to the side to avoid looking at someone's face and seeing double. She appeared to be constantly alternating between the two eyes on testing, except that she could get that stereo test when she worked hard at it. She could never keep her eyes together within 12 inches of her face, though, and often she saw two things at distance when she knew there was only one. Her tracking was poor. The two eyes had trouble staying together as they moved across a page of print, or shifting from one target to another. It was no wonder that despite being bright as she was, she had not learned to read, although many of her friends had.

MOST CHILDREN'S VISION PROBLEMS ARE LEARNING RELATED, BECAUSE THEY USUALLY START WITH NEAR VISION WORK: UNLESS SPECIFICALLY TESTED, THEY GO UNDETECTED

Basically, children with vision problems can be considered in one of two groups.

The first has made successful adaptations to using their eyes up close to succeed in school. The second group has not been able to adapt to near stress, and they are not succeeding in school despite trying hard, or they have given up trying.

We have seen how children with a constant crossed or walled eye are okay in school with one eye working well. We also know that myopic children are often great readers and good students. They went nearsighted to allow lots of close work without discomfort, and in the process lost their distance vision. These children can be helped but they do not need to have their myopia reversed or controlled to be successful in school. Nevertheless, this is the group that will be identified in regular screenings and given distance glasses. It is more useful if they can be given bifocals and separate reading glasses to keep their vision from becoming worse.

The second group of children have learning-related vision problems with many symptoms and signs that are never known to be visual unless astute teachers and parents watch for them. They make up the rest of the 25% to 45% of kids who fail school screenings in research studies that use more complex assessment measures than just a distance eye test (Fischbach et al. 1993; Orfield, Basa, and Yun 2001; Harris 2002). They are the ones that are visually handicapped in myriad other ways. They suffer from what behavioral optometrists call "soft binocular problems," which can show up as trouble learning to read, difficulty focusing on assignments, slower processing, and lower grades and achievement scores.

We will look at what behavioral optometrists examine when they want to identify a child with a learning-related vision problem or a child who has made an adaptation such as school myopia or using one eye for near and one for far in order to compensate for a visual problem with near work. Proper treatment and testing is taught in all optometry schools, but not all optometrists do these tests often. Ophthalmologists, who are specialists in eye disease and surgery, do not often do all of them either.

These tests are for the speed and accuracy of the convergence and divergence systems of the large eye muscles, the focusing system of the lens, and the oculomotor tracking of the eyes across a page of print, or saccades from near to far or side to side, as in desk to blackboard, or book to notebook.

Besides these three major categories for testing, there are visual perception and visual motor tests that address processing of what is seen and how it is used by body and hands for sports, balance, and handwriting. Those are the diagnostic measures to identify the causes for the signs and symptoms that any parent can watch for. See chapter six for a detailed list of signs and symptoms for parents and teachers and what they each can mean.

THREE VISION PROBLEMS ANY TEACHER CAN SPOT

Three pictures stick out in my mind of children that I was testing in a cohort study of first through third grade students in that inner-city Boston public school. They were all beautiful, bright children with eagerness to learn. Their parents had agreed that we could evaluate and film the students to illustrate vividly the importance of helping children with vision-related learning problems. Almost all the children seemed to have visual trouble with some aspect of close work, but the following kids exemplified the three categories well.

One leaned way back to read the series of numbers and the grade-level text we gave them. He was farther than twenty-four inches from the page.

I asked why, and he said, "I see two if I get any closer."

Another child rubbed one eye and kept her hand over it. Clearly, she was likely experiencing double vision when she used two eyes.

A third child leaned very close, measured at four inches on my ruler, with his head bent down over the page. Struggling to stay on the proper line, he kept his hands poised to touch, though he was instructed not to touch the page, but to just use his eyes to track. All three were eager to please, trying their best, wanting to succeed.

I did get one picture of the rare visually successful child. She sat up erect, and read with expression and eagerness. She held the book at a slant parallel to her face at about twelve inches. She was not stressed or trying very hard, and she was having fun.

Teachers will see these variations every day in their classrooms, and parents can observe them if they are there when their struggling child does homework.

Another picture to watch for is the dreamy child doing homework but dawdling through it because it is not comfortable or fun or easy. He or she is taking two hours when it should take only one, trying to salvage some of the homework time for his or her own inner purposes, rather than efficiently finishing the work and going off to play.

WHAT'S HAPPENING IN THE EYES OF THE CHILD WHO STRUGGLES?

What is going on in the eyes and the brains that are intricately connected to the eyes of the children who struggle? Sometimes they achieve, but the cost is high to their time for fun, their posture, and their visual development. What is going on is a learning-related vision problem with focusing, converging, tracking, processing, visualizing or using the information to produce some work with the hand/eye/brain combination (Cook 1992; Scheiman and Rouse 1994; Streff and Gunderson 2004; Wunderlich 1991; Dawkins, Edelman, and Forkiotis 1990).

Children tell me all about it when they come to my office for exams. Sometimes kids in this category see double, and sometimes they get headaches on school days but not on weekends, unless there is homework. Sometimes they are having trouble learning to read because the words are moving around on the page. They may also be failing to track from left to right. Often the words alternate between blurry and clear. Sometimes the child cannot even sit still to be tested, even though he is supposed to be sitting still in school and learning to read. Too often, children experience all of the above.

Other children who struggle to avoid these problems may be reading but not comprehending the way their parents and teachers wish. They are overburdened with the effort of holding it all together visually in order to just say the words, so that they have no energy left to think about what they are reading.

The excellent behavioral optometrist Dr. Francke, known for his spare and pithy statements, said, "If the mechanics of the situation take too much energy, there is not enough left over for the content of the situation" (Francke 1977). That is why some children do not achieve the potential that is expected based on the oral IQ testing of their early years. Their vision, through which they must learn and express and create, has not caught up with their innate wisdom, truth, and intelligence. Everything gets processed through vision, though, in school.

Some children compensate for their poor functional vision by becoming what we call "auditory learners" and then they have to speak the words in their head or with their tongue silently in their mouths, and that takes extra time. If the child is exceptionally intelligent and a good listener, he may learn enough in school to do well despite his trouble with close work and reading.

I have seen a few of these students arrive at Harvard with straight As from high school, and yet faced with the volume of reading in a demanding college, they do not have enough hours in the day. They suffer a real handicap that needs vision training, glasses, and sometimes extra time on tests to help them get through. Those who can just simply see are faster thinkers, faster readers, and faster workers.

VISION THERAPY OFFERED IN SCHOOLS

At a wonderful charter school in Howell, Michigan, run by several behavioral optometrists, vision therapy is available for all children who do not exhibit visual readiness to read. Dr. Steve Ingersoll is the creator of their method of developing visual cognitive function in children with learning and attention problems. The school is called the Livingston Developmental Academy. I have had the good fortune to hear this doctor speak twice. He lectures on how subtle neurological delays impact visual development, behavior, and educational results. His organization, called Smart Schools Management, Inc., can be contacted in Michigan for more information on what is being done in their several public charter schools (Ingersoll 2005).

The Smart Schools' philosophy is that no child should be taught to read until he is visually dominant. Many children have not gotten there by kindergarten or first grade. They need vision work and visualization work before reading will come easily. This group began their school with many children who were failing in other schools, yet their pass rate on the statewide testing is now 100%. They spent a few years working up to that, but now there is a long waiting list of parents who want their children, some of whom do not have learning problems, to have the opportunity to attend such a stellar school. There will be more discussion of this school in chapter three.

I visited another charter school in Minneapolis, Minnesota, run by Bob and Kathy DeBoer of the A Chance To Grow foundation, called the New Visions School, which teaches children with various types of learning disabilities and developmental delays. The children are given functional eye exams and receive vision therapy when it is needed as part of their "Boost Up" treatment program that also includes occupational and physical therapy, speech development, and neurofeedback therapy, as well as special tutoring.

The DeBoers founded the school because their own daughter had severe fetal distress and oxygen deprivation at birth. She was never expected to walk. With the neurological training they provided, she learned to walk at three and later graduated from high school and holds a full-time job. In the process of working with her, the DeBoers learned enough to start spreading the treatment to others and finally set up their charter school (Moroz 2001). There is more discussion of this school in chapter five.

Both the Livingston Developmental Academy and the New Visions School have been able to acquire adequate space for all the various programs they have and funding from their states as public charter schools. There may be a number of other such schools in the nation doing similar work, but they are far too rare. Certainly, the Boston public school where I ran an optometry clinic for seven years did provide quite a bit of extra help for its many LD (learning disabled) children, including our free vision clinic, which was a pediatric teaching venue of the New England College of Optometry.

When I retired, that clinic closed, but another school system in Framingham, Massachusetts, obtained the services of the optometry school and received some funding from their community. How it was done is described at the end of chapter six in a report from Kathy Majzoub. At that time, she was the Framingham school nurse who was instrumental in establishing that clinic. The clinic takes referrals from all the Framingham public grade schools.

One of the major things I learned by working in my Boston school clinic for seven years was that the number of children who need help is huge, and screenings are not a good way to spend the time of a clinic in a school. Teachers, parents, and the children themselves can spot the learning-related vision problems, and those are the children who should be seen when there are limited budgets and limited time. All children with academic problems severe enough for an IEP must have a full behavioral optometry exam. There are many more who need them also, who might be just getting by when they could be stellar learners if their vision worked for them.

WHAT ARE THE SIGNS THAT VISION DOCTORS IDENTIFY AND REQUIRE THERAPY AND/OR GLASSES TO CORRECT?

The College of Optometrists in Vision Development (COVD), a professional organization for behavioral optometry, developed a 19-item vision-related quality of life checklist for students and parents to assess vision problems. This checklist has been highly correlated with the Stanford IX test results on children in an Arkansas school. Ninety-one students from third, fifth, and seventh grades and their parents volunteered to participate. The parent/guardian checklist scores and the third graders' self-scoring were the most highly correlated with the academic results (Vaughn, Maples, and Hoenes 2006).

The nineteen points on the COVD's (visual) quality-of-life checklist include the following:

1) Headaches with near work
2) Running together of words when reading
3) Burning, itchy, or watery eyes
4) Skipping/repeating of lines when reading
5) Head tilting/closing of one eye when reading
6) Difficulty copying from chalkboard
7) Near work/reading materials avoidance

8) Constant claims of, "I can't" before trying
9) Poor use of time
10) Difficulty completing assignments on time
11) Up/downhill writing
12) Misaligning of digits/ columns of numbers
13) Low reading comprehension
14) Close holding of reading materials
15) Omission of small words when reading
16) Trouble keeping attention on reading
17) Poor memory
18) Clumsiness, knocking things over
19) Frequent loss of belongings

Another place that is doing excellent work with the help of behavioral optometrists is the state of Kansas. A major training program for optometrists in the state was developed to provide the services that the schools were demanding once educators realized that children with convergence problems, if treated by vision therapy, were able to catch up in reading, when others who did not get the vision therapy did not (Sullivan 2001).

THE MAJOR AREAS FOR DIAGNOSIS OF CHILDREN'S VISION PROBLEMS

Let us examine further the significance for learning of the vision problems in the categories we briefly mentioned earlier.

Focusing (Called "Accommodation" by Optometrists)

First, it is important to be able to focus at near, since adults persist in teaching children to read from books with small print at earlier and earlier ages. This way of learning reading is highly stressful for children who do not have exceptionally well-developed visual systems. Chapter six discusses an in-school visual readiness program that can be used for children who do not have adequate visual development. By kindergarten, most children have learned to see far before they have learned to focus on tiny things up close.

The Italian educator Maria Montessori, whose writings have inspired hundreds of Montessori schools across the United States, instinctively knew that visually dominant children who would take easily to reading small print were not the ones who needed her help. It was those still underdeveloped visually for whom she devised tactile ways of learning the alphabet with sandpaper letters and taught to put words together with letter blocks that they could handle (Montessori 1967; Hainstock 1968). This connected the tactile system with the visual system to build near focus ability. It also provided large letters so that stressful near focus was not necessary.

The smaller the letter, the more one has to focus the eyes. This is why a number of children who have been put on computers as early as two or three years old by their eager parents who have been buying "educational programs" for them end up in my office. They are getting nearsighted in just one eye, or they have developed other negative functional adaptations to the pressure on an immature focusing system. The one-eyed choice is efficient for a child hooked on computers. He can focus one eye much easier than coordinating two eyes together at near.

The problem is not just focusing too close, too young. It is that vision is traditionally learned in real space where light bounces off objects. The computer and the TV are backlit, which is not what human baby eyes are expecting and needing for vision development (Pearce 2003).

A child with such a background needs to have vision therapy and reading glasses to regain his binocularity and recover from his one-eyed computer myopia or beginnings of a wandering eye. This is not an easy process, because he is happy with what he has chosen to do unconsciously with his eyes. He does not want to be forced to use the other eye. It is his far eye and he can still see far with it, while the other serves very well for his hours playing on the computer. In a matter of years, though, he will not see far with that eye either, because it will be pulled along into the process of myopia once he is in school. Neither he nor his parents know what he is missing, until he fails a school screening for distance sight.

Sometimes the addiction to screens (computer or TV) causes focusing problems learning to write. The tiny hands on the mouse do not learn from that mouse normal eye/hand coordination in more than a rudimentary way. The eyes fixed to the TV screen while sitting in a little TV chair are not being used in activities involving the body, eyes, and hands. Those activities are what little children need to develop their bodies and, yes, their brains and their eyes' focus shifting ability as well.

Signs of poor focusing will be many, but the most common ones I see are the following. The child complains of headaches. Sometimes even an MRI has been done and there was nothing wrong. The child may continually rub his eyes and the pediatrician does not think it is allergies. Often the child will cover one eye or turn his head sideways a bit, which allows one-eyed viewing on the book. Or he might dislike reading because he says it makes him tired. Or she will not remember what she reads, because the effort is so great. Frequently, the child will have very poor handwriting, even though he may have a proper pencil grip, a good teacher, and parents ready to help him.

The problem of handwriting was never something that I connected with poor focusing ability over and above poor eye/hand coordination, until I became significantly presbyopic (a middle-aged poor focuser). I had trained out of all my nearsightedness. That myopia used to help me see clearly up close. I did not think about my handwriting being more and more illegible as a result of writing in my doctor's notes without my reading glasses on. When I finally had to wear them off and on during eye exams to avoid headaches by the end of the day, I found that I was writing more neatly. It makes sense to look for farsightedness or focusing problems in children with poor handwriting, and not just assume it is a problem for the occupational therapist alone to cure.

Convergence (Also Called "Eye Teaming")

If children do not participate regularly in outdoor activities that coordinate their eyes, hands, and bodies in free space, they are very likely to have trouble converging on the target they are trying to look at accurately with both eyes together. If they do not get a lot of practice with near eye/hand work, they may have trouble converging at near. If they do not spend most of their time in free space away from screens, they will not develop the peripheral awareness that helps the brain to converge accurately.

Sometimes children are born with eyes very wide set and eye muscles that do not converge as easily as other children's eyes, but this is rare.

Usually children with convergence difficulties can converge but not for long, or not always at the same place they want to, or not when they are tired, or just not often enough. They may habitually point their two eyes just beyond the target or the page. Almost all children with convergence problems learn in vision therapy how to converge accurately and sustain it. Optometry and ophthalmology research shows that being taught to do this improves reading quite significantly (Sullivan 2001; Atzmon et al. 1993). Convergence problems are also intertwined with focusing (accommodation) problems that can be cured with therapy and glasses (Birnbaum, 1993).

Not all convergence problems are about inadequate ability to converge the eyes. Some occur when children overdo the convergence and look closer than the target. They are not really crossing their eyes, but they are looking between themselves and the target, and so by the time the crossed-over line of sight from each eye gets to the target, there is no precise, two-eyed fusion. They do not see double because the disparity between the two eyes is not enough and the brain puts it all together in a slightly less clear view than a person with normal vision would get. This blur causes them to try to focus harder. The harder they focus, the more the image blurs, because they drive their eyes to overconverge even more. What these children need to learn to do is relax their eyes and look far. Plus glasses also help them to do that.

The fact that more focusing effort (not always the same as focusing results) can cause too much convergence is one of those intricacies of eye function that hardly anyone knows unless they are working in the field of vision. In the visual system, there is a neurological synkinesis between focusing and converging so that the more you focus, the more you converge. There is a delicate balance called "clear, single, binocular vision" that should occur in which focusing and convergence are coordinated at the same place in space, such as a page of a book. Sometimes children—up through second grade especially—bob their heads up and down when they are reading aloud in their attempts to find focus. Failing to find the perfect place, the child often holds the book so close that sustained convergence is no longer happening and he will use mainly one eye.

Often children who develop one or the other of these poor convergence patterns go nearsighted. Instead of vision therapy, they are given distance glasses, which do not help them up close, where the problem started.

Tracking and Fixating
(Called Oculomotor Skills by Optometrists)

A third aspect of vision that children have trouble mastering is tracking from left to right in the way English and European languages are written, or right to left when reading Hebrew. Tracking across a page or saccading from one target to another to shift fixation are oculomotor (eye/brain/movement system) skills that have to be learned. Babies start to learn tracking when they keep their eyes on their mothers while sitting in an infant seat or standing in their cribs, or while watching their hands as they learn to creep left and right, left, right, cross, crawl.

Children also learn these skills by catching and throwing balls, watching others in motion during games of everything from hide-and-seek to soccer, sitting in their bedroom windows and watching the world go by on the street, or looking back and forth at the faces of their parents in conversation. There are also many ways to teach these skills when they are not learned properly in early childhood. (They are discussed in chapter three.)

A small number of children can learn to read in a kind of global way without being good at tracking, and they will read well with comprehension to themselves, even though they fail tracking tests and may not be good at reading aloud. I have seen only a few children like this. Behavioral optometrists do notice these kids and think about the visual mystery there.

The majority of children, however, need to track and converge well to read well. Tracking failure correlates highly with reading failure, and tracking failure is now a rampant, epidemic problem in the early grades because the culture of childhood is not providing experiences for children to learn these things. There are also the epidemic neurological problems that cause poor tracking, which are discussed in chapter two.

Efforts in School and at Home Are Needed to Grow Children with Proper Focusing, Converging, and Tracking Skills These skills of coordinated vision are learned with play in free space with the hands, body, and eyes working together. Happily, play is something an

American Academy of Pediatrics study has shown to be essential for "mental, physical, and social/emotional development" (Eklind 2006; Ginsberg 2006). They could have added that it is good for vision development, too. Electronic media have become substitutes for watching the world go by and other old-fashioned activities of childhood, such as playing in the woods, by a stream, around a lake, and watching the animals and birds move in nature (Louv 2005). When families and schools cannot provide nonscreen play, no one is helping children's vision development, unless they see a behavioral optometrist for vision therapy. It is harder and harder for children to learn visual skills on their own in the culture of today without special efforts of teachers and parents (Wunderlich 1991).

Eye/Hand Coordination

A fourth skill that children can miss learning is eye/hand coordination. Optometrists test for this in many ways, and both ODs (optometrists), and OTs (occupational therapists) have noticed the problem increasing in the last fifteen to twenty years as computers have become more a household fixture, as television has taken over many households, and as children are no longer required to help with household work such as cleaning, cooking, laundry, and gardening.

Training children in all the hands-on household activities takes time. With two parents working outside the home, that time may be given up to what parents determine are less taxing activities with their children, such as TV watching. That may be a big mistake in child development (Getman 1962).

Sometimes the early bird on the computer has motor development problems with catching, throwing, balancing, eye/hand skills, and sports, which makes him more and more a computer recluse and less likely to learn to build a space world in his mind for visualization, experimentation, conceptualization, imagination, and creation. From Faraday to Einstein, the greats in physics of the last few centuries were hands-on observers of matter and motion, light and wind, substance and color. Theories were suggested, and mathematics came after observation to prove them true (*NOVA* 2005).

Computers were born out of hands-on skills, also. So were rockets. So were all the important inventions of the last century. Sadly this century's children, who are getting too much computer time too early, are not developing good eye/hand, observation, or conceptualization skills. Playing with a mouse doesn't cut it.

If today's children are lucky, the schools will take over the task of making little fingers skillful. Montessori schools help. A few public schools and astute physical education teachers try to address the problem in their own ways. There is also an organization of private schools called Waldorf Schools, in which eye/hand skills like rope climbing, stitching, crocheting, knitting, and illustrating dramatic stories are part of the curriculum in the early grades. The Waldorf program's success for training really good eye/hand coordination and a space world for the brain was made clear to me when I fit a high school freshman for contact lenses who had gone through sixth grade in the local Waldorf school.

If patients have never worn contact lenses, it takes a lot of time and tremendous learning and will for those individuals to get the first lens into that innocent eye. I have seen strong men crumple over this job and need to spend days at home practicing. Most young adults have a very hard time placing the lens in the eye without aiming too low or too high, bumping their lids, or squishing the lens back over their finger. This young, Waldorf-educated girl, however, whipped out her index finger, propped the lens on it as instructed, held her lids open with a finger from each hand, and the lens was placed delicately and accurately the first time she tried. Another Waldorf child was a very quick learner, too.

Other children have needed a long time to train, plus home efforts by contact lens-wearing parents, and even with those, some kids have decided they did not want lenses in their eyes after all. These cases were all folks with light to moderate myopia, so that seeing up close was no problem for them.

If putting contact lenses on were the only purpose for eye/hand skills, the problem would not be serious at all. Unfortunately, eye/hand coordination is necessary for innumerable activities and careers. It is required for sports and laboratory classes in high school and college. In addition, many lines of work, from automechanics to surgery, require those skills, not to mention the obvious printing, handwriting, and drawing required in school.

Let us not forget musical, craft-related, and domestic skills. Because shop, cooking, and sewing classes have been eradicated from most high schools, teens have no hands-on practice and may not know how to do these things well unless they can learn at home or from a book by visualizing what the book is telling them to do and then managing it with their hands.

In the past, the old adage that "all you really needed to know you learned in kindergarten" might have been true, but now, unfortunately, kindergarten is all about learning phonics and reading as soon as possible to get ready for the high-stakes third-grade tests. It is better that we as a culture, and all of us as parents and grandparents, offer up what skills we have for the next generation and be sure they are taught in the schools or in our homes.

I was taught a great many skills when I was a child but not nearly as early as I taught my own children, because my children and I were fortunate enough to have an Auntie Andre, married to my brother Steve. Her mother had died when she was three, and she very quickly learned a lot of household tasks. She was a wonderful cook and came to visit several times a year. The children went canoeing and camping with her and my brother and learned to love rivers and woods and cooking, diving, and dancing with her.

On one visit, she gave our first two children and me a lesson that changed my whole parenting style. She wrapped my two-year-old and four-year-old in aprons and stood them on a chair and a footstool to make dinner including chicken, potatoes, greens, homemade bread, and a pie. It was a project for the entire afternoon, but what pride they took in cooking with Andre! That lesson taught me to teach my kids everything—not just the academic, school-oriented things. Auntie Andre also taught them tumbling and dance movement, and so I started having them do yoga with me and Lilias Folan on TV, which long ago aired at 5:30 p.m., just when my dinner was in the oven.

If Television Is Sometimes Useful, What Is Wrong with It?   Our culture is trying to foster early learning, but it is often through nonspace, flat screens, which are not the real space of three-dimensional light, real objects, and real people. New York City optometrist Dr. Richard

Kavner, in his excellent book *Your Child's Vision*, reports that the average family was watching six and a half hours a day of television, the average child was watching four hours a day, and over a million children were still watching at midnight (Kavner 1985, 130). This was before computers were so affordable and before the computer game boom had exploded on the market with many early learning programs, which seduced parents away from the tried-and-true, hands-on, eyes-on, ears-on work of family living.

I really found Kavner's report of TV times hard to believe, so I polled my vision therapy patients at the Boston public school clinic in the late 1990s. In most cases, patients reported that the TV was turned on as soon as they were home from school at 2:45 p.m., the family took about 15 minutes for dinner, then the TV was back on, and they watched until bedtime at 9, or 10, or 11 p.m. (!), which I thought was late for children, who should be getting more sleep. That would be six and a half hours a day or more, with only 15 minutes at dinner for parent/child interaction. Sometimes there was no family talk even at dinner if the mother had a late work shift. Insufficient sleep, incidentally, is one of the new diagnoses that pediatricians are holding on alert.

Screen time (TV or computers) is still a large preoccupation for all the children who come to see me at Harvard University Health Services or in my private practice, so that I know there is no time for eyes and hands to work together, except on homework. A lot of children who can read have trouble with handwriting or printing. Parents often wonder what their child would do without TV or computer games. I tell them to get eye/hand skill-building toys and complex puzzle games and a tape player for listening to books on tape while the child draws, works with clay, or builds a model. That way, the imagination is at work visualizing the story, and the eyes and hands could be learning at the same time.

This is the way whole generations of kids spent rainy days with radio adventure programs. They would never have dreamed of just sitting and listening. But they could visualize the radio stories and keep active with their hands at the same time.

Television needs to be limited. It steals the child's creativity right out of his eyes and brain. The schools and pediatricians all agree. They might be thinking of motor development, brain-wave patterns, adequate sleep, and the sights of violence and explicit sex. However, the biggest problem I see is that children do not learn to visualize in a healthy way.

Healthy visualization does not happen with TV or computers. The mind is provided pictures—with no room for visualization or imagination. Also, seeing violence or pretend violence that they cannot understand simply fills their brains with worrisome pictures—not with their own creative visualization from delightful, clear, and telling descriptions in the best children's literature by writers who treasured the English language and its power to grow the mind. This brings us to the fifth visual skill that children often lack in our current culture of child rearing.

Visualization

Visualization includes everything from finding one's way home from the grocery store on foot or by car to enjoying the fast-paced action of a mystery story or the beautiful words of a classic poem. When I was teaching high school English back in the late 1960s, I observed that something had already affected children's imaginations. I found that my students had a very difficult time visualizing characters in a book and did not see pictures in their heads from descriptions of action. I thought it was television, of course, providing the pictures for them and not allowing them the development of their imaginations.

Richard DeMille (son of Cecil B. DeMille, the famous director of those imaginative, classic movie extravaganzas) was worried about this way back in the 1960s. With his own experience as a TV director, science fantasy writer, and psychology professor, he wrote *Put Your Mother on the Ceiling: Children's Imagination Games* (1967). He felt that the skills of divergent production (thinking of a variety of ideas) and evaluation (making judgments about the quality value of the ideas) were not going to be learned accidentally.

His worries were sound, even though he never foresaw the six and a half hours of eyes and minds captive to TV or the three to four hours of Game Boy and computer game playing, in which so many children of our century would be tied up and bound. He was still worried, though, that children in schools would not be able to do what we now call "mindful learning" (Langer 1997). His games were designed to teach visualization—rapid, creative, original, and enormously useful in every endeavor.

I think the best way to teach children to visualize is to read to them when they are very young. At first, parents will read from books with beautiful illustrations because it starts children off knowing what good visualization is. However, by the time they are reading chapter books in the second grade, children need to be good at "seeing" what goes on in the story. Therefore, chapter books should be read to them before they enter school.

Sometimes parents stop with picture books and assume the child will read by himself when he learns, but what we know is that the best readers come from homes where children are read to every day. If parents feel they are not good oral readers, the public libraries have dozens of good books on tape that children can hear instead.

Perhaps many children now who are reading the Harry Potter books are learning to visualize again. Many are certainly reading again, thanks to the unique imagination and visualization skills of J. K. Rowling.

Computer games have the same limitations for visualization that the TV does, and they really use such limited hand skills that they do not build strong fingers connected to a highly skilled fine motor system in the brain. A professional violinist and violin teacher has also been concerned. Ann Miklich of Boston says most of the children she teaches have poor small-muscle motor development, so holding and playing a violin is more of a challenge than it should be. She is also concerned about their overall visual development for note reading. "They were not always that way," she remarked.

At a workshop I gave, the Cambridge Schools' occupational therapists also told me that small motor skills with hands are not being developed well by school age. Neither is trunk strength. The older therapists had seen the changes occur over time.

Visual/Perceptual Skills

Another major visual area that behavioral optometrists focus on in visual training is perception. These skills include a number of defined types of perception, such as right/left awareness, directionality, visual discrimination or matching, visual closure, visual form constancy, figure/ground discrimination, and visual motor integration.

When children lack these skills, they will have problems that will affect performance in school (Kulp 1999; Solan and Ficarra 1990). They might have trouble differentiating similarly shaped letters or words with similar beginnings or endings; finding the correct key on a key ring; reading the correct numbers in their math problems; or confusing right and left, front and back, above and below, in and out, and so on. Writing out their work in an organized fashion on paper will be difficult. Math problems that they could do in their heads might be missed because they cannot line things up spatially on a page, so the correct numbers are in the correct columns. Map reading might be very hard for them to comprehend. Finding their way around their city and neighborhood might be difficult.

My approach to teaching these skills is to include them with all the other skills children learn in vision therapy, whether or not they have been tested as missing. I combine them with focusing, converging, and tracking training. The doctor quickly learns from doing an activity with a child what is missing in that child's perception, and that is then addressed with puzzles, parquetry, games, and activities that should be part of every child's growing-up play but is not in our time. Much more is said about this issue in chapter three, which is on reversing poor development of vision once it has occurred.

In the 1960s, Headstart was born to help provide these early learning experiences in impoverished areas. Books such as *Teaching Montessori in the Home* (Hainstock 1968), *Give Your Child a Superior Mind* (Engelmann and Engelmann 1966), *How to Raise a Brighter Child: The Case for Early Learning* (Beck 1967), and *Thinking Is Child's Play* (Sharp 1969) helped parents learn what could be done for their children in the home. Maya Pines wrote her *Revolution in Learning: The Years from Birth to Six* (1966), and the early learning movement was launched.

The assumption was then that somebody would be in the home. People really believed there would be shorter rather than longer working hours in a "cybernetics" future. Many more excellent books full of games and advice for teaching children were published. There were no personal computers then, and life was simpler. Fewer mothers worked outside the home, and there were fewer single moms needing to earn a living while raising children. It was possible to raise a family on one income then, and the women's movement had not been launched yet, which later pulled large numbers of economically secure women into the workplace during their child-bearing years. This left less time for training the children. Daycare did not always make up the difference in developing good visual/perceptual systems.

A renowned behavioral optometrist, the late Dr. Gerald N. Getman, was thinking about the early learning problem slightly ahead of the pack. He published his very useful volume from his Minnesota practice research in 1962. It was called *How to Develop Your Child's Intelligence*. Of course, it involved developing all the vision skills that have been discussed in this chapter. Many optometric studies have shown since then that visual/motor and visual/perception difficulties are highly correlated with school difficulties (Hoffman 1982; Kulp 1999; Solan and Ficarra 1990). It makes sense for parents to be sure that eye/hand activities and perception games are readily available and used by their kids.

Peripheral Awareness

Peripheral awareness is a major visual skill that involves one's visual processing with what is called the "ambient" visual system. This is the system of retinal cells and visual pathways that tells us what it is, where it is, and if it's moving, without looking directly at it. It is also the system that manages seeing the whole picture, knowing where players are on the basketball court, knowing where the end of the line or sentence or page is, and building the good habits of "street smarts," such as noticing what is going on around you and who is in your environment at all times.

The ambient system is one of two visual systems in two separate parts of the brain. This is not generally known, but it was discovered in the 1960s by Trevarthen and Sperry at Harvard (Trevarthen and Sperry 1973; Trevarthen 1968), and it has been reapplied to much of the thinking around dyslexia and attention deficit disorder. The concept of two visual systems needs to be understood by parents and teachers because children need to have both systems working in the proper balance in order to have good overall vision.

What behavioral optometrists often find is that some children are very good at central vision up close for reading but totally lack awareness of their surroundings. They are likely to become nearsighted, and they will never be competent in sports if they do not learn to use that second processing system, the ambient system. Other children have trouble with the close-up focusing, but may be quite good on the playing field. They need the close-up exercises and reading glasses to see well at near. Other children with inadequately developed visual systems have major limitations in both areas. Too much stress always diminishes periphery. It always does (Streff and Gunderson 2004; Shipman 1954; Marrone 1991). So does head injury (Padula 1988). This is discussed further in chapters four and five.

The ideal is to have children in a balanced processing mode so that both ambient and focal systems are reciprocally working together. The reason for this is that the eye movements are controlled in a part of the brain that is informed by the peripheral retina. Therefore, that peripheral information is used to decide how to move and focus the eyes for tracking and central viewing. Using just the central system for focusing and converging is a habit of children who are struggling with near work or going nearsighted. This hunkering inward might seem to help them cope with near work, but it causes visual discomfort and lessens efficiency. They become overburdened with homework and have no time for play. They have lost the periphery, the "ambience," both literally and figuratively.

This should not be a surprising fact to anyone. We have known as a culture for at least 100 years that excessive reading without breaks or reading in poor light or flat in bed tends to bring on nearsightedness more frequently than moderate reading with breaks and good light. It was reading under the covers with a flashlight that drove me and a surprising number of my older patients into myopia. The flashlights were to keep the light from showing under the door when one was supposed to be asleep, except that the book was just too interesting to stop reading. I thought I had invented that trick, but amazing numbers of people from my generation used that same ruse to stay up later than they were allowed.

Being sick and flat in bed watching television for a few weeks with strep, bronchitis, or pneumonia has also driven a few children I know into nearsightedness. The problem is that eyes in a sick body are strained, and then doubly stressed by staring centrally at the TV. There is a constant focus at one distance, with no chance to move around, and the body is too sick to process both central and peripheral vision so it just shuts down the periphery to zero in on the screen. Books on tape would be much better for the sick child's eyes, which could then look around the room, out the window, at the dog on the foot of the bed, and so on.

It is the job of behavioral optometrists to educate our patients about the many facets of vision development of which the public and the general culture of childrearing is unaware. The traditional eye as a camera concept of vision, or the old theory that it is all in the genes—all nature and no nurture—or the belief that school failure has nothing to do with the eyes, are all ideas whose time has long passed by. We are in the 21st century, and it is everyone's job to help all of our children become what they are meant to be. Children's vision is a very good place to start.

The following are three major points about vision development that researchers and behavioral optometrists have known for decades, but that have not yet trickled down into the general knowledge of parenting and teaching:

1) Vision is developed through movement (Gesell 1949).
2) Vision is an adaptive process to suit what we use it for (Carr and Francke 1976; Birnbaum 1978; Nicholson and Garzia n.d.; Rosenfield, Ciuffreda, and Novogrodsky 1992; Norton, and Siegwart 1995).
3) Vision can be helped or hurt by lenses, and changed for better or worse depending on how we treat it (Costanza 1994; Friedhoffer and Warren 1988; Sherman 1993; Streff 1977; Hung and Smith 1996).

We need a new paradigm of what vision is all about, how good vision is developed, and what poor vision is and how it handicaps a child or an adult. We also need to realize that one *can* change the way one sees and processes the information obtained from the eyes, which are really just part of the brain. Once we know that, we can upgrade our children's vision, which will truly change their lives for the better.

2

THE BEST VISUAL SYSTEMS ARE MADE, NOT BORN ON WAVES OF TOXICITY: IF WE FAIL TO UNDERSTAND THIS, IF WE FAIL TO HELP AFFECTED CHILDREN, SCHOOL LEARNING WILL SUFFER

If you imagine that the government or your pediatrician will protect your child or grandchild or students effectively from toxic chemicals or electromagnetic pollution in the environment, think again. We are all on our own to learn what must be done, though there are some excellent books and organizations now to help us. This chapter reviews some of the hot topics in this area that we, who work in the field of behavioral optometry, are thinking about for our learning-disabled (LD) patients. These topics should be bedtime reading for all parents and grandparents who take care of children. Indeed, they should be on everyone's plate at breakfast. Who is responsible for not allowing our society to poison our children and their environment? We all are.

Toxicity affects children's vision and learning because it assaults the nervous system, which is intimately connected with visual processing. There are things we can do to prevent toxicity, and to treat and rehabilitate kids whose visual systems have taken a hit from environmental poison. The main areas of concern are toxins in vaccinations, toxins in the food and water supply, chemicals in manufactured household products, fumes in the air, and frequencies from electromagnetic fields.

The children that behavioral optometrists see with learning-related vision problems are often found on what has been called the "autism spectrum," which a number of experts believe to be, in good part, a phenomenon of reactions to toxins. It includes not just autism diagnoses, but the very prevalent ADHD (attention deficit hyperactivity disorder) and ADD (attention deficit disorder) symptoms. Parents with children on this spectrum of infirmities simply call it "the spectrum." A mother will call me and say, "I have a child on the spectrum, and he has had all his neuropsych tests, and there is a 'vision piece,' so we need to see a behavioral optometrist."

Some parents may not even suspect that their child is on the spectrum even if he has learning problems, though he is certainly not autistic. Upon questioning the parents, it becomes clear that the child had seizures after his shots as an infant, that he is hyperactive with attention deficit, and that he needs vision therapy for developmental immaturities regarding focus and convergence, eye/hand coordination, balance, movement, and tracking. Those are all diagnoses on the spectrum. The child may also have digestive, sleep, light sensitivity, or kidney problems. The vision problems, specifically, are also typical of patients with head trauma, strokes, or any other neurological injury.

Tracking is a big one. I remember asking my old eye doctor, Amiel Francke, in the mid-1990s if he had any advice regarding vision therapy with children. He had been examining children's vision since the 1940s.

"It's tracking, tracking, tracking that is the problem now. It didn't used to be. Something has changed," he said.

Tracking means moving coordinated eyes attentively across a page of print, and across the midline of the body, to efficiently read. Optometrists call these skills "oculomotor skills." Failure to do this well can be just failure to learn the skill, or it can be a "soft neurological sign." That means there might be some neurological compromise in that child's visual system. Whatever the reason, children can be cured with vision training and practice. Much more is explained regarding vision therapy in chapter three.

Because the concept of the spectrum is so salient to today's vision-related learning problems, it needs to be explained. The spectrum includes, at the severe end, a full autism diagnosis, which now is more often than not regressive autism. This means the child was a normal baby but then something happened when the baby was between eighteen months and two and a half years that radically changed everything.

The next most serious disorder on the spectrum is pervasive developmental delay not otherwise specified (PDD-NOS). Then comes Asperger's syndrome (sometimes called "high-functioning autism"). After that, there is ADHD for which there can be many causes. Then finally, there is ADD, speech delays, tics, and other subtle neurological problems.

WHY IS THIS RELEVANT TO VISION AND LEARNING? TO TEACHERS AND PARENTS?

The vast majority of children on the spectrum have functional vision problems that interfere with school learning and success in relating to other children.

"Autism involves a global dysfunction in the sensory systems," says Dr. Randy L. Schulman, a Connecticut behavioral optometrist whose practice handles a number of children on the spectrum. She reports that the child with autism often exhibits the following symptoms that vision therapy can help cure: One eye turns out or one eye is frequently closed, stares habitually, looks through hands, flaps hands and objects in front of eyes, looks sideways at things, is light sensitive, is confused about depth or changes in the environment, rubs or pushes on an eye, has trouble with eye contact, bumps into objects, and feels his way around touching walls or tables (Schulman 1994). Adult patients have reported that prior to training, the room was not seen as a whole but just as parts at a time, or that vision was distorted.

Doctors Scharre and Creedon tested children diagnosed with autism and found high amounts of refractive error (need for glasses), exotropia (eyes turning out some or all of the time), some esotropia (eyes in), oculomotor problems (tracking and fixation), and focusing problems (Scharre and Creedon 1993). Other researchers have found significant balance problems and spatial awareness issues (Schulman 1994).

Optometrists who work with these children have developed some very good ways of helping get their visual systems ready for school

(Schulman 1994; Kaplan 2006). Besides providing vision therapy treatments and special training glasses, we do a lot of thinking about causes, and we suggest lifestyle changes and make referrals to other practitioners. That is our job when we see a child with autism or any other neurological insult that affects vision. We want to work on correcting symptoms, but we also need to help parents find ways to stop the continuing insults from the hidden, possibly toxic causes, the gastrointestinal illness suffered by many children with autism, and the frequent need for antibiotics because of continued disease.

In Dr. Schulman's, practice, "The patients who had the opportunity for other interventions," such as "body wellness, sensory integration," and often "auditory testing . . . made the most progress" (1994). She refers for nutrition, allergy work, chiropractic treatment, homeopathy, and cranial-sacral manipulation, and says, "There were no cases in which no improvement was made." This has been true of my own patients as well.

WHY DOES GENERAL HEALTH MATTER FOR VISION DEVELOPMENT WHETHER THE CHILD IS ON THE SPECTRUM OR NOT?

This is a book on vision, so why should it matter to worry about the spread of colds, flu, and other bacteria, parasites, and poisons? It matters because a period of illness during crucial developmental times takes a toll on vision development. When the body is fighting off toxins or illness, it doesn't have the extra energy for optimal brain learning, which in large part is visual learning. A trip with the family in good health always expands development in young children rapidly and noticeably because of the twenty-four/seven attention, new sights, and talk with parents. A week in bed creates a missing spot that slows development. In older children, it can cause myopia (nearsightedness) if the TV or books are used to entertain a child sick enough to be home from school or day care.

My old eye doctor, Amiel Francke, explained this when my own children were young. Then I saw it operate in one of my own patients. She had been kept free of myopia for several years with reading glasses and a few exercises. Then she got a respiratory flu followed by bronchitis and lay on the couch watching TV for two and a half weeks. She came in after she was well with a complaint of blurry vision at distance. She could no longer see through her reading glasses and needed something to see the blackboard at school. Sure enough, it was suddenly there—a significant amount of nearsightedness following round-the-clock TV during illness. Books on tape for listening are useful for ill children, to keep the eyes relaxed. The problems of TV for younger children are discussed in chapters three and four.

THERE IS AN EPIDEMIC OF AUTISM SPECTRUM DISORDERS FACING THE SCHOOLS NOW

Our culture has catapulted through many changes in the last twenty-five years that can each be partially blamed for the increase in autism (1 in 10,000 children in the 1980s and 1 in 150 in 2007). These numbers do not include the other kids on the spectrum. An excellent article that covers all the bases is, "How Recent Changes Have Contributed to an Epidemic of Autism Spectrum Disorders," by Patricia S. Lemer (2006), head of the Developmental Delay Resources organization.

Changes she discusses include the cessation of pediatric house calls from family doctors who know the children well, the overprescription of antibiotics, and an increase in the number of vaccines—from one to fifty in the last fifty years—before the child enters school. The antibiotics and vaccines all contain toxic materials. There has also been an increase in environmental toxins, an increase in food additives, an increase in screen watching, an increase in safety measures that restrict movement development, more pressure for academic achievement in the schools, more pressure for early reading, fewer and shorter recesses and physical education classes, less time for art and music, larger class sizes, less help from extended families, more households with two parents working outside the home, more fast foods, less free playtime, and more sleep deprivation—children need 10 to 12 hours a night and are not getting it (Lemer 2006).

The "total load" (Lemer 2006; nutritionist Kelly Dorfman's phrase) of all of these things is impacting all of our children. As parents, grandparents, and teachers, we need to do our best to decrease that load and improve nutrition to cope with stress that is inevitable in children's lives. Stress interferes with focusing and converging the eyes. This is explained further in chapters three and four.

A number of my patients' parents have made changes, and even with the best of environments, their kids are still on the spectrum. Some have children with autism, who were born perfectly normal. They suspect mercury in the form of the preservative thimerosal (46.6 percent ethyl mercury) in the increased numbers of shots children began to receive in the late 1980s. Others express concern about the live measles, mumps, and rubella vaccination cocktail without thimerosal that may have been too much for a child with a total load of stressors, including earlier shots with thimerosal, such as hepatitis B in the delivery room. They also feel that their children may have unusual sensitivities to the toxic aspects of shots (McCandless 2002; Sicile-Kira 2004).

After studying the information on the subject, I am inclined to say that for a mercury-sensitive child (one without the capacity to throw off and sequester toxic substances), the increased numbers of shots could have been a major player in developmental difficulties. Parents and teachers who are trying to help children on the spectrum need to know this theory and something about the recommended treatments, including vision therapy. New parents and grandparents need to ask their pediatricians for shots without thimerosal to be on the safe side. The information now available indicates that most of it has been removed from children's shots, but some of it has not. Even in 2006, some of my patients had to have shots specially ordered.

Patricia Lemer's advice to parents and their doctors regarding shots is to work together for a modified vaccination schedule. She recommends visiting www.donaldmiller.com for a sensible vaccine schedule. Never vaccinate a sick child or one who has just had antibiotics. Several of my patients have told me that they had worries about their sick children receiving vaccinations, but the doctors said it was okay.

Lemer's list also includes the advice to seriously consider all vaccine reactions such as fever, redness, or irritability as a forewarning of sensitivity. She recommends that acetaminophen never be used for these symptoms after vaccinations because it depletes glutathione, which is necessary to remove toxic metals. The signs should be seen as a warning regarding future shots.

Do not give booster shots without checking with a blood test to see if immunity is already there from previous shots. Immunity is all schools care about. Insist on thimerosal-free vaccines. Vaccinate for individual diseases. Do not allow your child to have a vaccine cocktail like the MMR (measles, mumps, rubella). Space out shots and administer vitamin C before and after every inoculation (Lemer 2006).

Christine Northrup recommends that nursing mothers take 3,000 milligrams of vitamin C before and after their babies receive shots (Northrup 2005).

THE MERCURY THEORY MAY EXPLAIN SOME PROBLEMS OF MANY CHILDREN ON THE SPECTRUM

Many believe a major cause of the sudden increase in children with disorders on the autism spectrum is the result of poisoning from ethyl mercury in the form of thimerosal shot preservative—especially as the number of shots has increased. The afflicted children could be genetically sensitive, or sensitive because of previous toxic insults, or both. Ethyl mercury is nearly as toxic as methyl mercury (which everyone has been warned to limit by restricting the consumption of large fish like tuna and sword). Pregnant women are also cautioned against mercury fillings during those nine months.

Mercury had been "grandfathered in" back in the 1930s as a shot preservative in the form of thimerosal, without ever being checked out by the Food and Drug Administration (FDA). The mercury theory is supported by the fact that during the 1990s, American six-month-old babies were exposed to a total of 187.5 micrograms of ethyl mercury through vaccination. In addition, newborns were given hepatitis B shots with the mercury, which was not removed until 2001, although in 1999 it was suggested that small birth weight babies should not be given the shot for six months.

Not the pediatricians, or the shot manufacturers, or the FDA, or the Center for Disease Control (CDC) noticed that two-month-olds' shots alone were over the top in toxicity. By age ten, there would be many more doses (Bernard et al. 2000). No one was keeping track of these mercury dose increases between 1988 and 1992 when the number of

shots doubled the mercury exposure amounts. When someone did figure it out in 2000, actions to decrease exposures were not immediately
taken (Kirby 2005, 173; Kennedy 2005).

The autism symptoms are identical to those of organic mercury poisoning (Bernard et al. 2001), and their increased prevalence parallels
the increased number of shots from 1988 to 1992. However, if spectrum
disorders are not from the mercury as many medical spokesmen still as-
sert (Harris and O'Conner 2005), we are all going to have to do some
very careful thinking about our environment for babies and pregnant
women. The best hope is that it is mainly the mercury and that everyone is now forewarned about how to protect their children.

THE SCOPE OF THE SPECTRUM EPIDEMIC AFFECTING SCHOOLS IS SO LARGE THAT EDUCATORS HAVE TO CONSIDER IT IN ALL OF THEIR PLANNING

The scope of the autism spectrum disaster is huge. There was one child
with autism for every 10,000 births in the 1980s. By the late 1990s, the
number was one in 500. By 2005, it was one child in every 166 children,
according to the CDC (Fisher 2004). By 2004, Fisher reports, there
were 94,000 children with autism in the public school system. In 1991,
there were only 5,000.

These numbers do not refer to the entire spectrum, just to the autism
diagnosis. We now have one in every six American children with a developmental problem, such as ADD or ADHD, speech delay, and tics.
Autism alone is found in four boys for every one girl (Kirby 2005, xiv).
This is consistent with the mercury theory because testosterone makes
it more difficult for boys to detoxify the mercury and other heavy metals, and estrogen helps protect the girls.

INCREASED NUMBERS OF LEARNING-DISABLED CHILDREN ARE NOW IN PUBLIC SCHOOLS

Carla Hannaford, a neurobiologist, reports that there are "between
three and four million school-aged children, mainly boys, who are

labeled with specific learning disabilities." That does not count pre-school kids, she says. There may be up to 500,000 preschoolers labeled LD, and "between 1,000,000, and 1,500,000 with speech and language" problems. Another 500,000 have emotional disturbances, 75,000 hearing problems, and 100,000 autism (2005, 144). Her data is mainly from the March 2002 U.S. Department of Education's Common Core of Data survey, which reports on children served in programs funded federally.

It would be useful to know if the major cause is not mercury, so we could plan whether or not this epidemic is going to be a continuing reality that schools have to face. I am inclined to believe that a large part of these problems was due to a mercury load on top of the total load of environmental stresses that have increased over the last 25 years. The story of mercury toxicity and the nonbiomedical treatments for afflicted kids, as well as the biomedical treatments to stop ongoing toxic damage, are discussed below, because educators and parents need to know this information. Optometrists have been studying it because toxicity affects vision.

HEROIC PARENTS AND THE INTERNET HAVE LIKELY SAVED MILLIONS OF CHILDREN

The story of the effort to remove thimerosal from children's shots is told in the page turner *Evidence of Harm* by science writer David Kirby (2005). I could not put it down. It sustained my compulsion to read on for all 460 pages. It is a horrifying and fascinating saga of discovery and political action by a group of astute parents of children with autism or PDD–NOS, including some MD and PhD researchers who had autism touch their children's lives. Many of them met on the Internet from far-flung cities. This will be one of the great stories of medicine in the twenty-first century. It may also be one of the more interesting and heartbreaking political stories of our age (Kennedy 2005).

These heroic parents were racing against time to get treatments for their children suddenly afflicted with regressive autism; to figure out that the cause could have been the mercury and then stop much of the mercury use in the shots in order to save others. In the process they woke us all up about other risks of mercury, as well. Mercury-laden inoculations continued to be shipped abroad, and some reports indicate there was a simultaneous outbreak of autism in those countries (Kirby 2005).

Some clinics, thankfully, will no longer use shots with thimerosal even for adults. Harvard University Health Services sent around an e-mail to say they are a nonmercury clinic, except for the dentistry department's amalgam fillings.

Margaret Mead once said, "Never doubt that a group of thoughtful, committed people can change the world. Indeed it is the only thing that ever has!" These turn-of-the-century heroines and heroes did change our world. They deserve thanks and praise from whole generations of children following theirs who will be safe from one major source of toxicity, as long as those future generations pay attention and work with their doctors to ensure safe shots.

Unfortunately, the families have been affected by enormous personal stress and financial disaster (the estimated cost of caring for and treating an autistic child is two to three million dollars from birth to adulthood), and pain and misery have affected the lives of the afflicted children. If it is from the mercury, we should see the numbers drop off in a few years, if we all avoid thimerosal and other sources of mercury. Many highly reputable doctors and scientists are convinced that mercury is a major cause (McCandless 2002).

New federal laws have eliminated the possibility that the government or the pharmaceutical industry will be required to help treat the unlucky kids now. When their parents die, the most severely afflicted will need to be institutionalized if they cannot be treated and sufficiently cured by then, so in the long run, society will pay the price. It pays it in the schools now, and it will pay later as well.

This massive developmental crisis in our culture has crept up on most parents and younger teachers unawares. Older special education teachers and occupational therapists know that there has been a major increase in problems. Old-time pediatricians know (Kirby 2005, 173). Grandparents know that it was not this way when they were in school.

Health care providers in my field were seeing more and more problems with children in our testing protocols and wondering why. I am talking about convergence, tracking, focusing, peripheral awareness, and the ability to look us in the eye. We thought it was a result of excessive television, lack of sleep, stressful lifestyles, and poor nutrition, which some of it was. We were shocked to hear about mercury in the shots. Thimerosal was taken out of eye drops in the 1980s. I was in optometry school then. There was much discussion about how toxic this mercury compound was to the human eye. Sadly, it was not taken out of children's vaccinations at the same time it was removed from eye drops and all veterinary inoculations.

Avoid Mercury (Amalgam Silver) Fillings for Children

It is also true that mercury in fish and mercury in the amalgam fillings that children and pregnant women have in their mouths could also be part of the toxicity of mercury story. This is a good reason for not allowing refined sugars into our children's world. Refined sugars cause tooth decay cavities that need to be filled by a dentist. If you get amalgam fillings, the standard in the U.S, there is mercury in them mixed with the silver. This may not be something good for a young child to be chewing against. One can find dentists who will do nonamalgam fillings, especially in baby teeth (called "composite" fillings), which will help protect children's brains when they are young. A few holistic dentists have stopped using mercury fillings altogether in their practices, so try to find one for your child, if you feel this concern.

Patricia Lemer of the Developmental Delay Resources has also reminded me that antimony trioxide used as a flame retardant in pajamas may not be good for sensitive kids. Lead is another heavy metal that is very toxic. It is discussed later in this chapter. It, too, causes problems like convergence insufficiency that affect learning and hurt the growing brain and nervous system, lowering the brain's potential for excellent school performance.

NONBIOMEDICAL TREATMENTS FOR THE VISION AND LEARNING PROBLEMS OF CHILDREN ON THE SPECTRUM

A lot of good people have worked on cures for the children on the spectrum. First, let us have a look at the nonbiomedical treatments, which have helped many children to be effectively mainstreamed in class-rooms. Children who have neurological problems from toxicity or injury can be rehabilitated. The four therapies that I recommend the most are vision therapy, applied behavioral analysis (ABA) therapy, neurotherapy, and homeopathy. This is not to say that I do not also refer out to MDs who work on the varied, individual biomedical problems of afflicted children if my patients are not already getting that type of care.

Vision Therapy Can Help Significantly One thing more parents of children on the spectrum need to know is that vision therapy can help. Every one of the spectrum children I have examined has had functional vision problems. These can be treated. If vision can be normalized, it will significantly help that child's rehabilitation. Children on the spectrum almost always have problems in the areas of light sensitivity, tracking, focusing, and converging the eyes in a coordinated manner for reading (as do many brain injury patients). Even more basic than those, they have difficulty just being aware of where they are in space and how to fixate on a target and aim their eyes where they want to look, so that they are not looking through people. These problems are manifested in behaviors like fear of heights, lack of correct judgments about depth in space, waving of the hands in front of the eyes, failure to look people in the eye, and inability to take part in reciprocal play.

Fixing these visual limitations is not the whole story of recovery, but as my patients' parents tell me, it is an important piece of putting their children's lives back together. It can be done in ways that allow the child to be treated passively as he plays, wearing training glasses, which children usually enjoy. One of the lens treatments uses a set of what are called "yoked prisms" with small powers, which move light in different directions. One pair moves the view to the right, one to the left, and one up and one down. This fascinates most children and stimulates the peripheral vision system, which is necessary for effective use of central vision and tracking.

There are also lens treatments with alternating low plus and low minus glasses. Later, children use aniso lenses, which are prescribed in pairs—in one pair, the right lens is plus and the left lens is minus, with the opposite being true in the other pair. Doctors John Streff and Amiel Francke explained these protocols for autism in two separate articles a long time ago, and optometrists have been using them ever since (Streff

1975; Francke 1975). The child is intrigued and pays attention to vision with these glasses on, exploring how things look with each eye. New visual brain processing happens. Practice in focusing happens. It is like a wakeup call to see differently.

Some spectrum children have damped down vision in order to emphasize hearing, because their senses are not integrated. Vision also needs to be strong and integrated or the child will continue with his ineffective visual behavior. If we do not move children ahead, they can deteriorate more and more each year in all areas, even if they were born functioning normally, before they regressed into autism.

Dr. Francke had such a case. The child was finally helped by orthomolecular psychiatry prescriptions of diet and vitamins (nutritional interventions for brain health). This modality was combined with passive vision therapy, including a series of low plus and minus lenses worn alternately in pairs, and then the aniso lenses (one eye plus, the other minus), while the patient performed a lot of visual gross motor, balance, and fine motor activities at home. The child was totally changed and able to attend a school for children with special needs. The regressive autism behaviors (in the 1970s they were much rarer and called schizophrenia symptoms or mental retardation signs) were gone, the mother reported, although Francke believed the child still did not have totally normal vision development, which required more work at home with the special aniso lenses and the gross motor activities. Nevertheless, the boy's whole mental, emotional, and behavioral status was radically changed.

Another treatment that is sometimes used to wake up peripheral awareness is to have the child wear glasses with one red filter and one green filter for activities that use white moving targets, such as cutouts of white paper clouds or birds. One family working with well-known behavioral optometrist Nancy Torgeson bought a large, fluffy white dog as one ever-present moving object (Torgeson and Frost 1998). Later, when the child is more visually aware, he can engage in balance activities with vision and a lot of other eye/hand visual activities, and then he can progress in more specific ways to get his two eyes to work together.

Many children with autism are strabismic, often with exotropia (one or both eyes drift out so converging the eyes is very difficult). It is interesting that after most brain injuries, patients have what is called "post trauma convergence insufficiency," a major reduction of peripheral vision, and trouble focusing—some of the same symptoms children with autism often exhibit. Dr. Melvin Kaplan's *Seeing through New Eyes*, a book about how vision therapy can change the lives of children on the spectrum, is a very important reading assignment for parents of afflicted children (2006).

Dr. Carol Marusich from Oregon uses yoked prisms and primitive reflex work (see chapter five) in her practice with children on the spectrum. There is a video that demonstrates her training available from the Optometric Extension Program (Marusich 2002).

Currently, I have a beautiful six-year-old patient who is very hyperactive and often inattentive, though obviously emotionally responsive and intelligent. He had seizures after the hepatitis B vaccine at birth, and later also after some other early shots. Besides some visual processing, tracking, and focusing difficulties, he had come with the beginning of a wandering eye, high hyperopia, high astigmatism in one eye, and amblyopia.

He also has major sleeping and eating problems, which is one of the symptoms of mercury poisoning. The nutritional protocols and the vision therapy can go a long way toward helping children like that six year old. So far, he is doing well in a school without rigid desk sitting required. His vision function is normalizing, and he is a good reader for his age.

Every one of the spectrum children I have worked with is a picky eater and many have light sensitivity and sleep problems. Some also have chronic bowel syndromes or kidney disease.

Neurotherapy   Neurotherapy has been used for a number of years with children on the autism spectrum. It is a good short-term treatment to investigate. There is more information on this therapy in chapter five. It is available in many cities and is being investigated in research studies at UCLA in California and Brown in Rhode Island. Many children in the Boston area who have ADD and ADHD diagnoses undergo neurotherapy.

The justification for neurotherapy is that we know in hyperactivity there is reduced brain activity in the premotor and superior prefrontal cortex (Hannaford 2005, 146). This reduced activity would be responsible, Hannaford explains, for symptoms of unfocused attention, lack of fine motor coordination, constant erratic movements initiated from adrenalin, and constant external unorganized chatter, which means that the inner speech that controls behavior is not operating.

Dr. Jolene Ross of the Advanced Neurotherapy Institute in Wellesley, Massachusetts, says that hyperactivity is the way a child increases the frequency of brain waves in the affected areas through his movements. Neurotherapy can train him to have more efficient brain waves in specific areas.

Ross emphasizes that the timing of all insults to the brain is very significant for what effects will be. This is because different parts of the brain develop at different times. Neurotherapy research is increasing tremendously in the kinds of injuries that happen in different parts of the developmental sequence. I believe that if this research could be connected with the inoculation decisions of the CDC, perhaps shot schedules might be less likely to cause harm in sensitive children.

ABA Therapy Combined with Movement   ABA therapy is considered the most effective developmental therapy for ASD (autism spectrum disorders) in young children (Sicile-Kira 2004, 94–99). It is often combined with diet therapy. This is not short-term therapy and it takes a lot of manpower, but it does succeed in actually developing an autistic child's ability to have normal behavior and responsiveness, so he can be mainstreamed into supported classrooms in a regular school.

Applied behavioral analysis therapy was developed by Dr. O. Ivar Lovaas at UCLA's Young Autism Project. He published a report in 1987 in which he told of nine children with autism diagnoses who were mainstreamed with the method. This was 47 percent of the group he treated.

I heard about Lovaas' therapy in the early 1990s because my daughter Amy, studying for an MA in dance and movement therapy in Chicago, had two part-time jobs as a Lovaas therapist. At the time, she suggested to the parents of her two students that combining movement therapy with ABA would be very effective with the children. The parents told her to pursue it. Both of the children she worked with were able to be mainstreamed in school, having started out with full autism diagnoses. Her monograph case study of one of the children, regarding the combination of Lovaas' and movement therapy, is available from wdainc1@yahoo.com (Kohler 1999).

In addition to the preschool therapy, she spent one year as the shadow teacher for that child in kindergarten.

HOMEOPATHY FOR CHILDREN WITH COMPROMISED BRAIN, VISION, AND HEALTH

There are also many effective homeopathic treatments. Chapter five includes a section on homeopathic support for children by a prominent Boston-area homeopath. An article by Amy L. Lansky, author of *Impossible Cure* (2004), explains how her son eliminated autistic symptoms with homeopathic remedies, in addition to the casein-free diet and some cranial osteopathic treatments (2006). The big changes happened after nine months of homeopathic treatment.

After a year and a half, the boy tested above grade level in school. He seemed totally normal to all but his parents, who said he was 80 percent cured. "The remaining 20 percent took another four or five years," during which he transitioned to new remedies until by fourth grade, no one could have ever discovered that he had been autistic. Lansky's book is highly recommended by the chapter five homeopath.

AUTISM AND ITS TREATMENTS ARE HOT TOPICS WITH ONE IN EVERY 166 (OR 150 BY LATEST CDC COUNT) KIDS AFFLICTED IN THE UNITED STATES

The issue of *Mothering* magazine containing Lansky's story was totally devoted to autism spectrum cures (January/February 2006). There are articles on the shot theory, recipes without wheat or milk, information about chelation and other biomedical treatments, and an overview of the most promising treatments including vitamins, diet, and ABA therapy. Autism is no longer a topic that is out of the mainstream. It is a mainstream problem and will continue to be a major educational challenge for our society, as one out of every 166 children in a generation move through their lives. An early 2007 CDC report (2007) recalculated the occurrence as one in every 150. In a report on "Autism in America," published in *Child*, the current epidemic was compared to the polio epidemic of the 1940s and 1950s (Mayor 2005).

BIOMEDICAL TREATMENTS FOR AUTISM: CHELATION, NUTRITION, AND SPECIAL DIETS ARE ALL OPTIONS

If you have a child with regressive autism (develops between eighteen months and three years) it could be from toxic metal poisoning, possibly from the shots. Chelation of the toxic metals out of your child's body with the help of an expert medical doctor may be the best way to give that child a second chance at life. If you are going to do chelation, it is better to do it sooner rather than later, and there will be many lab tests necessary. You may need to have that child on a special diet long before the chelation treatment begins. The book you want to read is *Children with Starving Brains: A Medical Treatment Guide for Autism Spectrum Disorder*, by Jaquelyn McCandless, MD (2002).

Dr. McCandless limits her practice to the 1 in 150 or 166 (based on different CDC statistics) children who suffer from autism and those other children on the autism spectrum who have other neurological damage, learning and speech problems, and attention deficit and hyperactivity. She does chelation to eliminate the heavy metals and their continuing toxic effects. She sees enough good results to spend her life doing this, and the patients keep coming.

Most children with autism, according to the folks who are actually working to treat these disorders, have an impaired ability to eliminate or sequester toxic substances in their bodies. This could be due to genetic weakness, or it could be the result of possible early immune injury and intestinal pathologies, which affect nutritional status and immune function. What chelation does is bind the heavy metals, and then, with the help of vitamin C and other factors, it flushes them out of the body (McCandless 2002).

There is one diet that, if used, has the best chance of working for many of the kids on the autism spectrum according to the books on the subject, the parents I have spoken with, and the speakers I heard at the DAN! (Defeat Autism Now!) conference in spring of 2005 in Boston. It is McCandless's prerequisite for patients who want to do chelation therapy. Sometimes the diet and vitamins work without chelation.

FAMILIES AND SCHOOLS NEED TO KNOW ABOUT THE DIET THAT HELPS SPECTRUM CHILDREN

This diet is called the GF/CF diet. This stands for gluten free/casein free, which means wheat and other gluten grains (rye, corn, oats) free and dairy free. What these substances do is irritate children who have compromised immune systems by causing an overproduction of cytokines that produce inflammation. Dr. McCandless (2002, 255) believes that this diet is especially important for the children who received the hepatitis B shots as newborns, "very likely triggering the processes of (beyond genetic) immune impairment, very early gut injury, increased infections, antibiotic use, yeast overgrowth (Wunderlich, 1998). and 'leaky gut.'"

Chelation works better if "the gut" is in its very best possible condition, according to Dr. McCandless. That involves a special diet that is casein (dairy) free and gluten free. Eliminating the milk products, part of the GF/CF plan, has been the second most effective biological treatment for autism, according to a small parent survey. The third most effective treatment according to the survey was eliminating chocolate! The first, of course, was chelation (Pangborn and Baker 2005, 10).

In the spring of 2005, I had the opportunity to attend the DAN! Conference in Boston run by the Autism Research Association. I met one of my best former optometry students there. She was staying home with her little boy with autism, and she had put him on the GF/CF diet, which, she said, really changed his behavior and ability to function. If he went off for a taste of bagels and cream cheese, he was sick again. The good news about these diets is that a lot of children who are not on the spectrum also have sensitivities to these foods, and the marketplace is providing more and more things for them to eat, including gluten-free pancake mixes and breads. One brand called Pamela's baking mix is available from Amazon.com in eight cartons. This type of mix is the only way my family can feel good and able to concentrate after eating pancakes.

The manual cited above, *Autism: Effective Biomedical Treatments* by Jon Pangborn, PhD, and Sidney MacDonald Baker, MD, went through several printings leading up to the comprehensive manual ready for the DAN! Conference in April of 2005. These books and a number of others available on the DAN! website have been helping spectrum kids when no doctors in their area could. Now there is a list of "DAN! doctors" who can guide parents through the dietary and biomedical treatments that might be needed for their children (Autism Research Institute 2005).

There is a new approach to enhancing nutrition for children who cannot eat a healthy diet or swallow pills. It uses transdermal creams that allow complete absorption of nutrients through the soles of the feet (*Developmental Delay Resources* 2006).

TOXINS IN THE FOOD AND WATER SUPPLY?

Inoculations and their toxic risks can now be questioned, controlled, and timed by the parent, if a compatible pediatrician or family doctor can be found. Lead can be avoided. Most other environmental toxins cannot. However, the food and drink we allow into our homes is truly all up to us.

Toxins in food and drink come in the form of pesticides on produce and grains, nitrates and hormones in meats, food dyes, additives like MSG, hidden sugars or fake sugars, trans fats, preservatives in packaged foods, lead in the water supply, and mercury in fish. Some adults can eat anything and maintain high functioning brains and high energy. These things affect some children less than others, just as the shots did.

Sometimes parents who are unfazed will have children who are supersensitive. Their development will be hurt unless the parents can provide for them. When fewer packaged snack foods and sodas are allowed in the budget, there is more money for more organic and fresh produce. It is probably true that all children's brains (and that includes the retina of the eye and the entire visual system that connects with every major part of the brain) function better without many chemicals and additives.

When children are having problems with learning and come to me with their parents to assess their vision, I almost always hear that they are picky eaters, have a terrific sweet tooth, or both. The family does use a lot of packaged snacks and desserts. Eliminating these takes work.

The unfortunate fact is that we may have the best of intentions, but fresh, organic food is more expensive and harder to find. Whole Foods, Trader Joe's, Stop and Shop, Wild Harvest, or independent health food supermarkets are not in every neighborhood or city. Busy families do not always have the extra money or travel time to get to the places that have the organic meats and produce.

Consider for a moment the problem of just milk, which older generations of Americans grew tall on. If it is not organic now, the issue is hormones in the cows, not just dioxin in the grasses they feed upon. Since 1993, the FDA has allowed recombinant bovine somatotrophin (rbst) to be given to cows to increase milk production. This raises the level of IGF-1 hormones in the milk supply. Although it is a necessary hormone in normal amounts, it has been linked to breast cancer, bone cancer in children, and colon and lung cancer (Landrigan, Needleman, and Landrigan 2001). Organic-certified unpasturized milk is not available in some states, even from the famed Alta Dena-certified dairy in California.

Skim milk is the best way to go if one is using the traditional milk supply, because many toxins—specifically dioxin—are stored in milk fat. However, children need good fat for healthy brain development, so doctors do not always want them on skim milk. They reason that there is also dioxin in breast milk, but they want children breast-fed for a year at least because of the other benefits for bonding, brain development, and immune system support.

I often wonder if the big problem with dairy and wheat for growing children is not really the natural item itself, but what has been laid upon it by pollution sifting into the food chain and added chemicals in our farming, preserving, and selling processes.

I read of a lengthy soaking process years ago in a book by Dr. Bircher-Benner from his famous clinic in Switzerland (Bircher-Benner 1977). This may not really get rid of all the pesticides, but every bit helps when a child's health is at stake. Some produce, such as green beans, apples, grapes, peaches, pears, spinach, and winter squash, are the ones that should be bought organic or avoided, according to Landrigan, Needleman, and Landrigan (2001). Even small amounts of pesticides can affect brain development and hormone function in children. I'li remember that when I am serving meals to my grandchildren.

THE ADD AND ADHD DIETS THAT ELIMINATE TOXINS AND SUGARS MAY HELP CHILDREN FOCUS BETTER

ADD and ADHD children often have trouble focusing on school work and tracking, which is why optometrists care about what these therapy patients eat if it turns out that they have food allergies and sensitivities to preservative chemicals, colorings, flavorings, and sugar. A trial diet sometimes clears up many visual problems. Long ago, one of my daughters was prescribed a special diet with a variety of supplements by the brilliant biochemical geneticist, Dr. Mary B. Allen. Her chronic chest congestion, functional vision problems, and cranky disposition all disappeared. That was before the age of shots and the spectrum. Dr. Allen treated the Krebs cycle in the mitochondrian of the cell to produce more energy for healing, seeing, and smiling (Allen 1976).

Not all children with ADD and ADHD are mercury sensitive from shots, though clearly some may be. They could have had many things go wrong: a birth trauma, a temporary reduction of oxygen at birth, a serious illness with high fever, anesthesia during the birth process or an early surgery, or a cesarean section that prevents infant reflexes from being stimulated in the birth canal (see chapter five). They might have had a fall off the diaper changing table, down a stair, or off a swing, leaving their cranial sacral balance of cerebral spinal fluid flow less efficient, and circulation to the brain worse on one side or another.

A hit on the head can also cause shearing of learned connections (see chapter five). Premature birth, seizures after shots or with high fevers, poor child training by parents or caretakers, poor nutrition in utero and after, medications necessary for allergies or asthma, and excessive sugar eating are other aggravating factors (Armstrong 1995).

There are many books on nutrition and diets for children with attention deficit and hyperactivity problems. A good look at the different possible protocols is found in *The ADD and ADHD Diet*, by Rachel Bell and Dr. Howard Peiper (1997). This book is a useful manual for parents wanting to change a family lifestyle to help their child with the overwhelming problems of inattention. Allergies are a big part of what needs to be controlled—both to foods and to pollen in the air. Paying attention to the acid alkaline balance of foods is also a useful tool for helping children with ADD or ADHD. The Akai water purifier can be used to set the correct alkaline balance for pure, filtered drinking water.

Many of these ADD and ADHD children have candida overgrowth from frequent antibiotics, so certain nutrients are needed as well as a careful elimination of foods that candida thrive on. Candida thrives on sugars. All of the above can cause children to be less attentive, to have vision tracking problems, and to perhaps need increased nutritional support. Glasses and vision therapy will help them focus, track, and converge their eyes better, which really enhances their ability to attend to desk work and classroom discussion.

WONDERS CAN BE WORKED WITH PROPER NUTRITION, EXERCISE, AND VISION THERAPY

In a book called *The Myth of the ADD Child: 50 Ways to Improve Your Child's Behavior and Attention Span without Drugs, Labels, or Coercion* by Thomas Armstrong, PhD (1995), six of the fifty ways to help the child involved diet and exercise. Florida Pediatrician Ray C. Wunderlich Jr. has written some helpful books on nutrition for kids (Wunderlich and Kalita 1984), one of which is still available online, regarding treatment of the candida problem in the intestines that many of the spectrum children suffer (Wunderlich 1998). He also wrote a book for optometrists and others recommending behavioral optometry treatment for children's learning problems (Wunderlich 1991).

PARENTS AND SCHOOLS MAY WISH TO CONSIDER THE ARMSTRONG DIETARY RULES TO CUT DOWN ON ADHD TRIGGERS

Rule Number One from Dr. Armstrong

All children, not just ADD children, need protein at breakfast, not high carbs. His suggestions include a bean burrito, scrambled eggs, boiled egg, oatmeal with nuts and raisins, potatoes with eggs, pancakes without syrup but with yogurt, and so on. Baking mixes without wheat or gluten can be used for all pancakes, muffins, and waffles. He says

> It turns out that the effects of a sugar-laden high-carbohydrate breakfast of sweet rolls, or syrupy pancakes, or waffles dripping with jam, or even toast and butter, are particularly fierce on some biologically sensitive kids with attention and/or behavior problems. (Armstrong 1995, 68)

Armstrong cites research done at George Washington University School of Medicine in Washington, D.C., to prove his point. The hyperactive and nonhyperactive kids were given either two slices of white toast and butter or two scrambled eggs, and on alternate days, a nonnutritive drink sweetened with aspartame or sucrose. Armstrong notes, "The hyperactive kids who ate the high-carb breakfast and the sweet drink did more poorly on attention measures than any group. They also had the highest blood sugar values. However, if they had the high-protein egg meal and the sugar drink, they did better than all the others."

Rule Number Two

Rule number two is to "Eliminate foods with artificial flavorings, colorings, preservatives, dyes, and other additives, and foods with natural 'salicylates' like oranges, apples, apricots, berries, and grapes." The hyperactive child is not necessarily allergic to these foods, but there is a chemical sensitivity to them. A number of people have told me that their child progressed with leaps and bounds once these foods were eliminated. This is called the Feingold diet, developed by Dr. Ben Feingold, an allergist from San Francisco. To eliminate preservatives and additives is a huge task. It would seem that one should always cut down radically on the amount of preserved and chemically enhanced foods, but to eliminate all of these things takes a commitment of the whole family. The nice thing about better, less-toxic nutrition is that it can treat many systems simultaneously: concentration, skin, eyes, and overall health. It gets the energy needed for particular systems to run well to the places where it can be used.

Rule Number Three

Remove allergens. A 1985 *Lancet* study (Armstrong 1995) reported that hyperactive children who were fed a simple diet without colorings and preservatives did well. When these were added, they were hyperactive again. Certain foods were also problematic. The major offenders were "soya, cow's milk, chocolate, grapes, wheat, oranges, cow's milk cheese, chicken eggs, peanuts, maize, fish, oats, melons, tomatoes, and ham." Some children with ADD are suffering from allergies to many things. The symptoms of the allergies include irritability, hyperactivity, fatigue, inability to concentrate, stuffy nose, dark circles under the eyes, puffiness around the eyes, abdominal pain, and headaches."

SOME VISUAL PROBLEMS ARE MISDIAGNOSED AS ADHD

Some learning-related vision problems are caused by dietary toxicity, but others can exist in the child with the perfect diet. It is important that we do not put all our eggs in one curing basket when we have a hyperactive child with ADD. Many optometric studies have shown that visual skills problems like poor focus, tracking, and convergence are often misdiagnosed as ADHD (Damari, Liu, and Smith 2000; Farrar, Call, and Maples 2001).

FEEDING MOTHERS AND CHILDREN MORE SAFELY

Here is a quick thumbnail list of how to feed children and mothers more safely for eyes, body, and health—and this includes school snacks and lunches.

- **Avoid "trans fats."** These are saturated fats created by processing, not found in nature. They may be called hydrogenated fats. Only a few margarine brands are without transfats. Instead of margarine, I blend up three cups olive oil with one pound of organic butter. It spreads thinly and tastes delicious.

- **Forgo snacks or carry your own.** Fill baggies with raisins and walnuts or almonds, seeds, and dried fruit, or organic vegetable sticks, if there are allergies to nuts. Many packaged goods are loaded with trans fats, which is one more reason for not buying packaged desserts and snacks filled with chemicals. Some products still have indigestible, fake fat that can cause intestinal upsets.
- **Avoid processed meats with nitrates.** Try for naturally smoked or nitrate-free processed meats. Processed food with nitrates can become carcinogenic when cooked because the nitrates are converted to the toxic nitrites (Landrigan, Needleman, and Landrigan 2001). Using organic meat or game meat is the best way to live if you are a meat eater.
- **Avoid peanut butter, for younger than three year olds and pregnant women.** It may trigger allergies when children are older. Most schools do not allow peanut butter sandwiches to be brought to school any longer, and eating peanuts for kids is no longer without risks of anaphylactic shock from allergy. There is a mold that can contaminate peanuts, but according to Doctors Landrigan and Needleman, in their book *Raising Healthy Children in a Toxic World* (2001), the aflatoxin produced by *Aspergillus flavus* mold is carefully screened out of Jif, Skippy, Peter Pan, Smuckers, and Arrowhead Mills peanut butters.
- **Buy fish carefully.** They should be bought from places without mercury, PCBs (polychlorinated biphenyls) and dioxins, or years-old chlorinated hydrocarbons from the long-banned DDT and chlordane in the water contaminating the fish. Wild fish from the Northwest rather than raised fish or the fish from the Great Lakes and the Hudson River are less likely to be toxic. Little fish, not the big fish at the top of the food chain, are less likely to be toxic (Landrigan, Needleman, and Landrigan 2001). Check the greenguide.com for a wallet guide on which fish are good to eat. Avoid eating the skin and fatty layers of fish, which hold the toxins. You can also check www.waterkeeper.org, the website of the Waterkeeper Alliance, or the state or local health department for a listing of contaminated areas and guidelines for safe fish.

The PCBs (banned in the 1970s) and the mercury still coming into the inland waterways are very real problems for freshwater fish. That is because of "1,100 coal-burning power plants that spew roughly 50 tons of mercury into the air," which poisons our lakes, rivers, and streams. These are antiquated power plants. The EPA (Environmental Protection Agency) put out the information that "one in every six women of childbearing age now has unsafe mercury levels in her flesh, organs, blood and breast milk, putting more that 630,000 American children born each year at high risk" for lower IQs, neurological damage, kidney damage, liver failure, fatal heart disease, aggressive behavior, autism, dyslexia, and blindness. Most tuna now exceeds the accepted level of mercury. The waterkeeper's newsletter has an interesting piece of information regarding how "absurdly poisonous" mercury really is: "A single teaspoon can poison a 50-acre lake so that its fish cannot be safely eaten" (Waterkeeper Alliance n.d.). What will the grandchildren and the great grandchildren eat?

- **Reduce white wheat flour and sugar intake.** Joan Ifland's book, *Sugars and Flours: How They Make Us Crazy, Sick and Fat and What to Do about It*, has helped numbers of my patients (Ifland 2000). The book includes useful recipes and lists for emergency supplies to store in the cupboard or freezer to help avoid the bad snacks consumed when there is too much hunger to wait for dinner to be cooked. The mother who wrote the book said her doctor's diet cured all her children of their so-called learning disabilities and herself of an overweight problem. Patients of mine have told me it changed their lives, too. One woman said she used to be exhausted by dinnertime and now she was going strong at 10:00 p.m.

  Refined sugars and flours are dangerous to the pancreas in our modern world of epidemic diabetes, with even Type II being found among children, which used to be an elderly person's disease. Children need an even amount of energy and blood sugar, not sugar highs and then big drop-offs in energy after the pancreas has been overstimulated. Most of the children I see with learning problems have a problem with craving sugar. They believe they are not eating sugar, but they get donuts, Pop Tarts, or sugared cereal and half a quart of orange juice for breakfast, cookies for a school mid-morning snack, desserts every night after dinner, a dessert and more juice at school for lunch, cookies after school, and candy as a treat for energy if there are after-school sports. This does not even count the sugars in canned foods that the school lunches have used, or the high-carb load of potatoes and carrots, which are the vegetables that most children will eat.

Children Need Sufficient Protein to Protect Their Energy Metabolism for Eye Work in School, the Growth of Their Bodies, and Their Brain Development

The other problem with sugars is that they are high in calories and cannot substitute for the needed protein that every child must have to make the enzymes daily that run energy metabolism in the mitochondrian of living cells. It is enzymes, along with vitamins and coenzymes, that will determine if he has the energy for study, good vision, sports, health, and being kind. Protein also provides the building blocks for body and brain growth.

Children who do not get sufficient protein cannot absorb enough water to keep their brain supplied (Hannaford 2005, 157), and research shows that they have limited brain growth also (Shinaur 1975).

More than a few parents have told me that orange juice for breakfast gives their child the protein he needs along with his sugared cereal or toasted pastry. They may be confusing the idea of protein with calcium added to some juices. Orange juice is not a protein food. Eggs, meat, poultry, milk, kefir, yogurt, fish, tofu, cheese, beans, chick peas, and nuts are protein foods. Sometimes one has to resort to protein shakes made with protein supplement powder stirred into juice if children are picky eaters or absolute vegetarians.

Dr. Richard Kavner is a Manhattan behavioral optometrist whose book, *Your Child's Vision*, includes a chapter on how to feed children best for sight (1985, 148–171). He states that children need 2 grams of protein for every 2.2 pounds of body weight (153). That is roughly double what adults need per pound of body weight. Pregnant women, though, are supposed to have 70 grams of protein minimum (Hannaford 2005). Up to 90 grams is good. Children need a high-protein breakfast because the morning is when most of the work gets done in school. A high-sugar breakfast will not deliver even amounts of energy through the morning, and so the eyes will become fatigued and less efficient visual processing will result.

Carefully Guard against Lead Poisoning

More parents know more about the problems of lead than mercury. Lead is a brain toxin and also causes functional vision problems such as an inability to properly converge the eyes. That is why it was removed from gasoline and paint—to save us all from extreme lead levels. They used to be high in all Americans, as much as 18–20 ug/dl in the blood. With the removal of lead from paint and gasoline, the levels dropped to 2.8 ug/dl. However, some children are showing up to 10 ug/dls in their blood tests, and this is now known to cause learning problems (Landrigan, Needleman, and Landrigan 2001).

So you bought a house with the lead removed and you are thinking you are risk free. That is not the case. The lead pipes carrying water through your home could still be contaminating your drinking water. Lead in the water from lead pipes in the home or the city water mains is a problem, unless you can find a filtering system that screens it out or you buy bottled water. I know obstetricians that require their patients to begin drinking bottled water long before they are trying to become pregnant.

The Massachusetts Water Resources Authority found some homes with lead levels that exceeded federal standards—4,500 homes to be exact (*The Boston Globe* 2005). The Conservation Law Foundation has also listed homes with lead pipes and brass plumbing fixtures that contain lead that still need to be tested. The best prevention from lead contamination is to install copper pipes, but when that is not possible, you can run the cold water for a few minutes. This will free the pipes of water that is sitting there collecting lead, so you will have a better chance of getting a pure glass of water from the city. Most cities do have lead-free water.

I find fascinating the theory that the fall of Rome resulted from what was considered then to be an engineering advance. The old stone aqueducts were lined with lead. At the same time people were drinking the poisoned water, they also used lead as a sweetener in wine! Such small events for the fate of whole civilizations to turn on (Landrigan, Needleman, and Landrigan 2001)!

Now your pipes are free of lead or you have put a lead filter on your faucets to protect you from the city's input pipes. Your kids are not getting any mercury-laced shots. You think you are safe now? Not yet. The earlier lead removed from paint and gasoline still lurks in some of the soils around your house where you might want to plant a vegetable garden.

I was shocked to learn that the land in front of my renovated, circa 1880s condo building is off limits to children, because the soil is so heavily laden with lead. There is a wrought-iron fence enclosing the front yard that they cannot climb and, thankfully, a preferable park next door. When the condo association planted tulip bulbs there last fall, we were all advised to wear heavy rubberized gloves so as not to absorb it through our skin or under our fingernails. Have your yard tested before you ever let a child dig in the dirt there.

When author Herbert L. Needleman, MD, was a researcher at Harvard Medical School, he did a study of the lead found in children's baby teeth from the towns of Somerville and Chelsea, Massachusetts. These children were followed for IQ, attention, and language development, and 10 years later, half of them were found and questioned about high school graduation and reading disabilities. The higher the lead originally found in their baby teeth, the worse the problems. Kids with high lead were seven times more likely not to graduate from high school and six times more likely to have a reading problem. Juvenile delinquents in one study had more lead in the blood than the normal person (Landrigan, Needleman, and Landrigan 2001).

Kids that I see with a history of lead poisoning have functional vision problems, such as difficulty converging the eyes at near. This also interferes with learning. Testing houses and kids for lead is a smart move, it seems. Testing their eyes is also a smart move because functional vision can be improved with glasses and/or vision exercises.

A purification system to get rid of lead and chlorine is produced by the Japanese company Akai. It also eliminates bacteria and viruses. I have one sitting on the sink in my home, attached to an extra cold water faucet, which I had installed. The water tastes very good. Prior to having this system, I had water delivered in five-gallon containers from a mountain spring. This is the only way anyone in our household drank enough water. I believe that without good water, we instinctively did not want much of it. This may be why some children will not drink water instead of juice and soda.

At a school in which I ran a vision clinic, bottled water was brought into the school. All fountains were turned off, and each teacher would get water from the central office and dole it out in small paper cups when the children were thirsty. They were doing their best to prevent lead poisoning from the ancient water pipes in the school building and the city, which the taxpayers would not pay to replace. Schools are supposed to test their water and do something to fix the problem if it is filled with lead.

ENVIRONMENTAL TOXINS

Something in the Air May Be Toxic

Many toxins are those carried in the air from both inside and outside allergens and pollutants. The worst source is cigarette smoke. Children raised with second-hand smoke are much more prone to have upper respiratory infections. Also, there has been some evidence that it causes convergence problems with the eyes. All pregnant women know now that they should not smoke or be exposed to second-hand smoke. (Women who smoke while pregnant give birth to babies with low birth weights and IQs that are an average of nine points lower than babies born to nonsmokers.) Second-hand smoke has also just recently been found to be correlated with breast cancer. That is the number one air pollutant that should be eliminated in the house. According to a 1994 article in *Pediatrics*, cigarette smoke contains 2,000 to 4,000 chemicals. These could damage developing nerve cells in young children (Hannaford 2005, 159).

ADD AND ADHD CAN START WITH CHEMICALS THAT DERANGE THE ABILITY TO DIGEST FOOD, CAUSING FURTHER ILLNESS FROM MALNUTRITION

Chemical sensitivities and outright environmental poisoning are not found only in children on the autism spectrum. Our environment is becoming increasingly toxic, and pathogens move about the earth freely in people who travel far and wide. Some of the worst toxicity could be right in your own back yard. The following is the story of one of my patients, a middle-aged woman with a husband and daughter.

A woman who had been a vision therapy patient of mine off and on over a number of years started in 2002 to have major problems with her health, which increasingly worsened. She is a health care provider and one of the smartest people I know. Neither she, nor I, nor any of her doctors could figure out why she was having all these symptoms. These were increasing allergies, which included swollen eyes and intolerance to contact lenses and contact lens solutions, red rashes, and trouble sustaining attention when she had never had this before. Indeed, she had been a voracious reader. She also had digestive problems, a buildup of ascites (fluid in her abdomen), diarrhea, and so on. She dropped out of vision therapy a few years back because she had so many other worries.

It had crossed my mind that perhaps she was snacking on all the wrong foods and denying it, and had some intestinal parasite that she had picked up on her travels to various foreign lands. She did all those workups, though, and continued to get worse. Recently, we touched base again and she told me her furnace-poisoning saga. In the summer of 2002, a new furnace was installed in her rental house. It was a high-compression model that supposedly did not need to be vented up a chimney, but could go out the side wall of the house. This one was vented between her kitchen and her bedroom windows. She wondered why she was always sicker on the weekends. During the week she did not hang out in the kitchen or her bedroom.

She felt those years of 2002 to 2005 that she was allergic to winter. Things did get better in the spring, but all winter she would have a bad "intestinal bug," increasingly serious asthma, rashes, and the feeling that she had trouble concentrating. Then summer would come and she would spend time on Cape Cod at her mother's house, or travel to distant places. By Thanksgiving, she would be sick again and struggle through another winter.

However, in the winter of 2005–2006, things got totally out of hand. Every year she was a little bit worse, but by Thanksgiving 2005 she could eat only vegetables, but no nightshades (tomatoes, peppers, eggplant, and potatoes). She went to a nutritionist and got supplements to keep her going, but for Thanksgiving and Christmas dinner, all she could eat was squash, beets, carrots, green beans, salad, and a spirulina drink. She could not eat any grains or typical protein foods like eggs, meat, fish, cheese, or nuts. If she did, her eyes swelled up and the lids felt too tight. She had three or four "drop to the knees" asthma attacks each day and wake-up attacks every night. She had rashes all over her body if she ate any grains or protein foods, and frequent diarrhea. She had become so sensitive the previous year to her contact lenses and her plastic glasses that she went out without telling me and had her eyes lasered.

This was a woman sensitized by something. She tried to figure out what, and then remembered repeated calls to her landlord about the funny smell outside her windows over several winters. She smelled it again. She finally called in an environmental specialist who held up his meter near her bedroom window, and then to her kitchen window inside her house. She was being exposed, whenever the furnace was on, to high amounts of carbon monoxide, and the gases from nitric oxide, and formaldehyde, among other things. Her landlord has since put the furnace flue up a chimney and replaced all her carpets with wool because she is sensitized to chemicals in building products as well as all of those good foods that she needed.

When autism spectrum children, who may have been sensitized by mercury at early ages, have symptoms, they often have the same inability to eat normal food. They shun protein, they get intestinal candida overgrowth, rashes, diarrhea, and all the mental and physical symptoms that go with major gut imbalances

What these poisoning experiences do to people is sensitize them to all the other little toxic things that abound in our modern air, water, building materials, and foods. Medicine calls them universal reactors. My patient became a canary in the cage of a house with an experiment in the safety of new style furnaces that supposedly did not need chimney vents. She wrote a lot of letters. The state of Massachusetts has just ordered all managed buildings to have carbon monoxide detectors near every bedroom.

Several months ago I saw another patient with a different furnace story. The new forced air heating ducts were not metal but soft and gave off formaldehyde and other toxins. She was sick most of the winter whenever that furnace was on.

It is important that all of us parents and grandparents keep a wise eye out for these problems in all of our children and a wise mind in figuring out how to feed the suffering kids. They will not get well if we fail to give them the nutrients they need for their "starving brains." If children are born vegetarians and refuse meat and dairy, we need to provide for them. One of the best books I know for vegetarian eating is *Rainbow Green Live Food Cuisine* by Gabriel Cousens and the Tree of Life Chefs (2003).

We also need to remember that for most children, excellent nutrition free of toxins and allergens will be the major insurance policy against illness and visual learning problems.

PROBLEMS WITH PERFUME?

The last time I was at my holistic dentist's office, I picked up a pamphlet called "The Hidden Dangers of Fragrances," printed by the Environmental Health Coalition of Western Massachusetts. I was glad to see it because I have always been unable to wear perfume or to be around it. I was feeling justified looking at the title. I opened it up and there was a picture of the car freshener that I inherited with the second-hand Toyota that I bought a year ago. I never smelled anything, so I didn't take it down. Now it is on the list of those things that are regularly "coating nasal passages with nerve-deadening agents and impairing our sense of smell."

Additionally, according to the EPA, exposure to fragrances is associated with the following health problems. Those in bold are the ones that are reported frequently on optometry case histories: **asthma** and reactive airway disease attacks, **fatigue, eye irritation, sinusitis,** rhinitis, skin problems, dermatitis, kidney and **liver damage, chronic illness,** nausea, vomiting, abdominal pain, **blood pressure changes,** cancer, death from respiratory failure, and major effects on the nervous system, such as **headaches/migraines, depression, dizziness, irritability, confusion, panic attacks, anxiety, memory loss, impaired concentration, drowsiness, insomnia, impaired vision, spaciness, twitching muscles,** and **loss of muscle coordination.** Each of these is a symptom that may occur in individual patients seeking help with their vision problems. Unfortunately, people rarely realize that these symptoms could be related to sweet-smelling poisons in the air or, for that matter, the nonsweet smelling poisons in food, paints, and cleaning supplies. The town of Shutesbury, Massachusetts, now bans fragrances at town meetings. A number of doctors post a ban in their offices for new patients to see because no fragrance has been approved for chemical content.

The more you can prevent toxic chemicals, allergens, and pollution from entering your child's personal space, the healthier she or he will be in every way. We have now an epidemic of children's asthma, and we know that 72 percent of asthmatics have bad reactions to—of all things—*perfume*, not to mention all the other pollutants in the atmosphere. Asthma rates are up 40 percent in the past 15 years. The CDC reports that nine million children under 18 have an asthma diagnosis.

When I ran a vision clinic in an inner-city Boston school, I noticed that one of the major jobs of the school nurse was to bring asthma medication around to the children each morning. It took her a couple of hours because of the number of children. Many of the children who were doing vision therapy with us also had asthma, and in my private practice, many more children have asthma than would be expected. That health problem often seems to co-exist with visual problems that are related to learning, perhaps simply because the medications that are required often have some visual function side effects, especially relating to focus and convergence of eyes during close-up activities like school work. Likely also, the energy for efficient vision is diminished when a child has a breathing problem or is worrying about one.

I might not have become so conscious of these things if I did not see a number of patients with environmental sensitivity syndromes coupled with visual fatigue problems. They are the canaries in the coal mines of our modern lives, and it is very hard for them to get well. My oldest daughter is one of those canaries who has recovered and has the strong body of a professional dancer. However, for a number of years she was quite ill, though somehow she kept going and we had no idea how sick she was because we were half a continent apart. I sent her to a number of specialists. No one could find anything wrong, except one doctor who said it had to be some kind of environmental poison. I flew to Chicago, where she was a dancer and graduate student living in a single room with a gas hot plate and refrigerator. I was looking for toxicity.

Graciously, she gave me her bed for my stay, which was right along-side an old white dresser that she had bought secondhand. She had had it for several years in another apartment where the owner sprayed regularly for roaches, whether or not they were there. I felt very ill by the next morning and told her never to sleep without her windows open. I was sure it was a gas leak. There was a very funny smell in her apartment. No one had sprayed for bugs, though, she said. She could not smell a thing because she was always "stuffed up." I took all moth repellents out of her closet and told her not to use any aerosol sprays. I insisted she call the gas company the next week, but there was no leak in the entire building, she reported. I gave up and sent her vitamins.

It was not until a few years later when she married and moved her white wooden dresser into her husband's apartment that the problem was solved. He also had a nose and could smell the old bug spray from her first apartment, which was all over the inside of her dresser, including all the cases of music tapes in one of her drawers. The exterminator contracted by the owner to do regular work in that apartment building had sprayed inside of my daughter's drawers, and likely all over her clothes, and she never smelled it because of her stuffy nose. That dresser was removed from her life. She was lucky to find an excellent nutritionist who put her on a radical health food program with vitamins and got her well. She is still sensitive, though, and needs to keep her environment clean. She moved from Chicago to Asheville, North Carolina, partly for fresh air.

Eveyday Chemicals May Hurt More than They Help

That pristine green lawn, which should be a great place for a romp with the toddlers, may not be the place for that. Grass treated with pesticides and weed killers is not a safe place for children to play. Have a scruffy lawn and healthy kids? Or maybe if you just get grass seed it will be safe? No—look out. Many seeds are treated with mercury. I couldn't believe this. I learned that it is very common that seeds carry fungicides, and many of these are mercury based (Landrigan, Needleman, and Landrigan 2001). The Toxics Action Center of Boston found that 17 of 32 pesticides typically used by a large chemical lawn improvement company were potential or likely carcinogens, so they have taken the step to boycott the company (Toxics Action Center Member Update 2005).

Mildew-resistant paints sound like a good idea for the bathroom and kitchen. But look again. Mercury is the mildew protector (Landrigan, Needleman, and Landrigan 2001). Many cleaners, dishwashing soaps, laundry detergents, waxes, and polishes leave residues that, over time, add up to significant toxicity for children on the floor, touching everything. There are companies that make environmentally friendly household products. With sensitive children around and the future of the planet in mind, we might all benefit from looking for these in the health food stores and special sections of supermarkets or contacting one of the companies that sells them.

Instead of bug sprays and mothballs, there are wonderful products with moth pheromones as the lure that attract the pests into a triangular tunnel interiorly coated with thin, nontoxic glue. They truly save our clothes and our kitchen food storage without poisoning the air or surfaces of our home. The brand I found, called Safer, was sold in the local hardware store. The single-best thing one can do, though, to keep children safe from the spread of disease and toxins is to teach kids and caregivers to wash their hands, even after playing on the floor, playing outdoors, or playing with a pet. Then wash the toys, too. Also wash everyone's hands before washing the vegetables and fruits. Toxic chemical dust will then not be ingested, and colds will be fewer and farther between (Landrigan, Needleman, and Landrigan 2001). Wash hands for as long as it takes to sing one verse of "Happy Birthday" to be sure they are clean.

What Are Electromagnetic Fields and Why Protect against Some of Them?

There is one final area of unseen, stealthy pollution that I only recently became quite conscious of when a good friend had to move out of the greater Boston area because of a particular stress on her system. This is the silent, invisible pollution of electromagnetic fields.

Recently, a parent of a hyperactive patient on the autism spectrum called me up to see what I thought about the problem of high-tension wires right next to a house she and her husband had seen with a realtor. He felt it would be bad for their child. I told her to err on the side of caution and read the interesting book by Dr. Glen Swartwout called

Electromagnetic Pollution Solutions (1991). Complete protection from electromagnetic fields (EMFs) is probably not possible anymore in the cities, but things can be done to minimize the stresses on the child's developing body and brain from the things we bring into our homes. The fact is that in the last 20 years, the electromagnetic fields in the home have increased with each new appliance: VCRs, computers, printers, home xerox machines, extra TVs, microwaves, DVD players, tape recorders, cell phones, digital alarm clocks, battery-operated watches, touch-on lights, air conditioning, heating pads, electric blankets, and so on. These produce EMFs.

What are EMFs? These are low-frequency electromagnetic fields. Our bodies also produce these because there has to be polarity to move molecules across cell membranes. These EMFs are part of the communication system for our nerves and, as Carla Hannaford has reported, "They provide the body with a specific rhythm of vibration" (1995, 147–150), which should be learned in utero. While in the womb, babies entrain their own rhythms from the mother's heartbeat and breathing, as well as her own EMFs from her organs. The vestibular system develops and is myelinated in utero by five months under the influence of those natural rhythms (Hannaford 1995).

The vestibular system is one of the areas in which many children now have problems requiring occupational therapy. Now pregnant women are bombarded with more EMFs than ever before, from the job environment, the home, as well as ultrasound machines. All of these things can upset natural biorhythms that nature was counting on. Research at Stanford has shown that the cell's sodium potassium pump is disrupted by EMFs! This pump is unfortunately needed in the nervous system for learning, among other things (Hannaford, 162).

EMFs are measured in our brains by EEGs or in our hearts by EKGs. EMFs are utilized when we have an MRI. Hannaford argues that while most research has focused on cancer-causing EMFs, not enough has been done on the subtle links with our learning potential. The EMFs from the alternating current from our appliances pass through our bodies. I was shocked to think about the fact that electric current of sixty cycles per second has a magnetic field that changes direction twice as often or 120 times per second. There are effects on us from this that few people are really thinking about yet.

Some researchers have, and the message is this: They should be avoided in all reasonable ways, because they "affect our ability to learn" (Hannaford, *Smart Moves*, 1995, 147–148).

> The small frequencies in the home are called ELFs (extremely low fields). "Prudent avoidance" is the recommendation of researchers, especially with children.
>
> There is a greater likelihood that these natural rhythms may be disrupted if the mother spends hours a day at a computer, in a highly electrified office with fluorescent lights, near electrical appliances, ironing, blow drying other peoples' hair in a beauty parlor, or sleeping under an electric blanket. (Hannaford 1995, 149)

There have been stories of children with leukemia being cured by going to their grandmother's house away from the nearby high-tension wires that emit large amounts of EMFs. Because electromagnetism is the main force that governs interactions between molecules in our bodies, another electromagnetic field superimposed upon our own can cause interference. There are many stress-related diseases that can be influenced badly by interference from EMF fields outside the body. Where we sleep matters, it seems, according to the experts. And sleeping with a lot of electromagnetic equipment in the surrounding area is likely going to interfere with some of the natural recovery processes of the night.

Swartwout, a behavioral optometrist specializing in environmental issues, lists things like allergies, accidents, arthritis, anxiety, muscle cramps and tension, indigestion, hypertension, headache, diabetes, hypoglycemia, depression, and vision problems as being stress-related diseases that are aggravated by EMF pollution (1991). There are several types of EMF pollution that invade a child's space and that can be minimized. My suggestions here are those that I believe can be reasonably implemented by me or anyone else. I base this on the researches of Glen Swartwout.

Anything near the bed should not even be plugged in at night, even if it is turned off. That means we can use hot water bottles instead of heating pads and electric blankets. We also need to put our digital clocks across the room and take our watches off when we sleep. Do not buy touch on lights or sleep on heated water beds or beds with metal head-boards and frames if you have a choice.

Everyone seems to instinctively know that carrying a cell phone on one's body is definitely not good for pregnant women, and children should not sit closer than ten feet from the TV. This is true. Computer work may not be that healthy either during pregnancy or for children. I also have cases of adult men who have had total breakdowns in health and vision after being software engineers for years, as well as college students who have been computer game addicts for several years. Optometrists have seen computer work as a problem for eyestrain, but EMF stress can also be a huge factor if the new flat screens are not utilized. There are some shields that can be purchased to help deflect the rays from that machine and also monitors that are totally safe.

Dr. Swartwout recommendeds the following measures to protect against computer EMF stress if you have an old computer without the thin, flat sceen.

1. ELF Armor, which absorbs the magnetic field around the cathode end of the CRT and "reduces the magnetic field by 77 percent."
2. The NoRad DB60 Computer Shield that absorbs 99 percent of the electrical portion of the EMFs. It also cuts glare for the eyes.
3. Radiation-free monitors put out by the Safe Computing Company. They are called Safe Monitors and would solve the problem without shields. Swartwout says they are already being used by Harvard Medical School, Yale Medical School, the U.S. Congress, the EPA, New York State, General Electric, Cray Research, Intel, and the United Auto Workers Union (1991, 70).

There is also a device for the layman that can be connected to a computer, called the EmdexC, that provides data analysis and graphs as well as assesses the fields. The noncomputerized one is the Tri-field Meter. New Biopro Technology chips are useful for cell phones and computers. Because improvements are always being made, there will be something newer as you are reading this. Investigate what is best for your setup at home, and remember that computer use for children before they are needed for school work is not a good idea for the developing brain or development of vision.

Only plastic frames should be used on glasses, according to Swart-wout, because he says the metal frames, which attract electromagnetic pollution, short circuit the connections between the two halves of the brain, if they are not balanced. Many people have one very dominant side, and that could result in headaches and other signs of EMF stress, like fatigue and confusion. My old eye doctor never allowed any of his patients to have metal frames. I am not that adamant on the subject. I suggest that it would be prudent to avoid metal frames for computer use, and, of course, better for everything if that is possible.

Most of us have always known that microwave ovens put out too many EMFs to be really healthy, besides reducing the food value considerably, but I did not have a clue that clock radios are even worse in terms of ELFs than a color TV.

Teen Brain Toxicity from Early Drinking

This chapter has taken up many of the toxins that few are aware exist. It also focuses mainly on young children. Teenagers still have plasticity in their brain development, though, which most people do not realize. They also have their own set of toxic risks that parents have a hard time controlling. There are, of course hard drugs, which is not a topic for this chapter. I hope it never happens to any of my reader's children. The long-term visual and school consequences are there to be worked on by a behavioral optometrist. I have had a few patients who are in college or graduate school, who are now clean but did a lot of drugs at one point in their lives. Their visual perception and visual systems are not what they should be or could have been. Recall that pathways from eyes are everywhere in the brain.

What is not generally known by teens is that so-called innocent high school drinking is bad for the brain. Dr. Christine Northrup discusses the reason for the 21-year-old age limit on alcohol. It seems to be the age at which the brain can handle alcohol, recognize rational limits, and refrain from risky behavior. Besides that, there is still a great deal of neural plasticity in the brain until around age 21 (2005).

Northrup tells it like it is: "Binge drinking between 14 and 21 decreases the size of key memory areas of the brain, normally the hippocampus by 10 percent. University of Michigan study data shows 43 percent of 8th graders surveyed said they had used alcohol in the past year. Of 10th graders, it was 65 percent. Of 12th graders it was 73 percent (2005, 506).

This does not even include the recent problems with college binge drinking long before students are 21, while they are trying to learn with incomplete memory development in their under-21 brains. Of course, if they have children during any of the drinking, we now realize there is a whole pattern of fetal alcohol syndrome.

If teenagers realized the prohibition against drinking was not just because of driving or other life and death issues, but incremental chipping away at their developing brains' memory circuits, there would be less of it. Excessive drinking can cause toxic amblyopia, too.

There are a couple of thin books I have referred to in this chapter that perhaps should be in every home. One is *Raising Healthy Children in a Toxic World* by Philip J. Landrigan, MD, Herbert L. Needleman, MD, and Mary Landrigan, MPA (2001). It is available from Amazon at a high price, though it is out of print. Libraries should have it. The replacement for it is *Chemical Free Kids* by Allan Magaziner, Linda Bovie, and Anthony Zolezzi (2003). Another useful book is *Electromagnetic Pollution Solutions: What You Can Do to Keep Your Home and Workplace Safe*, by behavioral optometrist Dr. Glen Swartwout (1991). One that is appropriate if you have a child who is considered hyperactive or who has an attention deficit disorder is *The ADD and ADHD Diet*, by Rachel Bell and Dr. Howard Peiper (1997). Finally, Carla Hannaford's *Smart Moves* (1995 and 2005) has a wealth of information about the development of the child's nervous system and brain and how important movement is for its development.

The subject of toxicity in the environment is very complex. Those who feel the calling to do so can find numerous other sources and organizations to provide detailed knowledge on all of these topics. I did not even mention nuclear waste, which is now a huge problem for the state of Washington, because old storage tanks have started to leak underground (Stahl 2006). I am hoping that children raised with vision and without "nature deficit disorder," as Richard Louv calls it (2006), will step up to save our planet, our bodies, and brains for the sake of all of our grandchildren.

(3)

POOR VISION DEVELOPMENT AFFECTING SCHOOL SUCCESS IS EPIDEMIC, BUT SOME SCHOOLS AND MANY PARENTS ARE REVERSING IT WITH VISION THERAPY

Tolstoy once said that all happy families are the same, but each unhappy family is unhappy in its own way. I think this concept applies to vision development as well. All successfully developed visual systems are pretty much the same, but each one that is not, is unsuccessful in its own way. This is why it is endlessly interesting to do behavioral vision exams on children and adults. This is also why it is challenging, fascinating, and very satisfying to intervene to upgrade a child's visual abilities and see those changes translate into new school success, often with a side benefit of sports success. I wish all children who needed vision therapy could get it. When they don't, they suffer in school as a result.

WHAT IS THE SCOPE OF CHILDREN'S VISION PROBLEMS THAT EDUCATORS HAVE TO FACE?

Because 80 percent of learning involves use of the eyes and their brain connections, every child will do better if his or her visual function is efficient and strong. As a society, we need to be sure that vision is working for all of our children. Vision therapy with behavioral optometrists can do that for our kids if for any reason there is a breakdown in the way a child's visual system develops. Unfortunately, breakdowns in vision development are more common than any of us would like to think. These breakdowns affect our whole education system.

American schools for lower-income children are in crisis. In spite of demanding policies for performance with rigorous test requirements, achievement gaps are growing, dropout numbers are increasing, and there was little progress in the last two decades of the twentieth century (National Center for Educational Statistics 2001). I submit that a very large part of these school failures are visual function failures. If we upgrade vision, we will change that in the twenty-first century. This supposition is supported by vision research (Krumholz 2000; Orfield, Basa, and Yun 2001; Sullivan 2001; Harris 2002; Zaba and Johnson 1996, 1999, 2001; Damar, Liu, and Smith, 2000; Seiderman 1980; Atzmon et al. 1993). Some of what we know about vision and learning and how vision therapy can help a child with a visually related learning problem is discussed in this chapter.

These problems are not about seeing 20/20 on a chart or needing treatment for a lazy eye. We are talking about efficiently using the eyes to read, write, and perform math, in a nation where only one-third of all fourth graders are reading well, according to a National Center for Education Statistics study (1998). In poverty areas, success levels are lower (NAEP 1998; Zill and West 2000; Leventhal and Brooks-Gunn 2000).

There are a number of typical vision failures that are occurring, which are detrimental to a child's learning process. These include poor tracking (oculomotor skills), convergence insufficiency at near or far, convergence excess at near or far, diplopia (double vision) at near or far, intermittent strabismus (crossed or walled eyes), myopia (nearsightedness), anisometropia (the need for significantly different prescriptions for 20/20 with each eye), accommodative (focusing) infacility or insufficiency, ill-sustained accommodation, astigmatism (different prescriptions for different axes of the eye), various types of visual perception deficits, and so on.

These diagnoses go on insurance forms, clinic records, and letters to schools. However, there are endless combinations, permutations, and reasons for these in individual patients. It is always such an intriguing process to figure out why the visual system adapted the way it did, what purpose the adaptation is serving, and how to get rid of it by finding another way to help that child with vision training, therapeutic glasses, and lifestyle changes.

Important recent research by optometrists in several parts of the United States shows an alarmingly high incidence of untreated vision problems in schools serving poor children. Research also shows that the vision screenings the public schools have used for decades to assess student vision are inadequate for identifying the critical problems shown in the new research. Ideally, there should be large-scale research and treatment programs serving all children who are not measuring up to their grade levels for learning (Johnson, Blair, and Zaba 2000; Duckman and Festinger 2000; Orfield, Basa, and Yun 2001; Harris 2002).

Parents need to be made aware of the fact that vision problems do affect learning and that sometimes just reading glasses can make a huge difference. Other times, vision therapy will turn a child's life around. Behavioral Optometrists can be found to help their children.

VISION PROBLEMS ARE NOW RECOGNIZED AS VERY RELEVANT TO LEARNING

Significant efforts are underway to identify kids who are suffering academically because of subtle vision disabilities. Parents Active in Vision Education (PAVE) has worked with the National Parent Teacher Association, publicizing the need for adequate vision testing for children in academic trouble (PAVE San Diego n.d.). The College of Optometrists in Vision Development (COVD) published *Optometric Guidelines for School Consulting* (Hellerstein et al. 2001). This publication was a significant step toward preparing optometrists to play a much-needed role in solving the education crisis. The American Optometric Association (AOA) published two manuals on testing children in order to identify learning-related vision problems (1998, 2002).

The COVD, OEP (Optometric Extension Program), and PAVE developed interactive internet programs (2002 at www.digevent.com/events/visualconnection.html) on vision and learning. A national study is underway to improve school screenings, and local efforts have begun in many states to ensure that kindergartners all get proper vision testing. There have been research projects in Kansas (Sullivan 2001), and Oklahoma (Maples 2001) to upgrade school success by upgrading visual skills. A pilot study in Boston's Mather K–5 School with the support of then principal, Kim Marhall (Orfield, Basa, and Yun 2001), has shown promise for in-school programs to upgrade vision. A double-blind study in Baltimore (Harris 2002) showed significant improvements in learning after visual/perceptual training.

Even though large multicentered studies have not been done to prove that vision affects school learning, the information now available from optometric research really should convince us all as a society to invest in a much more expansive effort to upgrade every child's vision. Here is what we already know about visually related learning problems and the value of treatment:

1. Near point vision problems interfere with learning (Rosner and Rosner 1986, 1987)
2. Visually related learning problems can be identified if certain tests are done (Birnbaum 1993)
3. These problems can be treated with therapy and/or reading glasses (Birnbaum 1993; Orfield, Basa, and Yun 2001; Harris 2002)
4. If the problems are identified and treated, recent research as well as clinical experience suggests that test scores and grades will go up (Atzmon et al. 1993; Harris 2002; Sullivan 2001; Seiderman 1980; Orfield, Basa, and Yun 2001)

Given the enormous costs (National Center for Educational Statistics 2000) of repeating grades ($7,500 at the turn of the century, often $10,000 or higher now), summer school programs, dropouts, and inferior levels of academic achievement, vision treatment would be a minor expenditure. We know treatment could eliminate significant problems that otherwise are impossible to resolve within the school. This does not even factor in the savings in social and emotional consequences of vision difficulties for the child. We know that juvenile delinquents fail functional vision exams at about a 74 percent level or higher (Zaba 2001).

VISION AND LEARNING CONFERENCE AT HARVARD

A national symposium on "An Educational Barrier We Can Actually Eliminate: Visual Problems of Children in Poverty and Their Interference with Learning" was held at Harvard Graduate School of Education in April 2001 (Mozlin 2001). The presenters were doctors of optometry who had either been doing planned research or managing vision treatment programs in inner-city or rural poverty schools. Many of the papers presented have since been published in the *Journal of Behavioral Optometry* (Maples 2001; Mozlin 2001; Zaba 2001) and the *Journal of Optometric Vision Development* (Orfield, Basa, and Yun 2001; Harris 2002; Duckman and Festinger 2001).

This symposium was a significant step towards communication of what behavioral optometry can offer to help children learn. The highlights of research findings presented at the conference, added to the literature reviews and works by hundreds of caring practitioners in the past 25 years, clearly link vision problems with learning problems. This chapter explains the following little-known research findings regarding children's poor vision development:

1. Screenings, unless they are very thorough, do not identify functional vision problems. If they are very thorough then the numbers of children with problems are huge.
2. Children who have untreated functional vision problems are more at risk for failing school, dropping out, getting in trouble with the law, and growing up illiterate.
3. Vision therapy can change academic outcomes on tests and grades, and sometimes reading glasses alone can do a great job.
4. Vision treatments might be the most efficient, least costly interventions we could possibly make for improving a whole generation of children's academic abilities.

CURRENT SCHOOL SCREENINGS ARE NOT ADEQUATE AND FOLLOW-UP IS POOR

An important area of discussion at the Harvard meeting was the factual data on how widespread vision problems are among children in cities or rural poverty areas and how difficult it is to get treatment for them unless it occurs in the school. In a study by Rochelle Mozlin, OD and Irwin Suchoff, OD of 625 at-risk students in Bronx and Manhattan inner-city high schools, 53.2 percent of the teens failed the screening, and

44 percent needed glasses (Suchoff and Mozlin 1991). In spite of extraordinary efforts to get out-of-school follow-up exams for these teens, only in 17 of the neediest cases did the teens actually keep appointments for eye exams.

When they looked at the highly hyperopic (farsighted) children (+2.00 or more uncorrected), 78 percent were in special education. Previous school screenings evidently had not been effective at identifying refractive hyperopia or getting glasses for kids who really could not focus at near. It has been well researched (Solan and Mozlin 1997; Cool 1988). Mozlin explains, that children in poverty can be expected to have more significant visual difficulties. Factors include lack of prenatal care, poor nutrition, and low birthweight for starters. These difficulties will also take a greater toll on school success, because many economically deprived children have other health and well-being issues as well (Birch and Gussow 1970; Shinaur 1975).

EVEN GOOD SCHOOL SCREENINGS ARE NOT ALWAYS EFFECTIVE IN HELPING KIDS

Although I am personally in favor of good school screenings, there are problems in that they are never complete and parents think of them as a complete eye exam. In 29 out of 32 states that require screenings, there is no requirement for parental follow-up (*AOA News* 2006).

I believe all children with learning problems need a thorough functional vision exam. Learning problems are the red flag for a screener. These children will very likely have a functional vision or visual/perceptual problem. If they have a full behavioral optometry exam, it will be identified. They may have other issues also, but there will be a vision piece in that learning problem.

Foster care children in New York provide a specific example of how our society is failing to meet the visual needs of poor kids with our current screening set up. It was not the fault of the social service agencies, Robert Duckman, OD, said, because they met their legal requirements to get kids screened. Existing screenings clearly did not do the job of either identifying problems that could interfere with learning or leading to appropriate follow-up care (Duckman and Festinger 2001).

This study of 351 foster children showed that 39.5 percent had a visual acuity failure. Of those, 86.2 percent had refractive error, and 22 percent had refractive amblyopia (lazy eye). Only 4.6 percent had ocular health problems, a little over half of which were moderate to serious, but 10 percent were strabismic (crossed or walled eyes) when ordinarily the overall prevalence is only 1 to 5 percent (Moore 2001; Duckman and Festinger 2001). There were also many nonstrabismic binocular problems, which had gone untreated because they had not been identified. For example, less than one-twentieth of the vergence problems had been identified. Of the 36.8 percent (128 kids) referred for glasses, 70 had never had them, and many no longer had appropriate prescriptions.

Duckman concludes previous screenings were not getting proper follow-up or not picking up the problems in many cases. For other children, new problems had occurred in a one-year time period. It is very true, from my experience, that a child can go seriously myopic or develop very poor focusing ability or visual stress symptoms in the space of less than a year's time. This is why I worry that the push to get kindergarten screenings will not solve learning-related vision problems, because they develop after kids are forced to look at small words with underdeveloped eyes. They will help find the kids who are amblyopic, strabismic, and highly hyperopic or highly myopic. Just picking up the high hyperopes would be a good service when we consider the Suchoff and Mozlin findings on the high school kids in New York (1991).

HIGH PERENTAGES OF CHILDREN IN POVERTY ARE MISSING VISUAL SKILLS THAT ARE NECESSARY FOR SCHOOL SUCCESS

The high incidence of problems among children in poverty was a universal finding among presenters at the conference. My own findings from a New England College of Optometry pediatric teaching clinic in the Mather school in Boston showed extensive vision problems. Eighty-five percent of the children qualified for free lunch during the years of the project (1993–1999), which means most of the children were economically disadvantaged with all those attendant risks. The shocking news that came out of that study was that only 54.5 percent of 679 first- through fifth-grade children who took the Garzia and Richman Developmental Eye Movement Test (Garzia, Richman, Nicholson, and Games 1990) passed all subtests.

Considering all 801 children evaluated at Mather, traditional distance acuity testing, which is the usual screening in most schools, turned up 19 percent who did not see 20/30 or better at distance. But 41 percent failed using the more thorough California screening, called the Orinda criteria (The Orinda Vision Study 1959; Peters 1984), with a near acuity test added. When the Developmental Eye Movement (DEM) Test for tracking (Garzia and Richman, 1990) was added, 53 percent failed. This means that 125 of the children who passed the other parts of the tests still failed eye tracking. In total, 24.5 percent of the children failed that oculomotor (tracking) evaluation (Orfield, Basa, and Yun 2001).

Simple acuity (clarity of sight) failures increased at Mather by second and third grade, not just at distance, but also at near point, illustrating that children's vision problems develop over time, so exams need to be done yearly. Hyperopia (farsightedness) at 19.5 was the major refractive condition at the Mather school. Myopia (nearsightedness) was found in only 6.5 percent of the students tested. Farsightedness can cause difficulties for children who are living with stress that interferes with focusing abilities. Recall that farsighted kids need to focus at distance, as well as near (Birnbaum 1993; Scheiman and Rouse 1994; Scheiman and Wick 1994).

READING GLASSES MIGHT HAVE TO BE PRESCRIBED AND AVAILABLE IN SCHOOLS TO SALVAGE EARLY LEARNING

Farsightedness and poor focusing ability often need to be treated with glasses for near work (Moore, Lyons, and Walline 1999). Of 37 Mather children beginning special education programs in the fall of 1997, 34 failed at least one part of the screening that included tests for acuity at distance and near, refractive error, eye health, eye muscle problems, and the DEM (Orfield, Basa, and Yun 2001).

Follow-up, as well as thorough testing, should be done in the school for children who cannot afford to have it done privately. The Boston Mather clinic provided exams and vision therapy but originally had no intention of providing glasses. However, the first year, only three children out of about 30 filled their glasses prescriptions. The traditional medical system, leaving follow-up to parents, did not work to provide for these kids. Over the six years, 22 more parents filled our clinic prescriptions on their own. Another 25 got the glasses for $25 or $10, either at the optometry clinic dispensary or at the school in the next few years.

One day a child came to me and said, "My grandma wants to know if we can get the glasses now and pay the $10.00 over the next five months, $2.00 each month." After that, they were dispensed free at the school, and 116 out of 118 families accepted (Orfield, Basa, and Yun 2001).

The Boston project found the largest percent of failures of near acuity among second graders. Distance acuity was worse among second and third graders. The kindergarten and first-grade primers give way to smaller print by second grade, too, which could add to the visual stress, possibly causing intermittent blur at both distance and near (Birnbaum 1993).

CHILDREN'S VISION PROBLEMS HAVE BEEN CORRELATED WITH SCHOOL FAILURE

The Boston study's statisticians, Dr. Frank Basa and PhD candidate John Yun, produced a regression analysis with a significance of $p = 0.000$ (less than one chance in 1,000 that the correlation was by chance), correlating the DEM horizontal subtest with standardized math and reading scores. DEM tests on 448 children who also had reading and math scores at the proper times revealed that 23.2 percent of the variance in seven-year-olds' reading scores was correlated with DEM horizontal percentile scores. For ten-year-olds, that test was still correlating clearly with 19.55 percent of the variance in reading scores. By fourth grade just as much of the variance in math was predicted by this test as in reading (Orfield, Basa, and Yun 2001). This means that approximately one-fifth of the reading problems and math problems in crucial grades could be the result of (because they are clearly correlated with) failure to have the expected level of visual tracking skills measured by this test. Fortunately, tracking, fixation, and other related vision function skills are teachable in vision therapy (Cohen 1988).

If any single educational test could so clearly identify such an easily remediable problem that is correlated so significantly with reading failure, money would be invested in correcting that problem.

The Baltimore inner-city study (2001) headed by Dr. Paul Harris of the Baltimore Academy for Behavioral Optometry, was a masked and matched, double-blind vision therapy study. An account and results of the first two years of the study were published in the summer 2002 issue of the *Journal of Optometric Vision Development*. At the Harvard conference, Dr. Harris reported a huge prevalence of functional vision problems with a different battery of tests than those used in Boston. Only 14.7 percent of all the children in one school passed in all areas of the vision testing. Only 26.4 percent in the other study school passed in all areas prior to treatment.

There were two control schools as well. The Baltimore study clearly shows, as did the Boston one, large percentages of children with certain near point visual/perceptual problems. This was true in four different schools. Harris' screenings with a variety of tests showed failures in third graders on eye tracking measured by another tracking test, the King–Devick Test, of 56.6 percent in one school, 69.6 percent in another, 17.4 percent in the third, and 33.3 percent in a fourth school.

Dr. Harris also used a symptom questionnaire. It showed the top five visual complaints to be things any of our children might suffer from and we might not even consider them related to vision, but they are:

1. headaches in 84.3 percent,
2. "using finger to keep place with reading" in 78.1 percent,
3. eyes tired with reading/school work in 70.8 percent,
4. loses place when reading in 70.2 percent,
5. rubs eyes during the day in 52.8 percent.

Dr. Harris also noted that on certain tests, third graders scored worse than first graders relative to graded norms, as was found also in Boston. Vision not only develops by gradual learning of skills. It could also deteriorate because of stress on an already poorly developing system.

A comparable study for middle-class kids has not been done, but behavioral optometrists who see them have continually busy practices, so this is not just a problem of poor children.

Oklahoma's W. C. Maples, OD, found that vision problems identified in the Beery Visual Motor Integration Test, the Wold Sentence Copy Test, and the Developmental Eye Movement (DEM) vertical subtest were more strongly correlated with problems on the Iowa Test of Basic Skills than either ethnic or economic background (2001). These tests are usually not performed in a child's eye examination unless it is with a behavioral optometrist, but they reveal a lot about how that child functions visually.

Another visual measure thought to be significant in relation to learning for children who needed but did not receive glasses was refractive error with a type of astigmatism common in Native American children tested. This type of astigmatism makes it harder to see clearly at near without reading glasses (Maples 1996; Harvey, Dobson, and Miller 2006).

SOCIAL AND EMOTIONAL PROBLEMS ALSO CORRELATED WITH VISION PROBLEMS

Social, emotional, and educational problems have long been correlated with vision problems. Three studies by behavioral optometrist Dr. Joel Zaba and PhD colleagues in Virginia present the case (Zaba and Johnson 1994; Johnson and Zaba 1999; Johnson, Blair, and Zaba 2000). At the Harvard conference, Dr. Zaba urged visual treatment intervention in all areas concerned with juvenile delinquency, illiteracy, and at-risk student populations (Zaba 2001). The 1999 Virginia study showed 74 percent of adjudicated adolescents failed at least one of his screening subtests.

There was an 85 percent failure rate among at-risk students in an elementary through high school population in the 1996 study. Illiterate adults failed Dr. Zaba's vision screening tests at the rate of 74 percent. It is tragic how much education failure seems so obviously related to easily correctable, but normally unidentified, visual skills failures or the need for glasses.

INTERVENTION IN THE SCHOOLS DOES WORK, ESPECIALLY WITH DAILY VISION TRAINING CLASSES FOR SEVERAL MONTHS

As part of the "See to Learn Program," the Kansas State Legislature supported a vision therapy research project in cooperation with the

Kansas Department of Education and the Kansas Optometric Association. Dr. Joe Sullivan, OD, presented the results at the Harvard conference. This study was funded by the state of Kansas and "evaluated the effectiveness of optometric vision therapy in improving reading skills of third-grade students with convergence insufficiency" (Sullivan 2001).

Thirty-six third graders with a diagnosis of "convergence insufficiency" in the treatment group had fifteen weeks of vision therapy and improved one year in reading levels in 10 months. They also, of course, improved their convergence skills by a factor of 1.87 ($p = 0.0002$), as well as numerous other visual skills improvements. Those in the non-treatment control group did not improve their reading grade level at all. The control group also had convergence insufficiency but received no vision therapy.

After 15 weeks of therapy for core vision skills (accommodation, ocular motilities, vergence, and motor), the children with the therapy had almost doubled their convergence ability. Post-testing for convergence and reading skills on both a Visagraph machine and the Qualitative Reading Inventory showed such significant improvements that the Kansas legislature decided to fund a much larger program. Training of optometrists to do the tests and the therapy throughout the state was begun.

The Harris controlled, double-blind vision therapy study in Baltimore (Harris 2002) with 75 children also showed that the therapy improved test scores. Each child received a minimum of 70 sessions of in-school vision therapy, four days a week by trained vision therapists. To accomplish this, a school would have to devote 40 minutes a day for between four and five months to upgrading a child. This is much less costly than years in learning disability (LD) classes.

After the 70 sessions for each child in the Harris study, the reading scores in grade level terms increased on the average of 1.82 years and 1.42 years in the two schools that received the therapy. This was in a school system where on the average, after second grade, the children only increased their skills half a year each year compared to national norms. How inexpensive, compared to all the other treatments we offer our special education children for years!

In Boston, an average of 15.5 visits per child significantly improved specific optometric skills the most in those who tested the worst in the beginning. Those who tested normal on a particular skill improved less or not at all. Those with the worst initial findings made the most progress. This is quite different from results in educational interventions, where those who test the lowest often improve the least. This was a retrospective study and averaged few visits for vision therapy (only once or twice per week), but it improved visual skills and even had some significant effects on school performance.

Boston children at the Mather School who had vision therapy or who received reading glasses achieved modest gains over nontreatment, randomized comparison group children, especially in math percentile scores and teacher letter grades in reading. Specifically in math, 8.3 percentile points were gained per year for the glasses only group, 6.5 percentile points for those in vision therapy (some of whom did not get the glasses prescribed), and only 3.2 percentile points in the randomized comparison group, some of whom had no visual problems. Grades in reading were improved at a statistically significant level, though grades are admittedly a subjective measure.

A FAMOUS ISRAELI DOUBLE-BLIND, MASKED AND MATCHED STUDY SHOWS VISION THERAPY IS AS EFFECTIVE AS TUTORING TO IMPROVE READING AND HAS TWO OTHER BENEFITS

There is one highly significant, double-blind, masked and matched study that was done in an orthoptic (vision training) clinic related to the Sackler School of Medicine, Tel Aviv University in Israel. There were 62 children with convergence insufficiency problems divided into two treatment groups of 31 matched pairs. One group got 20 minutes of tutoring and one got 20 minutes of orthoptic treatment for convergence each day. Both groups made equal progress in reading, *but the vision group also eliminated their convergence problems and symptoms of discomfort in the eyes.* The tutored group did not. The study, headed by D. Atzmon, P. Nemet, A. Ishay, and E. Karni (an orthoptist, an MD, a PhD, and an MA), was reported in the spring 1993 issue of *Binocular Vision and Eye Muscle Surgery Quarterly* with a preface by Firmon Hardenbergh, MD, then director of the Harvard University Health Services Eye Clinic, where I work.

WITHOUT QUESTION, GOOD VISION THERAPY
IMPROVES VISUAL SKILLS AND VISUAL PROCESSING

I recommend that all children with a functional vision problem be given vision therapy first, because it will definitely improve their areas of visual function weakness. This in turn is likely to help reduce eye symptoms (Ciuffreda 2001) and improve performance in school (Harris 2002; Atzmon et al. 1993).

Behavioral optometrists engaged in private practice vision therapy seeing middle-class children have been achieving results for decades (Cohen 1988). However, large-volume studies have not been done, in spite of some excellent small studies on the efficacy of various vision therapy treatments for eliminating specific vision difficulties.

Allen Cohen reviewed the literature of vision therapy results in 1988 for the *AOA Journal*. There were many studies cited. Here are just a few: Robert Wold et al., did a study on the efficacy of therapy for improving vision in 1978. They reported on 100 consecutive therapy patients whose eye movements had been poor on an observational scale for scoring saccadic and pursuit eye movements. Only 6 percent of the children passed. Post-therapy, 96 percent passed.

In 1982, Daum prospectively studied young adults. They did daily therapy to improve convergence ranges. They were still improved 24 weeks after the end of the therapy. In 1982 also, Pantano reported on over 200 subjects with convergence insufficiency who did training and then were tested two years later. Most had no continuing symptoms. Those who had learned to integrate their focusing and convergence skills had the best results. Also reported in 1982, Hoffman found in a study with a control group that by improving focusing skills, children improved also in visual information processing tasks (i.e., visual perceptual skills) (Cohen 1988). NIH clinical trials of therapy for convergence insufficiency increased comfort and convergence abilities in the training groups (Scheiman, Cotter, et al., 2005).

EVIDENCE FOR THE EFFICACY OF VISION THERAPY
IS PILING UP

An excellent recent vision therapy study, the Amblyopia study, is from the National Institutes of Health's National Eye Institute. The clinical trial was done on 507 older children with amblyopia (inability to see 20/20 on a vision chart no matter what prescription is worn). There were 49 participating eye centers. Optometrist Mitchell M. Scheiman of the Pennsylvania College of Optometry was cochairman of the study with Richard W. Hertle of Children's Hospital in Pittsburgh. The study appeared in the April 2005 issue of the *Archives of Ophthalmology*.

The estimate of the doctors doing the study is that there are 3 percent of children in the United States who have some amount of vision impairment due to amblyopia. The results showed that the children who got patched therapy (either with patches or drops that limited the use of the nonamblyopic eye) combined with near vision activities improved their vision by two lines on the chart (53 percent), more than those who just received glasses (25 percent). The study concluded that vision therapy can help in cases of amblyopia long after ophthalmologists used to think it was possible.

Of course, the earlier the treatment, the better the recovery might be. This was a highly effective study, because there were no ancillary therapies to confound the results, and it was not trying to prove that vision therapy and patching were correlated with school success. They were only being correlated with visual acuity.

EDUCATORS AND POLITICIANS ARE BEGINNING TO REALIZE THAT VISION PROBLEMS AFFECT SCHOOL SUCCESS

Schools are beginning to realize that vision problems are correlated with lower test scores and can be remediated with glasses and vision therapy. If these near point eye strain and visual skills problems are treated, vision function is always improved, and there can be a realistic hope that grades and test scores will climb.

A bill was introduced in the Senate by Christopher "Kit" Bond from Missouri in July 2006 called the Vision Care for Kids Act of 2006. It is supported by both ophthalmology and optometry organizations. A federal grant program is at the heart of the bill—to support efforts in the states. My hope is that when the bill passes, states will set up requirements for thorough functional vision exams rather than a more superficial variety that might not identify the problems affecting learning. When the parents of children object to eye exams for kindergartners as they did in North Carolina (Greifner 2006), it might be more useful to require the exams by the middle of first grade for all children behind in reading, rather than for entry to kindergarten. Vision problems often show up as interference with reading, and symptoms begin when a child struggles to learn it.

It would be useful to have a large amount of funding for multicenter studies to prove once and for all the efficacy of vision therapy and reading glasses for helping kids learn. If test scores are going to be the measure of success in our society, then maybe we need to show the world in an enormous national study that test scores will be improved as children learn the visual skills necessary to read, write, and perform math. If I were a principal, though, I would not wait. I would forge ahead with testing, therapy, and glasses for all of my students who were slipping behind. The Harris and Atzmon studies would be enough for me.

If vision is a learned motor skill that is not being taught, and children are failing academic subjects, as well as becoming delinquent, illiterate, and learning disabled because they didn't acquire these basic skills first (Zaba 2001), then let us make sure that they do. If we know that low-powered, but necessary, reading glasses will not be obtained unless they are provided in the schools, then they need to be provided in the schools.

Dr. Stephanie Johnson-Brown pointed out in her Harvard presentation that, although we cannot control the stresses children are born into, the income of their parents, their health, the food they eat at home, or the support for learning that they receive after school hours, vision is one area that can be improved for children with school-based care (2001). When I was testing children in 2001 for the Reading Recovery tutoring program, I found that 100 percent of the children selected had at least one vision problem or needed reading glasses. It's that vision piece again, which is a big one.

The wealth of information available on vision and learning should make educators, local politicians, and parents jump up for action. It has not, except in a few towns such as Framingham, Massachusetts, which has a new in-school eye clinic, again staffed by the New England College of Optometry faculty and students. School nurse Kathy Mazjoub was instrumental in setting this up. Her story is in chapter six.

WHAT IS VISION THERAPY AND WHAT KINDS OF EYE EXERCISES ARE ASSIGNED FOR HOMEWORK?

Because it is unlikely that children of parents reading this book will get what they need in the way of vision training or even a proper screening in their local schools, parents need to be proactive themselves. They will need to find help to rule out or treat this most obvious block to learning for their children. That is how it has always been done since we have had modern vision therapy.

Dr. A. M. Skeffington and his optometric colleagues, like Dr. Gerald Getman, back in the 1930s and 1940s developed programs of testing and vision exercises that optometrists learned and offered to patients in their practices. Since then, many highly trained clinicians and research-oriented optometrists have elaborated and perfected this treatment modality that is likely the best first stop for children with learning problems.

Vision therapy consists of what some people call eye exercises or vision procedures. It is, in its most complex form, brain training for visual processing. This is not a book of eye exercises. I firmly believe that very few people can learn vision from a book, a video, or a computer program. It really requires the help of behavioral optometrists and their trained therapists in the office. Exercises to be done at home and in the office that are tailored to a child's specific needs will be demonstrated and supervised there.

For example, the patient may be required to shift focus from near to far with the biofeedback of doubling glasses to help line up the near targets vertically and then the far targets (which cannot be done without aligning the eyes properly).

Or the patient might look at a row of colored lights, flashing either in order or randomly, with a red lens on one eye and a blue lens on the other eye. Such glasses require the patient to use both eyes to keep both colors on at the same time because each eye sees only one color of light.

There may be a large box with a circle of lights that turn on, one at a time and randomly, and the child needs to press the button next to the light that is on before the next light will come on. The device keeps score. Speed at seeing and responding with the hands is learned. Other procedures train eyes to relax or converge against prisms. This could be called "weight lifting" for the eyes.

Sometimes a child will take home a tracking book and be required to circle letters in alphabetical order as he tracks through a preprogrammed paragraph of nonsense words to build up his speed and accuracy in moving his eyes across a page for efficient reading. If he does not end up with z in the programmed paragraph, he has made a mistake along the way. The parent times him, and the goal may be 30 seconds per paragraph, though he may have started at 2.5 minutes or slower.

All good vision therapy procedures have a built-in feedback mechanism that allows the patient to know when he is doing well. When a patient succeeds at a vision therapy exercise, he is learning new ways of seeing that are more efficient than his previous ones, and thus he is strengthening his visual system.

It is not just training eye muscles, but that is part of it. There are activities for shifting focus through alternating plus and minus lenses attached to a "flipper" stick, for placing pegs in a slowly rotating pegboard, or making patterns with parquetry blocks to match a pattern glimpsed for a split second.

Sometimes a tachistoscope that flashes words or numbers at one-tenth or one-hundredth of a second is used to speed up visual recognition. Sometimes 3-D glasses are used with 3-D targets sliding apart to increase ability to converge or diverge so as to keep the target single. Sometimes a similar type of slider is sent home along with a lens flipper for focusing shifts.

Other home exercises may be visual motor activities or visual memory activities. Now and then, bouncing on a rebounder while reading letters from four little charts in a specific order is done. Or the child might be wearing red and green glasses to read red and green letters while bouncing. Bouncing seems to keep both eyes "on." These are just a few of an endless number of eye activities that train skills that may never have been learned. One needs a professional to prescribe a child's program. Later in this chapter is a discussion of how to find one of these special vision doctors.

WHY ARE GLASSES PRESCRIBED IF YOUR CHILD IS DOING VISION THERAPY?

Most of the time glasses for reading or training purposes are prescribed to therapy patients, as well as carefully prescribed distance glasses if needed. Those distance prescriptions, often in an executive or flat-top bifocal, may be used to help hold down the progression of myopia, or help straighten the eyes with lenses and/or prisms in the case of strabismus.

Children who are having trouble reading but who can see 20/20 at distance are often a little farsighted with poor focusing ability. They usually need reading glasses. These may be of the tiniest amounts, from +0.12 to a +0.75 spherical prescription in glasses. They cannot be bought in the drugstore. They need to be prescribed carefully by optometrists who have experience with these lenses and can give a child a vision function examination to determine what is appropriate for their particular visual system.

Research and practice have shown that either no prescription or a strong prescription of +1.00 or more for reading in patients who are not farsighted at distance may not help. Lesser prescriptions of up to +0.75 do help (Greenspan 1975). The areas in which reading glasses can help include efficiency of reading, maintaining sufficient distance from the book to reduce stress on the focusing system, good posture, and less effort to focus allowing more energy for comprehension and visualization to happen.

OUR GRANDMOTHERS KNEW IT: POSTURE MATTERS

"Why should good posture matter?" I can hear parents wondering. While all normal children are born with lovely posture, many have become terrible slouches by the time they enter first grade. Some of that could be from primitive reflex problems (see chapter five) or nutritional deficits. Posture is important because good positioning of the head, neck, and torso allows better function of the neck muscles that turn the head down slightly for convergence while reading. Posture also matters for getting good circulation to the brain and keeping the back strong.

These low-powered plus glasses that improved posture were called "learning lenses" by A. M. Skeffington. Richard Apell, who ran the optometric clinic at the Gezell Institute in New Haven until 1989 when it closed, called these low plus spheres "developmental lenses." They have been helping children and adults to read more easily for decades and may have improved posture, too.

In my practice, I prescribe reading lenses for most patients and offer both children and adults vision therapy. I do not sell glasses, but I do insist that my patients use my prescriptions for contacts and glasses if they wish to work with me. Lenses themselves train the patient. Good prescriptions are life changing.

GLASSES ARE GOOD TOOLS FOR LEARNING TO READ

Glasses are tools. Parents need to realize that a pair of glasses does not mean that their child is going to have a permanent visual disability. It means for me, as that child's doctor, that I can push her visual system to learn some things with my prescriptions that she is not able to learn in another way.

Let us just take the simple problem of reading. Not so simple, the mother of a struggling child would say. However, a professor at the Harvard Graduate School of Education once said to me, "I can't understand why we cannot teach reading better. It does not take a great deal of intelligence to read, but there are so many failures."

"I think part of it is the eyes," I told him. It was at that point that I knew there needed to be a conference on vision and learning at Harvard. In another venue, a professor of optometry was giving a lecture to an audience that was certain the eyes had nothing to do with reading failure. It was all "language deficits," they believed.

He said, "Okay, everyone. Let's try a little experiment. Now, put your palms up over your eyes. Yes, good. No cracks. No light coming in. Now, look down at the course outline but keep your hands tight over your eyes. Who can read it first? Shout out your name." The point was made. Eyes matter, and if they are needed, glasses matter.

The eyes are involved in reading whether we like it or not. They are not the whole story, just as language is not the whole story, just as time to practice and books in the home and failure to creep and crawl for proper visual motor development are not the whole story. The fact is many children—especially poor children—suffer in all these areas: poor visual motor development, poor language development, a lack of books, no reading practice or hearing of stories in the home, and poor near vision skills.

Before television, a poor family that wanted to push its children onto a path of success would have somebody read aloud and treasure every library book and the few other books that they could have to use. That is very unlikely now. Everyone, rich or poor, has a TV, even if they do not have a phone, as I learned when I would try to call parents of children in that inner-city Boston school's vision therapy program.

Those economically disadvantaged children were watching between five and six hours of TV, based on my poll of vision therapy kids, so they were not developing language that was more complex than the little sound bites of TV sitcoms (see chapter seven for the Powers study results on TV versus reading vocabulary). The children were not training their eyes to do anything complex because those eyes were occupied by staring at TV. Staring at TV is not tracking, not converging, not eye-hand coordination, not shifting focus, not peripheral awareness development, not perceptual motor development, and worst of all, not visualizing. They were getting the basics of language but not the high level that they would get from good books, and they were not developing their visual motor systems or their visual imaginations.

This may be why a number of children pass the verbal parts of IQ tests but fail the performance IQ. They may then be labeled with a "right brain learning disability." Whatever the label, it is a failure of brain training in the home through activities that need to be done by all children to develop their bodies, eyes, and brains, as well as their sense of beauty, joy, and competence.

Here is the data on reading problems in this country put out by the Reading Is Fundamental (RIF) organization, with offices in Washington, D.C.[1]. By age three, children from privileged families have heard 30 million words more than those from poor families. More than 80 percent of "low-income" daycare centers lacked book corners but had TVs. The median hourly wage for parking attendants is higher than that for child-care providers. Forty million adults in the United States cannot read well enough to read a simple story to their children. Less than half of all families read to their kindergarten children daily.

A middle-class child is exposed to an average of 1,000 to 1,700 hours of one-on-one picture book reading. The average child in a low-income family has been exposed to only 25 hours. The RIF organization cares and has donated 300 million books to children since it was founded 40 years ago.

The language piece is clear. What is not so clear is that being read to stimulates visualization. Visualization is necessary for comprehension. Looking at picture books with a caring adult and pointing to the pictures stimulates eye fixation, convergence, and tracking—all skills needed to read. These were the skills lacking in the children of that inner-city Boston school—with 85 percent poor enough to have a free lunch and breakfast in school and reading scores well below the national average. The poor results on the children's ability to track on testing with the Developmental Eye Movement Test meant that they had not had practiced using their eyes to track, fixate, and focus. *TV does not teach tracking.*

In my private practice and at the Harvard University Health Service, I see children of highly educated and motivated parents. These kids are having problems learning to read processing what they see on the chalkboard, taking notes, answering questions, spelling, or doing arithmetic. All of these problems relate to their eyes. If the eyes can be fixed, some tutoring in reading or math facts will complete the cure. Sometimes they do not even need tutoring.

ARE PRESCHOOLERS GETTING THE KIND OF VISUAL LEARNING THAT HELPS WITH NEAR VISION READINESS FOR SCHOOL WORK AND READING?

Lately, the makers of computer games are advertising that handling a mouse is good eye/hand training. However, good eye/hand training includes much more variety of movement in all positions with special finger work, and with two hands used together with complex objects, while moving in space. The changes on the computer screen might parallel but are not directly connected to the hand. Mouse training is mouse training.

Home vision therapy on a TV screen may help with perceptual skills or eye muscle convergence, but it is not what is needed for overall vision development in children who have had too much computer or TV time and not enough moving in space and handling objects under the supervision of their eyes. If TV or computer screens could teach vision effectively, we would have a lot more children with no trouble reading and writing, but we don't.

I hasten to say that I am not opposed to moderate computer learning for children whose vision has developed age appropriately—after they have learned to read at a ninth-grade level, and after they have mastered printing and handwriting. Preschoolers should never be on computers. I have seen too many cases of children whose parents were computer programmers and wanted their kids to have all the latest learning games for children on the computer. Numbers of patients developed eye turns in the preschool years after being perfectly fine until they started computer use. The reason: They were not able to converge and focus both eyes in the fast-paced computer world for tots. They decided to pick an eye rather than struggle.

Many adults and teens also have problems with excessive computer use. I had a mother come in who had "burned out" her eyes on computer solitaire. She was still holding on to binocular vision, but she was having severe asthenopia (eye discomfort) that her reading glasses helped only a little bit. Before the computer game binge she had had excellent vision. Two Harvard students were addicted to computer games. They had to do vision therapy and wean themselves off of their games; their eyes hurt so much from the hours of playing on top of the hours of computer work for their classes that they could not get their assignments done.

An expert teacher of Brain Gym (which is discussed at length in chapter five) says that she is getting a number of teenagers now as clients who need to be trained out of an addiction to screen life (computers and television). They are unable to relate to friends or teachers, and all they want to do is sit in front of their tubes. It takes a lot of work with Brain Gym neurological reprogramming to get them back into the world from being lost in cyber space or media unreality.

TV AND COMPUTER SCREEN TIME IS NOT EFFICIENT FOR LEARNING

Daniel R. Anderson, a psychologist from the University of Massachusetts in Amherst and researcher on the issue of television and children's development, says TV is not a very useful learning tool. He was quoted in the *Boston Globe* as saying, "The evidence so far is that any hour they spend engaged in real-life activities is an hour in which they are able to learn much more, relevant to healthy development." His research shows that toddlers need to see a video on removing a mitten six times to learn how to do it. They only needed to see it done once if they were shown the process in real space by a live person (Jackson 2005).

The same article mentioned research showing that only 6 percent of parents with children under two years old knew the American Academy of Pediatrics had said there should be no TV before age two for any child. TV blaring in the background is being blamed in some quarters for increasing the attention deficit problems of children and for generalized anxiety from scary sounds. Behavioral optometrists certainly would agree and some of us think it should be off limits until age four, at least.

What many behavioral (sometimes called developmental) optometrists know from experience with patients is that computer time needs to be limited until children truly need it by age nine for school, and even then, very infrequent use is the ideal until eighth or ninth grade. Fourth graders I see for therapy are being required to turn in homework done on the computer. Our culture has not learned to use its inventions wisely, and knowledge of the side effects of electronic media is not widespread.

SOME SO-CALLED "DYSLEXIA" MAY REALLY BE A FUNCTIONAL VISION PROBLEM OR A FUNCTIONAL HEARING PROBLEM: CAREFUL DIAGNOSIS MUST INCLUDE A VISION EXAM WITH APPROPRIATE FUNCTIONAL VISION TESTS

One of the main signs of poor vision development is trouble learning to read. Research has shown that fixing a convergence insufficiency can increase reading ability with no other treatment (Atzmon 1993; Sullivan 2001). I remember a second grader who was the perfect case of how effective vision therapy can be for reading. She had been diagnosed as dyslexic by a dyslexia clinic in her town. Her school was mainstreaming her with pullouts from the classroom for special work in reading. She had an eye exam with me and was put on a vision therapy program for the rest of the school year (about seven months). Her initial diagnosis was mild farsightedness with poor focusing ability, poor convergence ability, and poor tracking ability.

At the end of that year, she was reading above grade level. She had also improved to a normal level in all of those visual categories that same year. I had given her a pair of low power plus "learning lenses," in addition to the vision therapy. She did not always wear the glasses, but the vision skills stayed with her, and she graduated several years later as the top student in her fifth-grade class. She went on to a competitive private school with no record of dyslexia.

That is what vision therapy can do for kids who are missing significant visual skills and are being required to read before their visual system is ready. This child had a tutor, but tutoring alone will not cure those visually related learning problems that were holding back her reading development in seven month's time.

Dyslexia is a suspected diagnosis in children who have average and above-average IQs but are reading one and a half grade levels behind. Dyslexia is also a suspected diagnosis in children with convergence insufficiency. Children who have to struggle to get their eyes together to read won't be great at comprehension and remembering content. I am emphatically not saying here that all dyslexia is visually related or that vision therapy cures dyslexia. Although some so-called "dyslexia" is from visual processing problems and can be resolved with vision therapy, another type is from auditory processing difficulties and may need Tomatis therapy, a technique for training ears, not eyes, to hear different frequencies.

The Tomatis method was developed by Alfred Tomatis, who was a French medical doctor, born in 1920. Tomatis developed a theory that people cannot produce a sound with their voices that their ears cannot hear. The Tomatis method is very-well explained in a book by Joshua Leeds called *The Power of Sound* (2001). The "Tomatis effect" was corroborated by research at the Sorbonne in 1957, according to author Leeds. If children do not speak clearly, chances are they cannot process certain frequencies of sound clearly. This may also be true if they cannot sound out words. Therapy consists of listening to special tapes to train the ear to hear the missing frequencies, determined by testing. This is useful therapy especially if a child must rely mainly on phonics to learn reading.

THERE IS A SCHOOL THAT INTERVENES EARLY WITH VISION EVALUATIONS FOR ALL STUDENTS AND PROVIDES VISION THERAPY FOR THOSE IN NEED

A good example of the problems that delayed visual development can cause is the tendency to need to use phonics instead of the rapid ability to remember words by sight. This can be avoided, according to Dr. Steve Ingersoll, an optometrist and cofounder of the Livingston Developmental Academy in Howell, Michigan, and Smart Schools Management, Inc., that guides a number of charter schools all over Michigan. When children have not developed their visual ability enough to read at their grade level, the smart school puts them in vision training immediately. They also teach ways to read rapidly that emphasize visualization for meaning. All the children in Dr. Ingersoll's school read at grade level and pass the state exams. Ingersoll says this is because they do not teach reading until the child is visually competent to learn it (Ingersoll 2005).

Ingersoll, too, is perturbed by the changes in kids coming to school over the last 30 years. He says the older teachers have been noticing it. It is from TV, computers, daycare, reduced outdoor play, earlier academic demands, and, very likely, toxic chemicals. Because they have a visual motor delay, their cognitive abilities are not at a level necessary for reading and visualizing, but pressure is on them to learn earlier and earlier. As a result, they are failing to learn because of their compressed awareness, inaccurate eye movements, and poor visualization. The stress of failing to learn complicates further learning. Ingersoll's information can be found at smartschoolsinc.com, excelinstitute.com, and grandtraverseacademy.com.

The last website is for a new school being built with the following architectural principles: spaces that encourage neurological development, outdoor play, natural and full-spectrum light, open space that encourages movement, strategic use of color, and good ergonomics.

Another principle of the school is to make sure each child feels a good measure of safety, love, belonging, and fun during learning in the school setting. There are special protocols for students about treating others well and opportunities to become assistants to the teachers if they need a boost of self-esteem. The basic idea is that children do not learn in a stressed-out frame of mind (Ingersoll 2005). One of the problems interfering with near vision focus and learning is stress.

STRESS INTERFERES WITH VISUAL LEARNING SO SCHOOLS AND PARENTS SHOULD TRY TO REDUCE IT

When children are anxious, the part of the brain that learns is damped down in favor of the part that has to think about survival. Under stress, everything takes more effort, including brainwork. Under stress or medications for allergies or ADD, the eyes do not focus well at near tasks. It takes much more effort then to read. Behavioral optometrists prescribe reading glasses to reduce some of that stress and focusing trouble.

The problem with visual stress is that the brain does not interpret the cause of stress. When a child is worried about a test or getting an assignment done and is concentrating hard to focus with insufficient energy, the brain does not say to itself, "Gee, it is just his eyes that are bothering him for up-close reading, nothing to panic about."

It says, instead, "There is an unknown, frightful reason to be on guard, because the sympathetic nervous system is switched on," which it does whenever we are concentrating really hard.

Sympathetic nervous system fight/flight hormone outflow occurs and further prevents good focus of the eyes at near as well as good learning. Dilated pupils and unfocused eyes go along with sympathetic outflow (Birnbaum 1993). The amygdala part of the brain is activated, and that inhibits the prefrontal cortex needed for higher things. In addition, things learned during high stress may not be as easily retrieved (remembered) because of the negative sensations of stress attached to that learning (Pearce 2003). These problems exist for both poor and middle-class children under the pressure to pass high-stakes tests by third or fourth grade in public schools and in selective private academies where there is stiff competition among children.

What we do know is that many of the children who are dropouts and become incarcerated for difficulties with the law have myriad vision deficiencies that make it very difficult for them to learn to read well and succeed in schoolwork (Kaseno 1985; Barber 2000). I wish that, in this push to make sure that everyone is reading by third grade, there would be an equally strong push to see that everyone's eyes are ready to read by first grade. Instead, many schools are pushing reading in kindergarten in the hope that the child will have one more year to learn by third grade. The best kindergarten teachers will tell you that most kids are not ready that young (see chapter six for things schools can do to ready kids).

There is no concerted effort on the part of schools to see that the children's eyes are even slightly ready to do near work and manage focus and convergence shifts from book, to blackboard, to book again. Some of the wise old doctors in behavioral optometry and a few dentists, too, have suggested that when the second set of teeth are in, the child is neurologically ready to read. That is small comfort for a family with children who are diagnosed dyslexic or LD because they are not ready to read by age six. Some children miraculously are, and their eyes can do it even earlier, but this is not the average child. The average child will need some help at home.

VISION-FRIENDLY LEARNING TO READ METHODS ARE AVAILABLE FOR PARENTS

Neurological Impress Method

Parents can use a few methods to help their children learn to read that make sense from the point of view of a child's eyes. One is the neurological impress method of reading (NIM), developed back in 1969 by R. G. Heckelman, a clinical psychologist at Riverside General Hospital in Riverside, California. The details of this method can be found by googling NIM and downloading material on the method.[2]

The method consists of reading out loud with the child while tracing under the words with your finger. You read at a normal pace, which is likely faster than the child's speed. He tries to keep up and follow your finger. There is no stopping to correct his mistakes. It is done for 15 minutes a day on books a year or two below his grade level. He learns by hearing, seeing, and saying all at once, and feeling secure when not being corrected for mistakes. He gradually learns with the sound, sight, speed, flow, and expression impressed on his mind all at once. The value of this is that it integrates sound and sight together. We know that there are connections in the brain between all the senses, so that a proper teaching method would include using sight and sound together.

The Phonics Game

The phonics game is another approach that evolved from the research done at Yale's Center for Learning and Attention by Dr. Sally Shaywitz and coworkers. They believe the brain really needs to read with phonics in a phonetic language rather than using whole language as in a picture language such as Chinese. Their recommendation is that children who are learning disabled or dyslexic be taught phonics. Information on this game can be obtained online. The Lindamood Bell system, also, uses phonics in a powerful way to teach poor readers.

The child who does not pick up reading with a mature visual system may spend his life primarily as an auditory learner, which works in high school, but causes problems with the high reading loads in college. I have seen a few of these very brilliant auditory learners at Harvard, who have major visual problems sustaining the eye effort over the time that is needed because they are slower than most at reading. I am always wondering if well-developed vision when they were learning to read would have made them visual learners instead.

The Visual Memory Approach

There are others who say that visual memory and visualization is the problem and children must be taught to see pictures as they read, or they will be slow readers forever after. The Smart Schools programs in Michigan try to go this route instead of the phonics route by making sure that all the kids in need get vision therapy to ready their eyes for reading and then teaching visualization along with reading. They teach phonics also, but do not dwell on it. As a relatively slow reader myself, who has always had to fight against the habit of sublingualization that I learned very young along with phonics, I would recommend that if a child can get his eyes developed properly, he might learn most words by sight. That is vastly more efficient than to build habits of sounding them out. Vision is the most efficient sense. To have to run it through one's tongue and ear is a great deal slower, though it may be necessary in some cases of specific reading disabilities that relate to faults in the visual pathways.

As a doctor now who sees children who have had to learn to sublingualize in order to learn to read, I would say if there is a way to be sure that the visual system is seeing well enough to remember words before there is too much pressure to read, this is the better choice. Try for vision first. If that fails, go strongly with phonics.

Poor differentiation of sounds can complicate learning phonics. The bonding of voice and gentle sound from pregnancy throughout the growing-up years is an important way the brain grows and the child acquires the language of the parents' culture. Sometimes there is poor learning in this area and sound therapy is needed, just as vision therapy may be needed. Great help can be received from the Tomatis method for children who are clearly in need of learning to differentiate sounds better. They have a sound-processing problem different from a hearing deficit, just as a visual processing problem is different from poor distance sight.

SIZE OF PRINT AND DISTANCE VIEWING MATTERS WHEN CHILDREN'S VISION IS IMMATURE: THE SNAPP METHOD

It has been observed by behavioral optometrists that it is probably not the reading itself that is the problem early on. It is the small print up close that is the problem for underdeveloped visual systems. Marie Clay, founder of the Reading Recovery program, used "tall books" or "big books" across the desk or farther away to teach reading. The print in those books was significantly larger than the print in the regular readers used in the classroom. This has been a very effective program for teaching children who are falling behind to learn to read. Perhaps the distance from the book and the size of the print helped. There is also the Glenn Doman method, from his book on teaching babies to read (Doman 1964), which insists on large print because the eyes are not ready, though the mind is.

A very clever physical therapist in Arkansas, the late Ed Snapp, taught children to read by rapidly flashing large word cards at distance. When they learned them at distance, they were moved closer—still large print, still rapid flash. By the time those words got to the desk in front of them in a book form, they were very well known. Children could read the book. Sometimes when it has been tried on adult observers with advanced degrees, they have not been able to do the rapid visual processing that children who learn the method master (Ward 2006). There is more on this method in chapter six.

BOTH RESEARCH AND EXPERIENCE IN BEHAVIORAL OPTOMETRY OFFICES SHOW THAT VISION THERAPY CAN HELP A STRUGGLING CHILD, AND TEACHERS WILL NOTICE THE DIFFERENCE

Since most schools are not looking out for the vision development of our children, the best thing a parent can do is find a behavioral optometrist to assess their children's functional vision, and begin therapy and/or have the child use glasses to read if there is a problem.

Research shows vision therapy works to improve functional vision. If the child is regular about keeping appointments and does his home exercises, this therapy is extremely effective for making changes that cause the teachers to notice the difference. Regular in-office therapy works better than home programs, unless the parent can stay on top of the program every day. I think this is because it at least gets done two or more times a week in the office. The school programs that have worked best were those where therapy was done during one period every day.

Home programs can be just as effective if certain tools are purchased and if the parents regularly oversee the eye exercises. I have never seen a child manage a vision therapy home program on his own, though very motivated high school students can, and college students do all the time.

CASES OF PARENT-MANAGED HOME PROGRAMS THAT WORKED

Children doing vision therapy need a lot more direct, one-on-one supervision than adults. My patients come every two weeks for therapy usually, but there must be a daily program of exercises for their visual system that is administered by the parent. Some need to come every week, and others cannot come more frequently than one time a month because of distance. In those cases, the parent is usually a teacher or a health-related professional who I know will be able to manage the child and a home program well, or there is an experienced teenager to supervise the home program.

I am thinking of a family with a part-time nurse mother who was able to come an average of once every three weeks for about a year to work with her slightly delayed first-grade child. The delay was in reading and in all motor areas. Once the father brought the boy and said, "But don't you think that is just him? Won't he always be kind of a klutz, and be unable to learn to print?"

"No," I said. "If we can train adults with head injuries and athletes to learn better visual motor skills, we ought to be able to train a happy little boy like yours." So we did—the mother and I. I saw them for over a year, and at several follow-ups, the child was consistently fine. He was doing martial arts gracefully with good balance and peripheral awareness, and his printing and handwriting were perfectly adequate. His math skills were off the charts, and his reading was above grade level. We taught him to converge his eyes, shift focus, and track, as well as to do a number of perception and visual motor improvement activities. He also had reading glasses to cut out any visual stress learning to read or do arithmetic problems.

The basic message that hits me whenever I see a child through vision therapy is that vision skills are learned, and other learning is far easier if efficient vision is already in place. Vision can be learned at any age and should be taught as early as possible if gaps exist in visual development. It is a motor skill like riding a bike, I tell parents. Once learned really well it is not forgotten because it is always being used.

I am thinking of an 11-year-old boy in a demanding private school who had done about 12 office visits over a period of eight months. He had been a reasonably good student but was working so hard and feeling so stressed about it that someone told his mother it might be his eyes. Sure enough, there were a number of vision problems. He did do his home program, though he was not as regular at the office as I would have liked. The last time he came in, his mother reported that he was one of the only two students who got straight As that quarter in his entire grade at a competitive private school. I would have liked his vision to be even more perfect, and it will be if he keeps up with the therapy, but they are already very happy.

Within a month or two after vision therapy begins, many of the younger children will be off the charts in math, and making slower improvements in reading. Math is often a problem only because the child cannot line up items on the page properly, so he will skip a row of numbers in his arithmetic process. When the visual skills of spatial localization, focus, and convergence are learned quickly, the math is much easier. Older children take a little longer, but are still noticeably better academically with their vision system improved.

One family of two children did bimonthly office therapy; implemented a significant amount of home therapy, dietary, and exercise regimens; and had the children wear reading glasses. They were in to see me with "right-brain" learning issues, which include visual/spatial processing and can be directly improved with vision therapy. They moved out of state at the end of the school year, but all their test scores had been raised significantly and the LD diagnoses were gone.

A general rule is the more serious the problem, the more regular and frequent the office visits need to be to train out of it. Some students may need a reading tutor, because once the eyes are ready to read, the children will still be behind and need catching up on skills of actual reading. Some optometrists have in-house reading teachers doing some of their therapy. I leave reading tutoring to the reading specialists and I sometimes refer patients to tutors when they are ready visually. My job is to be sure the eye/brain complex can do that kind of work.

IT IS NEVER TOO LATE—EVEN TEENS AND ADULTS CAN IMPROVE THEIR LIVES WITH VISION TRAINING

My adult groups meet one hour a week, though it is possible for some patients to sign up for two groups at a time, getting two office visits weekly. This plan is extremely effective if the adult can find the time to fit the visits into his or her schedule, and it goes faster if a mild home program is also done.

There are adults (teens included) in the therapy program for many different reasons. Three of the major reasons for therapy in adults are (1) sports vision enhancement, (2) computer eyestrain, and (3) severe binocular vision problems, such as those of a strabismic who had surgery as a child but is "decompensating" and beginning to see double or having trouble staying focused for near work.

A fourth reason, myopia control and reduction, is discussed in chapter four. A fifth group of patients are those with head injuries who have post-trauma vision syndrome or more serious, field loss or strabismus. A lot of people who present with these problems have had head trauma or whip lash that affected vision, but it never occurred to them that their vision problems began after that accident. Others know they had major head trauma or they have double vision following a retinal detachment, and that is very demanding therapy work, which I find extremely interesting and successful for the patient.

THREE CASES ILLUSTRATE THREE OF THE USUAL REASONS TO HAVE VISION THERAPY

The First Case

The first case is of a graduate student who was a squash player on the team at a major Eastern university. He was losing all of his competitions. He came to me for vision therapy and computer glasses to save his distance vision one summer, and the next year he won all his matches, became the captain, and came in second with his team at the playoffs.

He continued to come every week before his matches because he said the therapy activities always readied his eyes for the competition of that fast-paced visual game. His therapy consisted of major work on peripheral awareness and near/far focus shifts. He was a rocket scientist on computers all day long, so he had lost that balance that is so necessary in high-intensity sports. He was also starting to develop a little myopia, which he wanted to eliminate. Reading glasses and therapy did the job. This was many years ago.

Now sports vision training is very common on numerous professional sports teams, and it does give athletes an edge. In the February 5, 2006,

New York Times "Play" section, an article by Gretchen Reynolds discusses how many sports teams, from Olympics to professional baseball, are using vision therapy to up the visual skills of their members. Vision therapy helps with sports almost before it works on learning issues. Parents are excited when their son or daughter is suddenly getting more hits and catching those fly balls on the softball team after three weeks of eye exercises. They are motivated to keep up the pace until the schoolwork improves.

The Second Case

A second case was a highly skilled computer worker who worked at home. She was having trouble, though, because her eyes were terribly bothered and sore, and it was hard to sustain the length of time that she needed to spend on her computer. She was farsighted and getting to the age where she needed reading glasses. She did four months of once-a-week office therapy with homework to restore the balance between her peripheral and central visual systems and improve her focusing ability. When she left, there was no longer any discomfort, and she was able to do the work she needed to do for as long as she needed to do it.

The Third Case

The third case was a young woman who had had four strabismus surgeries as a child. One of her eyes still wandered out often, and she would then see double. It was hard on her in business to have that happen when she was talking to a client. She came to try to get her eye to stay straight. After a little more than a year of once-a-week office therapy and some home activities, her eye was always straight. She went on to business school for two years. After receiving her MBA, she returned for one last exam before moving out of state. She had no wandering eye signs or symptoms of her formerly uncontrollable exotropia, even though during business school she had no time to see me or do any eye exercises. She reported no problems with the eye over those two years.

FINDING A BEHAVIORAL OPTOMETRIST

Stories of patients in my practice, thankfully, are not the only evidence we have of the efficacy of vision therapy for intervening in poorly developing visual systems. It has been done for decades in many optometric practices and is taught as a part of the academic program in all colleges of optometry, though very few optometrists actually do vision therapy in their offices. The doctors who do vision therapy usually have a membership or fellowship in the COVD, are members of the Optometric Extension Program, are fellows in the American Academy of Optometry Binocular Vision Section, or call themselves "behavioral optometrists," with offices where vision therapy is a major aspect of their practice.

Parents who wish to pursue more information or find a behavioral optometrist in their own city and state can check out the website www.vision3d.com for a great many recent and classic articles on vision therapy. There is a good short video put out by Parents Active in Vision Education (PAVE) called *The Hidden Disability: Undetected Vision Problems*, which was a Telly Awards Recipient.[3] As a behavioral optometrist who utilizes a number of ancillary therapies along with vision therapy, I am never bothered when I cannot prove vision therapy did the whole job when a child suddenly blossoms in school. I want the job done, and if it takes two or three practitioners or programs to get it done, then I will call them in.

Just today a child came back for a yearly check-up who had benefited tremendously from an ancillary therapy. He had been extremely hyperactive and inattentive a year ago. I had prescribed plus glasses for reading because he was esophoric and fairly farsighted. The family lived too far to do therapy. The mother is a Brain Gym practitioner, so I told her to work with those vision exercises plus a few other procedures and dietary and lifestyle changes.

In addition, I wanted her to take him to an osteopath that I know and trust to see if there were some cranial imbalances that could be fixed. After two visits with that doctor, his balance improved so much that he could suddenly ride his bike. He is now reading and much more attentive in school, his mother reports, and I could see this on his exam. Chapter five describes the therapies that I "call in" if need be.

THREE SIMPLE EYE EXERCISES EVERY PARENT SHOULD KNOW

Now and then I see a child whose parents tell me he is an excellent reader but who does not track well at all. The child skips around picking up the gist of the book, but cannot really read out loud. This is an observation made by several optometrists I know, as well as in my own experience. This may be what the fastest and most efficient of readers always do, but I think it is good to play it safe and make sure your child can track, converge, and focus if he cannot read well yet. Below are three simple ways to test and train your child for these specific skills. They all use a sticker on the end of a Popsicle stick or a pencil. That is your target, your tool.

1. Tracking. Move the target side-to-side in front of the child's eyes to see if he can follow it precisely for several minutes, at least. Ask him also to be aware of the periphery, to tell you what he sees out of the sides of his eyes without losing fixation on the moving target. If he cannot, this is a good exercise to do with him every day. When he masters it, move it in an X pattern, an H pattern, or in circles.

2. Focusing. You can also push the sticker on the stick up to one eye, with his other covered, and watch for the decrease in the size of his pupil if he is focusing properly. It will increase when you pull it away. Lots of kids need to learn that.

3. Converging. With both eyes open, you can push the sticker up to the bridge of his nose until you see one eye move out or he says he sees two stickers. That will help him learn to converge his eyes.

Track, focus, converge. Make sure your child does those procedures every day until he is really good at it. If there are any problems with learning or he starts squinting or rubbing eyes, though, you will need a further evaluation by a developmental (behavioral) optometrist. Also, don't forget that vision systems are built with movement in the light— preferably outdoor light.

In this chapter, the focus is on the facts regarding the huge numbers of children with vision problems, how they affect schoolwork, and what can be done about them. I mentioned one case of the highly successful graduate student athlete. What I have found to be a motivating factor for some children to do their vision therapy exercises is that very rapidly, they get better in sports. I recall a child with a huge convergence insufficiency who did therapy with me when he was in little league. Suddenly, he was hitting the ball a lot better, long before his schoolwork got better. He became an excellent high school athlete and an A student and went off to a top Ivy League college.

Children who are already nearsighted (myopic) are often brought to me to try to stabilize or reverse that process. Most of them are doing well in school. Myopia is a successful adaptation for children who are not able to shift focus from near to far and far to near efficiently, or shift from convergence at near to divergence at far smoothly. Nearsightedness allows them to read really well without too much focusing effort, and they can be good students and even bookworms. Chapter four deals with the problem of nearsightedness.

NOTES

1. Call toll-free at 1-888-725-4801 or visit www.rif.org for more information.

2. There is also a pamphlet on NIM that can be ordered from the following address: Parent Brochures, Academic Therapy Publications, 20 Commercial Blvd., Novato, CA 94947-6191.

3. *The Hidden Disability: Undetected Vision Problems* can be ordered from PAVE National Headquarters, 4135 54th Place, San Diego, CA, 92105-2303. Their phone number is 619-287-0081. Their website is www.pavevision.org.

4

CHILDREN DO NOT HAVE
TO GO NEARSIGHTED

Without Intervention, Myopia Usually Progresses, but It Can Be Controlled and Sometimes Reversed

I can still remember discussions with my brother when we first needed glasses at age 12; long wistful talks about the survival of the fittest and how we, with our nearsighted genes, were probably only allowed to survive childhood because of the invention of glasses. Otherwise, we would be run down by trucks or eaten by lions. Now, though, with our ophthalmic crutches, we myopes could all go forth and multiply. That was evidently the reason that more and more of us appeared every year wearing glasses. Or was it? Yet when I told my ophthalmologist that surely God had not intended that evolution should lead to a human race so rampantly nearsighted, he assured me that whether God intended it or not, that was the way things were and anyone who said otherwise was a quack. I wasn't convinced, but gradually, as I lost more and more control of my vision, I started to believe him. (Orfield 1994)

By the time I was in my 30s, I was wearing minus lenses that allowed me to see 20/15 vision, but I was " knocked out of space," as I described it when I was later let back into my world with vision therapy that reduced my myopia down to almost nothing. Back in my 30s I could no longer see the big E on the eye chart clearly at all without my glasses, and my peripheral vision in my glasses was so poor that I was terrified driving a car on freeways if the children were talking while I was driving. My glasses were over −4.00. Now I do not need anything at all to see distance, and most days I see 20/20. If I am really tired or have been working a lot on the computer, it goes down to 20/25, but I can always see the 20/30 row, which is what children need to pass the school screenings.

I never had laser surgery, and I do not recommend it to my patients. Patients from the small percentage of laser surgery subjects who have serious problems have come to me afterward. I was always glad I had not made that referral. I am also concerned about what will happen 40 years from now to those lathed and lasered corneas.

This chapter discusses good reasons for trying to control a child's developing nearsightedness, how it is done, why it works, and what one school system did that reduced its prevalence.

Note: If you have forgotten some of the terms like myopia (nearsightedness) used in this chapter, refer back to the beginning of chapter 1 for explanations.

What do you do if your child fails a school screening for myopia?

You see a behavioral optometrist and ask for treatment, not just compensatory lenses. Myopia can at least be controlled and often reversed if you start early and you and your child are motivated. Some lifestyle changes may need to be introduced, and learning activities with the eyes and hands will need to be part of that child's life.

This is not far fetched. Vision is a very flexible process. There is good evidence for saying this, which is discussed in this chapter:

- Behavioral optometrists work with myopia control regularly and get results.
- My own personal experience of training out of my nearsightedness illustrates this truth (Orfield 1994).
- A study done in a school system found that special teaching methods not only reduced the incidence of myopia, but also raised the Iowa test scores of the intervention group compared to the baseline group (Streff 1977).

- Animal research shows that we can change the refractive error in monkeys and chickens by putting contact lenses or spectacles on them (Hung, Crawford, and Smith 1995). For example, plus contacts will make them farsighted (Hung and Smith 1996).
- Short-term vision therapy in a school setting lowered refractive error (myopia and hyperopia) an average of one-third units (diopters) (Orfield 2001).

GOING MYOPIC

It is not fun to go nearsighted. Some parents may remember what it is like. Below is my story of going nearsighted in eighth grade and pulling out of it in my 30s. Patients who remember going nearsighted have told me it is similar to their experience, and patients doing vision therapy have been motivated by reading of my process of regaining clear distance sight and other skills with vision training (Orfield 1994).

REMEMBRANCES OF A MYOPIC PAST

When I was a child, I understood as a child. I did not know that when people are under stress they "zero in" at near, stop looking far, and stop processing peripheral light (Shipman 1988). I figured out, though, that it was much easier to read and cast my eyes down than to deal with the hallways full of teenagers in my large junior high.

I noticed in eighth grade when I sat in the middle of the auditorium that the people on the stage were blurry. I remembered that the year before they had been clear from the back of the auditorium where the seventh graders sat. I could still see the chalkboard, but I failed the school screening. My first glasses were −1.25 DS, OU, and with them I was given the power to see the veins on the leaves of the trees at astounding distances. Was this the good vision I had lost? After that I sat in the exam chair every year and demanded telescopic sight. I did not have words for the extra stress those glasses put on my accommodative (focusing) system. I just took them off to read.

I did not know how to react to that panicky feeling brought on by the loss of clear sight. The inevitability of visual deterioration was the worst of it, with no way to stop the inexorable process of eyeballs growing longer and longer, I thought. I strained harder to see in the same way one might focus in dim light on tiny print at near. Soon I needed the glasses for the chalkboard as well as the auditorium. There was no one to tap my occipital bone and tell me to "see further back in the head," "relax and look softly," and "hang on to the periphery." I felt I was an oddity, a genetic mistake, totally unlike all of my friends.

Most people in those days had clear sight (Pearce 1981). Now we don't, but our fashion frames have lulled us into thinking myopia, rampantly increasing as it is, is not such a loss. At age 12 in the fifties, though, it was socially and aesthetically catastrophic to become a myope. I was known as the "blonde bombshell" in junior high, but blondes were no longer bombshells in girls' glasses with little rhinestones at the corners.

Later, when frames were small black cat eyes, good looks were still elusive. With a prior self-image of beauty, I was suddenly caged in ugliness. I wore them only in class. The rest of the time I moved in a fog of vanity and became somewhat introverted. I stopped looking far. I felt my personality change behind my very eyes. My mother wondered what happened to her outgoing daughter.

I was athletic and had won a letter the year before I became nearsighted. It was much harder to catch a ball with my glasses on. Things were smaller and closer than they were without my glasses, and I was in a different place. Behind my frames, I was no longer in the world, but looking into it instead. There was fear of breaking glasses then, too. They didn't have prescriptions in plastic then, and the only contacts available to athletes were large, painful scleral lenses (large ones that covered the entire eye and stayed on with the help of the lids). Our babysitter wore them and my emmetropic (normal vision) mother looked at her coming up the walk, goggle eyed, and said, "Poor Susan."

My father was sorry that it was his "dominant" myopic genes that had made us so blind. He gave me a book by oculist Dr. William Bates on "better eyesight without glasses" (Bates 1940). At 13 or 14, I faithfully did the exercises for three months, hoping to eliminate my then -2.50 DS with cylinder myopic correction all at once. I surprised my

ophthalmologist that year because I did not get worse. He had predicted progression to age 16. In fact, I never did get worse until a
whiplash injury at 22 put me over the −3.00 DS mark (Roca 1971), and
during my second pregnancy, an appointment with an ophthalmologist
unaware of the effect of hormones on vision put me over the −4.00
mark at age 29.

Perhaps I even got better after "doing Bates," but it was not part of my
doctor's model of vision to take minus away from a myope. I would "grow
into it all soon enough," I heard him tell my mother. If perchance I was already fully grown, these would give me "extra help" when I learned to
drive. Or so we thought.

I did not know that depth perception is affected by minus or that when
one has to overaccommodate, convergence is pulled in more or recali-
brated. I just knew that space was so different in glasses that I wasn't sure
where things were any more. Once the driving instructor used his brake
when I was certain we could turn without hitting those pedestrians.

I did not suspect that the higher the lens power, the more the periphery is warped by the lens, because light is focused for the benefit of foveal
acuity (central vision) at the expense of ambient (peripheral) vision. Nor
did I understand that the more the periphery is warped, the harder it is
to see the center clearly, because you cannot judge how far it is without
peripheral cues.

All I knew was that I didn't feel safe driving. I could not see anything
out of the sides of my eyes, and I had to whip my head back and forth and
back and forth and was in great danger of losing sight of the middle of the
road. The driving instructor told me I had to keep my eyes straight ahead
or I would drive off in the direction I was looking. I tried to do that, but
it scared me so much I didn't take my test until I was 20.

I thought glasses gave me good vision, though, because I could see the
veins on the leaves of the faraway trees. I did not know that when you're
certain of what you see and where it is, that is good vision. All I knew was
that I didn't know what was there for sure without my glasses, and with
my glasses I wasn't sure where the "what" that was there was. But I was
a child.

While I never read in glasses, I took notes in them. I sat through high
school and college and graduate school in them. No one ever suggested
a bifocal in class or plus spectacles over the contacts to read. I told two

contact lens specialists in two cities that I couldn't read through my hard contact lenses. They both frowned and said, "You should be able to read through them," and that was that when I was a child.

The above describes the problems of going into the myopic pattern. It does not tell us how to get out of it. I did not even begin to learn that until I was 33, and took my daughter to a behavioral optometrist, and then decided to have an exam myself. This doctor, Amiel Francke in Washington, D.C., told me that I could get out of my myopia if I worked at it, and that it would take a long time with gradual lens reductions and the wearing of reading glasses that were weaker than my distance, but still were minus lenses. Reading with no glasses at all did not serve to make me better. I had done that my whole life, and gotten worse. I would have to gradually change my "space world," he said.

I figured out what this "space world" concept meant years later after many reductions in lenses and several months in office therapy when I was 39.

As I gave up lenses, I felt I was "pushing space out with my eyes." This new kind of looking occurred naturally. I wrote of it in my diary:

> I seem to have pushed the horizon away quite a bit and it is still sharp and clear. I was getting very puzzled about how far is far? How do we know the farness that we see is the same as the farness that someone else sees? Physical space can be measured but visual space cannot. It is in the eye and brain of the beholder. Whose space is the true space? In my mind's eye I can shoot an arrow into the air and say, "It came to rest I know not where." In the reference frame of related things I can see what time it lands and where. And so can anyone else in the vicinity. But what we each see when we say, "It went 50 meters" has no physical reality. It appears to me now that "On a Clear Day You Can See Forever." (Orfield 1994)

IF PARENTS AND CHILDREN ARE MOTIVATED, MYOPIA CAN BE CONTROLLED OR EVEN REVERSED

When I became a behavioral optometrist myself, years later, I knew I wanted to work to prevent myopia in children and reduce it for adults. Many children going nearsighted are brought to me so that I can try to stabilize their vision. If I see them before someone else has given them minus (nearsighted) lenses, and if vision is not too bad yet, I give them plus lenses for reading, instead, and put them in a vision therapy program. With those who have slipped into minus lenses, it is more complicated and individualized programs are necessary.

In my office, I also spend a lot of time reducing myopia in adults who are tired of being "knocked out of space" behind thick glasses or contacts, but who have no desire to try for a surgical solution. It is remarkably easy to do this with a motivated patient who can devote time to a home vision and exercise program.

My advice to parents is to make the time and space in their lives to work with their behavioral optometrist to stabilize the child's vision and have faith that it can be done. At the very least they will slow the progression of myopia significantly, so the child will not end up in super strong lenses. The stronger the lens, the less peripheral awareness the child has, and the more unreal his vision of space becomes.

At last count, there were an estimated 60 to 80 million nearsighted people in the United States (Sperduto, Seigel, Roberts, and Rowland 1983), but only a tiny percent have hereditary myopia that goes along with some genetic conditions, or gestational or birth injuries that interfere with normal eye development. The rest is functional myopia, sometimes called "school myopia," which can have one or more of several causes related to the *use* of the eyes and the *energy* the child has to meet his visual demands. That kind of myopia is a preventable disease.

The editors of the *Binocular Vision and Eye Muscle Surgery Quarterly* came to that same conclusion in their 1994 comments:

> There is little doubt in our mind (and also in those of many others) that with improving and earlier screening for refractive errors in children, ordinary myopia, certainly most "school myopia" (if not also many cases of "pathological" myopia) is a preventable disease. (Editors, *Binocular Vision and Eye Muscle Surgery Quarterly*, 1994)

School myopia appears at predictable times during the child's life, when eye stress is increased, and other stresses are limiting his energy for staying flexible visually. Now with early use of computers, there are some children by first grade going functionally nearsighted. In the past, the first cohort usually went down in third grade, when reading to learn became necessary, as opposed to learning to read. That created a significant amount of added stress on visual systems that were teetering on the edge of staying normal. The print in the books also became significantly smaller in order to fit more information on one page. Print size matters, as I discovered again typing this manuscript. When I used 12-pt. letters, my eyes hurt even with reading glasses. When I resized the text to 14 pt., they did not.

The next cohort of kids going nearsighted is usually fifth grade, when those who are great readers begin choosing reading over physical activities and read themselves right into myopia, sometimes with flashlights under the covers after bedtime. The next dangerous time is during adjustments to a new school such as middle school or junior high in sixth or seventh grade. These are stressful years, so that without help, by the next year (seventh or eighth grade) glasses start appearing in class to help students see the blackboard. Finally, junior year in high school is the last time of threatened myopia until college or graduate school. That year, college-bound kids get serious about the college board exams and the need to get the best grades possible for the admissions committees. Again, with no help, the system will often adapt into myopia.

Dr. Richard Kavner, author of *Your Child's Vision*, presents the following statistics that illustrate the epidemiology of myopia at the above times: There are 6 percent by age 10, 20 percent by eighth grade, 40 percent after high school, and 60–80 percent in college (1985). This is different from the records of Texas school children in the first half of the 20th century, when only 6 percent of children had visual difficulties of any kind (Pearce 1981). We are in a visually stressful world now. The longer we can keep our children from slipping into myopia, the less myopia they will end up having.

Nearsightedness is not nature's first choice. There is internal physiological pressure to do what is called "emmetropization" (normalization). Emmetropia is the ophthalmologic term for normal vision (Norton 1999) (Norton and Siegwert 1995). Most children are born slightly farsighted, we think, based on studies where infant eyes have been checked with an instrument that measures light reflexes off the retina. Others are born a bit nearsighted. This is all in flux in those early months. They move toward normal from both directions.

It is later that school myopia develops because of their response to near work stress. According to one study, it is the same children who were myopic in babyhood and then normalized that develop myopia later (Gwiazda et al. "Emmetropization" 1993). It is hard for the practitioner who sees the children after they are in the process of "adapting into myopia" to have any idea what the life story of their eyes has been. My job is to stop that adaptation by providing other ways to cope, including useful plus glasses to read (Francke 1988; Norton and Siegwert 1995; Goss and Uyesugi 1995; Goss and Grosvenor 1990) and eye exercises (Orfield 1994). Improving nutrition (Lane 1994), reducing stress (Forrest 1988), and increasing exercise (Orfield 1994; Kavner 1985) can also help prevent or arrest the progression of the nearsighted adaptation.

Many years ago, my old optometrists, Amiel Francke in Washington, D.C. (now retired), and Jim Blumenthal in Illinois (now in Phoenix, Arizona), explained the same to me, and we were able to prevent and reverse school myopia in all my children. I speak here as one parent to another, not as an optometrist, because way back then I was not an eye doctor, just a parent taking my girls to a behavioral optometrist. I was as motivated as any parent to have children who were successful in school, voracious readers, and who would be accepted into good colleges.

I have a first-hand understanding of parental hopes, dreams, and feelings of deep responsibility and internal pressure for our children's success. I was a stay-at-home mom until my youngest daughter was 10. It might be even harder if one is working at home because the children's success becomes a measure of one's "job performance."

My optometrists pointed out the obvious to me. Kids need long, golden afternoons to use their imaginations and their bodies in space, and they will be better off forever with efficient vision that such afternoons of play will allow them to develop and maintain. After grasping these concepts, and after my work pulling myself out of myopia, I surely did not want to be driving my kids into it. I figured that if myopia does not just drop from the sky, a hereditary time bomb, ready and set to obliterate distance vision, then something could be done to prevent it. So I had a countervailing force against my motherly anxieties, and I did what my doctors suggested with significant success.

One daughter finally went a bit nearsighted, first in one eye, then both, after she had finished law school and was living on her own in a new city, doing litigation work for a U.S. government agency. However, even this only came about after a whiplash injury that compromised her system (Roca 1971; Gilman and Bergstrand 1990). She now has distance glasses but rarely neds to use them. Another daughter started to go nearsighted in the eighth grade, as I had, but she did vision training and pulled out of it. She had always had reading glasses, but did not use them until she was threatened with losing her clear distance sight without glasses. She started again to go myopic her first year in college, while not wearing her reading glasses, and I had to give her the smallest myopic prescription that exists in a bifocal and tell her to sit in the front row. She stabilized wearing her reading glasses and that bifocal. She recovered good vision again after law school, but still keeps those minipowered glasses for driving, because she last renewed her license during law school and failed the driver's eye test.

At her most recent eye exam she was 20/25 in each eye and 20/20 with both together. That would give her a license with no restrictions. She warns me, though, that practicing law may be driving her back into that myopic pattern.

The third daughter started going nearsighted in ninth grade in a new school in a new city. She recovered and began again to adapt into myopia her junior year. At one point she could only see 20/80 with one of her eyes. She pulled out of it again with a great deal of athletic activity. She was always an excellent student, but her love for dancing, tai chi, and synchronized swimming in college held her vision stable. Now, as a professional ballerina, dance/movement therapist, and choreographer, who also uses computers to manage a business, she has an excellent 20/15 in one eye, 20/20 in the other. She was motivated to maintain her vision because our Dr. Francke in Washington had explained that she would never dance her best if she had to wear minus lenses. What he meant, I know now, was that her spatial awareness and movement would be compromised because of the side effects of those lenses.

HOW MUCH AT RISK OF GOING NEARSIGHTED IS YOUR CHILD?

There are a number of predictable factors that contribute to increased risk of making the myopic adaptation. Parents need to be aware of these.

If your child starts squinting, thorough testing with a behavioral optometrist would be a good idea before the distance clarity is gone. One of the first stages of myopia is to be blurry at distance after close work. The eyes do not recover as fast as they had previously when everything was normal. This testing will reveal what visual function patterns are driving the system into that adaptation. There is no such thing as a "simple case of myopia that does not require thorough testing." That was always a fantasy of my optometry students. There is also no such thing as the perfect training procedure or bifocal prescription for controlling and reducing myopia for *all* patients.

This is what makes treating myopia so fascinating for the practitioner who decides to "treat" it rather than simply "correct" (compensate) it with minus glasses. Glasses are tools, not crutches. You want a doctor who understands that distinction.

Risk Factors

It is useful for parents to have some grasp of what are considered by optometrists to be the big risk factors for going myopic. These factors are circumstances that create stress and thus lead to functional adaptations. The environmental risks need to be addressed, so that lifestyle changes can be instituted to eliminate as many as possible. The underlying functional problems can be treated with vision therapy and reading and training glasses, hopefully before "the horse is out of the barn" without preventive measures to rein it in.

Traditional myopia research has elaborated extensively on these risk factors. Reviews on the topic have been done by a number of optometrists (Sherman 1993; Grosvenor 1989; Rosenfield 1994; Gottlieb n.d.). There are no doubt familial tendencies (though not specific genes) that foster myopia (Goss, Hampton, and Wickham 1988; Zadnik, Satariano, Mutti, Friedman, Sholtz, and Adams 1993), whether from common natures or common lifestyles, including habitual eye use. Two myopic parents is a greater risk; one does not seem to be a greater problem than no myopic parents (Thomas 1992). Nonmyopic parents can still have myopic children if their lifestyle fosters it.

Mechanical forces on the eyeball from the oblique muscles during sustained focusing have been suggested as a major direct cause (Green

1980, 1981). The hereditary positioning of extra ocular muscles would make this worse in some kids. Near focus problems can occur that are associated with going myopic (Gwiazda et al. 1993). Inadequate binocular systems are associated with going myopic also (Goss and Jackson 1993; Gwiazda, Thorn, Bauer and Held, "Myopic children . . ." 1993). Preventive vision therapy and reading glasses would eliminate focus and binocular problems.

Some beginning myopes are clearly using overfocusing to hold the converging of eyes for single vision or experiencing overconvergence from focusing under stress conditions. There is a neurological connection, a focusing and convergence "synkinesis" that facilitates that type of adaptation. It is aggravated by reading too much, too close, for too long, without varying eye use with frequent breaks or protecting the eyes with learning lenses.

Experience with adults on computers going nearsighted for the first time has made it clear that fatigue of the eye muscles has to be considered (Costanza 1994; Sussman, Loewenstein, and Sann 1993). This is aggravated by weaknesses in nutrition, such as deficiencies of chromium because of too many refined carbohydrates (Lane 1981, 1982). Erratic sleep routines, lack of exercise, and "zoning out" on the computer without regular breaks all result in inefficient energy metabolism and greater fatigue than under optimal conditions.

Clinical observation suggests that head or neck injuries or blows to the eye can also be precipitating events (Roca 1971), as my daughter's whiplash injury was, in spite of excellent treatment. General stress is a major risk factor here also, one that will be discussed at length as the number one cause of myopia (Bowan 1996).

Frequently lifestyle imbalances, such as too much TV (Pearce 1992; Healy 1990), which is prevalent now among children (Nielson 1990), computer use, or excessive reading in poor light without looking far are major risks, also (Young 1961). All of these habits overwhelm the system with central vision, curtailing the use of peripheral (ambient) processing.

Posture is another risk factor. If the head is poked forward, many degrees of peripheral vision are lost. If a person converges best gazing down and his computer is straight ahead or up a bit, he will tend to tilt his head back in order to gaze downward at the computer. This causes extreme muscle tension in the neck and back and warps posture and frequently vision, as well. Neck, head, and torso alignment can be improved with help from a body worker and an ergonomic evaluation of workspaces (Alexander 1984; Harmon 1958; Francke and Kaplan 1978; Huxley 1982).

A variety of risk factors combine as the stressors in individual myopia cases, just as there are a variety of risk factors involved in anyone's development of heart disease. Dr. Dean Ornish's model for reversing heart disease is practical in myopia reduction. Based on the evidence that mental, nutritional, emotional and spiritual issues are all involved in the health of the heart, Ornish treats all of them (1990). Dr. Andrew Weil focuses on all of these also in his "8 Week Plan for Optimal Healing Power for the Whole Body" (1995). The eye/brain complex is a priority user of body energy, drawing on about 25 percent of available energy, so the health of the whole body is essential to having sufficient energy to keep the eyes flexible and strong. Fatigue, stress, malnutrition, emotional issues, and bodily limitations can all compromise one's vision.

To reduce myopia, we must keep in mind that the visual system, which flows throughout the brain, is neurologically connected to every other sensory and motor system (Cool 1993; Zeki 1993). The visual system affects and is affected by posture, balance, motion, memory, perception, and thought. It is much more than the tiny part of us that is our eyeballs, much more than the eye chart shows, much more than the brain connections with the central part of the retina (called the fovea) that we use for reading, computers, or TV.

The following are three principles, relating to diagnosing and controlling myopia, around which the rest of this chapter is organized:

1) The factor of general stress and near point visual stress. Reading glasses and therapy can reduce near vision stress. Sports activities reduce general stress and give the eyes a chance to look far. Endorphins, nature's calming hormones, are produced in vigorous exercise. Nutrition is also used to enhance energy to meet the needs of stress and can directly protect eyeballs.

2) Individuality of cause. Each child who is going nearsighted will have his own unique habits of eye use that are driving the process of losing distance clarity. Intervention is possible because change

is always happening in the eye and in the brain's programming for vision.

3) Imbalance between peripheral and central visual systems. Treatment, therefore, must revive the ambient system (peripheral vision) and integrate it with central vision processing. The central system breaks down into myopia if it has to do all the work. That is an improper use of the eyes and the energy drain is enormous.

STRESS AND VISION

Myopic patients going through myopia reduction often recall issues of emotional or physical stress that clearly used up their energy at the time of worsening vision. Stress is also a factor in the onset or worsening of myopia because it leads to sympathetic nervous system outflow, affecting the accommodative/convergence system and flooding the body with adrenal hormones that make it hypersensitive to the slightest stimuli. Adrenalin dilates the eyes and reduces focusing ability. Another stress hormone, cortisol, reduces the ability to stay mentally focused and remember, thus further increasing stress (Hannaford 2002) for people "trying to do their best." Dr. John Streff, who ran the Cheshire Schools Research Program on learning and vision for the Gesell Institute, found that myopic children scored much higher on the Sarason Anxiety Scale than those who were not myopic (Streff 2006).

I have noticed that when I give reading glasses to a "stressed-out" student with high normal intraocular pressures, their eye pressures reduce. That is good. Adults whose myopic glasses are too strong also show lower eye pressure after a lens change that reduces continual overfocusing. We know from research that a focused eye for near vision has higher pressure than an unfocused eye looking at distance (Kavner 1985; Bowan 1996).

It is very important not to let children read constantly. They need to look up and shift focus every ten minutes. They can put a bookmark in a few pages ahead to remind themselves to do that. We have known for decades that 75% of monkeys confined to cages where they had no far view went myopic very fast (Young, cited in Kavner, 1985). Outdoor sports tend to cut down on the prevalence of myopia by allowing regular shifts in focus at distance.

How Stress Affects Eyes

How could stress (including eye stress) have such an impact on eyes? What is the physiological mechanism? Some really bright people have researched it in the field of behavioral optometry. The stress concept, introduced by Skeffington and elaborated by Birnbaum (1984, 1985, 1993) and Forrest (1988), was further developed by Bowan, who combined Selye's "general adaption syndrome" (Selye 1976) and Lane's research on nutriture and vision (Lane 1982) to show how biochemical stress factors can affect the eye. Excessive and continual focusing at near, as mentioned, raises pressure inside the eye and stretches the sclera, especially when there is insufficient protein, calcium, and vitiamin C, all factors used up by stress (Bowan 1996).

A stretched sclera can mean a more myopic eye. This is because the sclera, what is called the "white of the eye," is a supportive tissue that actually envelopes the eyeball, except where the cornea provides a clear window for light in the front.

Some new research suggests that myopia is related to the stress on the body of refined carbohydrate diets. In the islands of Vanuatu, where school is compulsory for eight hours a day, only 2 percent of kids go myopic. They don't eat like American children. They have fish, yams, and coconuts. Scientists say it might be that the increase of insulin production from a blast of sugar, white flour, and refined cereals reduces "insulin-like binding protein-3," which could disturb the process of eye growth (Fox 2002).

Another effect of stress—that on posture in the form of the "tendon guard reflex"—has an indirect impact on vision. This reflex, an automatic result of stress causing sympathetic outflow, shortens the calves and locks the backs of the knees, pushing the balance forward onto the toes for "flight" or readiness to "fight" (Hannaford 2005). This postural adaptation triggers adjustments up the spine, which tighten the lower back and neck. Clinical observation of patients in chronic stress reveals the tight neck, along with enlarged pupils, and often beginning or worsening myopia. Many patients in vision therapy habitually stand with their knees locked. More information on reflexes and their effect on vision is included in chapter five.

It is interesting that myopic children have been shown to have an "insufficient accommodative response to blur" (Gwiazda et al. 1993). This means they have trouble keeping things clear up close. This is seen in practice all the time, and behavioral optometrists like to give plus lenses to allow them to see well at near, so they will not need to be nearsighted to see up close. For anyone who wants all the physiologic details, Martin Birnbaum's discussion of Skeffington's "nearpoint stress theory" (Birnbaum 1984, 1985, 1993) is a very good read.

The study by Gwiazda, Thorn, Bauer, and Held "Myopic children. . ." (1993) did establish that there is a significant difference in the recently myopic child's ability to accommodate (focus) to the stimulus of a minus lens. This is also true of recently myopic adults. The authors believe that "reduced accommodative (focusing) ability is found for a period after, and perhaps before, the onset of myopia, at whatever age it occurs." Once the patient has thoroughly adapted by going nearsighted, there will not be any more trouble focusing at near. The nearsighted eye can do that.

This near point focus stress and general stress theory, supported by research, explains the necessity of holding back on lens increases and using near point bifocals or reading glasses for myopia control. If patients don't get reading lens help early, or if they are not motivated to use it, other adaptations can occur. Below is a simple review of the theory so that parents and teens can clearly grasp it.

What Do Parents Need to Know about Visual Stress to Help Their Children Avoid It?

When we are under stress (or even just concentrating hard on a task requiring intense attention and information processing), studies have shown that our sympathetic nervous system—the fight/flight mechanism—turns on to try to help us. All of its power, though, is directed to setting the eyes to see far for flight and not for taking pencil and paper tests at near.

The world has changed, but the body has not. Children, for example, have to sit still while taking tests, worrying about grades, being told to hurry, and trying to focus their eyes on new tasks that they are just learning. There are also enough general stresses in most lives to activate the sympathetic system even without school tests. Some children and adults live with chronic sympathetic activation (Birnbaum 1984, 1993; Forrest 1988).

Near work unfortunately is more difficult when the eyes' focus is reduced and pupils are large, which is what sympathetic outflow does. This creates a natural tendency to be blurry at near (what optometrists call "natural cycloplegia," just as if there were dilating drops in the eyes), so the child or adult puts out extra effort to focus. This may use up energy needed to shift focus from near to far and make it hard not to get stuck in that same extra focus all the time, even at distance. The extra effort, studies show, is between 0.25 and 0.75 diopters of focusing (Birnbaum 1984, 1993), which is why low-powered reading lenses can reduce stress for children and adults doing near tasks, even if they are not farsighted.

All children sitting in desks using enough intense concentration to meet their teacher's expectations are at risk for the near point stress adaptation (i.e., myopia). The sympathetic system is activated by intense concentration as well as stress (Birnbaum 1984, 1993). Adults regularly pressured to meet deadlines have the same experience. Computers are particularly problematical because of the dot matrix print (even on the new flat screens), constant standard distance, need to look straight ahead instead of down at a slant, and often-cramped space without windows to rest the eyes in far gaze. Another problem with screens is that they use backlit radiant light and are not objects in space seen with reflected light. This is a different kind of seeing from what the human eye has been doing for centuries.

The Cheshire Schools Project with the Gesell Institute Improved Test Scores and Vision by Reducing the Sitting-Down Stress of Close Work

Many years ago, Dr. John Streff and colleagues from the Gesell Institute in Connecticut collaborated with five schools in Cheshire,

Connecticut, to change the way classroom learning was presented, so that children could use all of their senses with freedom of movement and learn through their own systems while having fun testing out their own speculations. Abstract concepts were not presented first. This would have reduced a lot of stress for many children. Teachers had workshops to prepare the problem-solving, free-space curriculum. The project lasted for six years. There were 346 children in the experimental group (with the new methods) and 476 in the control group.

In the school that adapted the best to the experimental program, there were only two children who went myopic during those school years. Overall, for girls in the control group, the prevalence of myopia was 30 percent and in the experimental group it was 10 percent. For boys it was less of a spread. Test scores on the Iowa tests were higher in the experimental group. The mean was the 90th percentile, which is extraordinary.

Dr. Streff found that children entering after third grade into the experimental groups remained like the controls. It was evidently important, said Dr. Streff, that the children were captured early. It seems that the self-motivated, hands-on, eyes-on, ears-on, movement-on approach before coming to conclusions resulted in fun learning, less stress, better test scores, less myopia, and learning habits that were not easily acquired after third grade (Streff 1972, 1997, 2006).

Dr. Streff spent half of every day assisting in the classroom, one grade level each year. His book with educator Ellen Gunderson, *Childhood Learning: Journey or Race?* (2004), presents this brilliant optometrist's contribution to thinking about how we can educate well and healthily.

Controlling Visual Stress with Reading Glasses or Bifocals

Plus lenses can substitute for the tendency of the eyeballs to develop into stronger plus lenses (i.e., nearsighted eyes). The +0.25 , +0.50, or +0.75 near prescriptions take the place of the amount of accommodation that is lost from stress or too much intensity (Birnbaum 1985). When people already wear minus lenses, they may need a cut of that small amount of power in a reading prescription to be comfortable for near work. This can break the progressive myopic cycle. If a small cut from the distance power is used for near work, patients may be able to use the reading prescription for most intermediate distances after a while and keep the strong ones only to drive. At that point, a new weaker minus or a plus reading prescription is in order (Orfield 1994).

Unfortunately studies have focused on magic bullets, such as +1.00 or +2.00 bifocals to control myopia (Grosvenor, Perrigin, Perrigin, and Maslovitz 1987). These may be too strong, except in cases of high amounts of esophoria (eyes aiming too close) (Goss and Grosvenor 1995). Doctors can look at the change in a refraction of increased myopia or astigmatism and get a good idea of how much plus is needed to stabilize the system. If a person is one-half a diopter worse, then maybe a reduced reading prescription by one-half a diopter would have saved his vision. Some patients are clearly helped by just a +0.25 or a cut of −0.25, which can often be obtained by wearing some older glasses to read. This only works if the balance of the two eyes' prescriptions remains the same.

The average worsening of myopia per year is −0.75 diopters, so it is not surprising that often, a +0.75 diopter reading prescription is required to stabilize the vision. When these patients' vision got worse, they had built the reading prescription that they needed right into their eyeballs by going more myopic. This made the old distance prescription less clear for far, but better for near. This is an unconscious brain process. Part of it can happen in the first weeks of adjustment to the yearly change to a stronger prescription.

For myopia control at any age, a reduced prescription may need to be part of the treatment, but "cold turkey" off of minus all at once is not recommended. Clinical experience indicates that a fuzzy 20/20 or 20/25 prescription for adults works best at first. Later they often clamor to cut more quickly. A 20/30 to 20/40 lens for most children is useful because it protects those who will not wear their reading glasses or a bifocal, and it will reduce blur in the periphery. They must, however, be clear at near without a lot of wasted energy output caused by too close a working distance stressing their eyes. Near blur has been shown to cause myopia (Norton 1999), so we don't want them blurry at near as we try to reduce their nearsighted adaptation at distance.

The Case for Minimal Prescriptions in Animal Studies

My old eye doctor, Amiel Francke, told me years ago, "You train a patient whenever you put a lens on him" (Orfield 1994). Training means brain training. Dr. John Thomas, an optometrist who has expertise in the field of myopia, has suggested that maybe the distortion created by high minus lenses in the periphery of a child's vision causes myopic degeneration on the retina and stretching of the eyeball (Thomas 1992).

This is not farfetched when you look at animal studies (Norton 1999). With chickens, an Australian group of researchers showed that "only peripheral field occlusion is necessary to induce a myopic shift, while the central retina is receiving sharp images" (Crewther, Nathan, Crewther, and Kiely 1984). These things were suspected also by Elio Raviola and Torsten Wiesel in this country. They believed that the retina exerts a control on eye growth by responding to the light patterns reaching it by "releasing regulatory molecules" (Raviola and Wiesel 1979).

The best prescriptions, then, would not be so intense in the central vision category that there would be excessive distortion of the peripheral vision to create an impetus for further elongation of the eye. In my own case, I believe I was able to train out of myopia partly because I never wore my glasses to read and I was too vain to wear them when I was younger, except when I really had to see in the movies or in school. My retina did not suffer a great deal of myopic degeneration, perhaps because it did not suffer from lack of peripheral light.

Controlling General Stress

Besides prescribing individualized reading adds and milder than 20/20 distance prescriptions, the behavioral optometrist will want parents to reduce the energy drain of general stress for their kids. The fact is stress of any kind causes myopia, because it reduces the ability to focus at near point and invites the adaptation to go nearsighted in order to see better up close.

Long golden afternoons are needed in childhood but seem to be a thing of the past, since children have been programmed into so many activities after school because both parents work. There is also the problem of more and more homework (Harp 1995). The emphasis on national tests for public schools and early private school admissions pose a problem also. The less-pressured alternative of public schools supplemented with private tutors when needed, and family travel, is less costly and more fun for the whole family. I will never forget the gratitude of an architects' family that I urged to go with public schools to have money for travel. They took a trip to France with both children the summer after the first year in public school.

It has been my personal and clinical experience that super nutrition sometimes takes the edge off life's stresses and allows stubborn people to continue in their current habits with fewer side effects. Many of the children and teens going myopic have erratic eating habits. I explain that the effects of stress can be mitigated by appropriate food intake and vitamin supplements.

It is well known that nutrition has an impact on all the systems of the eye (Cooper, Yolton, Kaminski, McClain, and Yolton 1993; Edwards, Leung, and Lee 1996; Lane 1982, 1994), the functioning of the brain (Shinaur 1975), as well as overall health (Todd 1985). Protein and calcium are major players in preventing myopic adaptations. Chromium picolinate helps metabolize carbohydrates to give the ciliary muscle more energy to stay flexible. Multiple vitamins and supplements of vitamin C are often recommended. When I did training with Francke, I was given a paperback by Ray C. Wunderlich, MD, on how to improve my nutrition (1976). An overall reduction or elimination of refined carbohydrates is highly recommended for all health issues, including those relating to vision and learning and development of myopia.

Visual Hygiene and Stress Reduction

We have noted how the Cheshire study reduced stress with more problem solving, less testing, and less rote learning. It engaged the children, and they did better visually and on tests (Streff 1977). Optometrist Harry Wachs and Piaget scholar Hans Furth's book, *Thinking Goes to School*, suggests many large space, hands-on activities to substitute for hard-on-the-eyes dittoes and workbooks in elementary school (Furth and Wachs 1974). It might still be available in libraries.

Years ago, the stress guru Dr. Hans Selye pointed out that some people experience some things as stressful that other people find healthy challenges or fun projects (1976). Children in the second group will do okay. Plus glasses, good light, and good posture for all near work will help the others. "The others" are the worriers, the overdutiful perfectionist children, the book worms, the children trying to keep up with important, busy parents, as well as those who get no help in the home because parents cannot read English well enough to understand the homework. All of these kids have enough pressure in their lives to make it difficult for them to stay relaxed visually. Many of them go near-sighted. In the absence of reading glasses, it is a useful adaptation.

There are some children for whom eye interventions to learn skills and reduce eyestrain might not be all that is needed. These are the ones going through big stresses like the divorce of parents; the death of a sibling, parent, or beloved caretaker grandparent; the remarriage of a parent; or a move away from good friends. Poor nutrition and lack of exercise will add more stresses on their health and metabolism. Helping children handle stress with nutrition—especially a good breakfast—and exercise after school pays off. Consider homeopathy, described in chapter five, or counseling.

The Right Kind of Food and Exercise for Stress

Some research has shown that a high-carbohydrate, low-protein diet is correlated with children going myopic. Other research shows that exercise will help prevent or control myopia, in that children who play sports have a significantly lower incidence of myopia. If your child is in a private school, he may be given enough sports activities as school requirements to help him handle the stresses of a competitive school. Competition in sports may also be stressful, but the body is designed to reduce the physiological effects of worry, fear, and pressure through physical activity. It is not designed to clear away stress by sitting at a desk, quiet as a mouse, taking tests, and tensing up one's jaw, neck, and shoulders. Nor is it designed for hunching over at a computer for hours every day.

Our culture has forgotten the old wisdom that really excellent food and a lot of daily exercise is absolutely essential for growing children. Besides building strong bodies with skills and awareness, it helps the body handle stress physiologically. Chemicals called endorphins stimulated by exercise support winding down from stress reactions of the sympathetic nervous system. They help the body restore the balance of the parasympathetic. If you want to think about the two systems, think about the sympathetic system as relating to fight/flight or "test the best," and the parasympathetic as relating to a cozy day in front of a fireplace, with nonstressful board games, books read aloud, and pleasant conversation.

When I was in a myopia reduction program my optometrist required all his patients to take up an aerobic sport. I chose swimming. I swam every day for a year for half an hour going as fast as I could go. That was half a mile most days. I had no allergies that spring, and I caught no colds or flu the entire winter. I also noticed that my eyes got better faster. They literally were better for several hours after my swims, and that lasted many hours during the day. I also walked at least one hour every day. One of my doctors at Harvard University Health Services tells me that research now shows exercise every day is essential—not just three or four days a week.

Children need to do walking outdoors, looking far, to keep their systems from going nearsighted. I often took mine with me on roller skates. The old rule, "Use it or lose it," applies to distance vision as well as cardiovascular health and the working of large muscles in the body. During one of my daughter's early bouts of poorly developing vision, our eye doctor insisted that she play outdoors three hours a day. This went on for three months until summer when she stabilized.

THE VISUAL SYNDROMES THAT LEAD TO MYOPIC ADAPTATIONS

Many risk factors for myopia can be eliminated by willing patients or their parents. Some, however, are part and parcel of the child's nature and cannot be changed. I am thinking of the perfectionist child and the worrier. A lot of my myopic adults admit to those personal qualities as children. However, specific visual factors can be treated by the behavioral optometrist. These are visual syndromes that occur at the onset or worsening of myopia. To understand these, a thorough behavioral optometry exam must be done. If one spots one of the syndromes initially, it is much easier to treat it than to treat myopia after minus lenses have been applied.

Any threat to the binocular system is a major impetus toward making the myopic adaptation. Long ago I was surprised to hear my eye doctor say that a myopic person got that way *because* of poor vision. I had always thought myopia itself *was* the poor vision. No. It is a resolution to the problem of performing with poor visual skills. What I see in my practice are very poor visual skills in all the kids who are going myopic.

There are two general categories of poor skills, although there are also many permutations and additional problems. One group is exophoric (eyes looking past the object of regard). There are many theories about why a child is exophoric in the first place, and some of that could be just placement of muscles on the eyeball, which might be the hereditary factor in myopia, if there is one.

A second group is esophoric (gaze meeting closer than the object they are trying to focus on). Each group has different problems that need to be addressed. Let us look at exophoria first.

Exophoria Sometimes Leads to Convergence Insufficiency at Near and/or Divergence Excess at Distance   Start with the child who looks too far. His eyes are too diverged relative to the target he wants to see. These kids going myopic have used their focusing mechanism to hold their eyes together in order to keep from seeing double at near, at far, or both. Recall that there is that synkinesis between focusing and converging the eyes. If the child focuses harder, the eyes will converge more. He can avoid double vision by focusing harder, but then his vision is blurred from focusing too much for the distance he is trying to see. If he does this, he has become nearsighted.

What he needs is vision training for proper convergence without overfocusing. Although minus lenses can be given to lock in his overfocus and make things clear at distance, if he reads through that same prescription he gets for distance, he will have to focus more to see at near when he was already overdoing it without glasses, and that can make him more myopic.

The problem with this adaptation is that he will some day reach age forty-five. At that point he will not be able to focus as much to hold his eyes together because of presbyopia (middle-aged reduction in focusing ability). Then, the best scenario will be that he gets prisms in his glasses and vision therapy. Otherwise, he may stop reading because of discomfort or double vision. He may pick one eye for near, the other for far, or struggle to keep focusing hard and get eye pain and headaches, and need to give up his computer job. I see a lot of these cases. They can be resolved, but they could have been prevented way back in that person's youth and childhood, when he learned without help to stop seeing double. As a child, he did his best. He decided to overaccommodate (overfocus) to hold his eyes together at near and/or distance to avoid strabismus and double vision.

This syndrome is a common precursor to myopia or worsening myopia. The cause of the exophoria could be anything from posttraumatic visual stress to what optometrists call the Skeffington/Birnbaum buffer against overconvergence (Birnbaum 1993). It needs to be treated rather than having increasing thicknesses of minus lenses applied. Training is needed and here is why:

Children are confused because of the way intermittent fatigue-induced diplopia (double vision) looks to them. With exophoric decompensations, they see crossed diplopia. In other words, their eyes see the right eye image on the left and the left eye image on the right. That is how the eyeballs are set up. Children with exophoria assume that in states of overlapping double vision, the right eye should be seeing the right image and the left eye should be seeing the left image, but it is the opposite of what they expect. They feel they must be crossing their eyes too much already, so do not try convergence power to recover the single view. What they don't know is that converging their eyes would bring the two views together. They give up on convergence.

The brain and eye complex have a failsafe device, though, to resolve double vision. Accommodation (focusing), which triggers accommodative convergence because of that synkinesis between the two systems, works. Soon they become more myopic, because they are in a state of overfocus constantly. They cannot release at distance because it is what holds their eyes together. They need therapy to stop the overfocusing and increase the convergence at distance and/or near, and with various biofeedback exercises, they can train their brains and eyes to do the right thing. Vision is a learned motor skill, but no one is teaching it to the children, and their daily activities that used to teach it are no longer what they used to be.

The Esophoric Shift Is a Tendency to Look Closer than the Target   The child who is esophoric is a little more difficult to cure with therapy, but therapy still does work. Reading glasses work well with this problem (Goss and Grosvenor 1990). The child is going nearsighted, not because of needing to focus hard to hold the eyes together (as the ex-ophoric child), but because he is overconverging. This child is looking too close, so that when the lines of sight of both eyes get to the plane in space where the target is, they have already met in front of the target.

There is blur if eyes are not meeting in space where they want to fo-cus or close to that point. Unfortunately, while minus lenses seem to clear up the blur a bit, they may just drive the child to more looking too close. Plus lenses for near can relax that focus and put the eyes in a po-sition in which they will not look too close. Plus lenses always need to be prescribed in a way that results in clear vision at near. There is no magic lens power that will help all kids going myopic.

Plus lenses do help esophoric kids to be more comfortable for near vi-sion, whether or not they are going nearsighted. They can help move their convergence back out to where they are in focus for near work. Vi-sion therapy can help get to the root causes of that adaptation in the child's awareness of what his eyes are doing.

One theory of how this syndrome develops is the concept of the esophoric shift after sustained near work. A brilliant optometrist, the late Dr. Martin Birnbaum of SUNY College of Optometry in Man-hattan, explained why. This tendency to overconverge (look too close) arises from the natural cycloplegia (reduction of focusing ability at near as if there were dilation drops in the eyes) created by sympa-thetic nervous system outflow (fight/flight impetus) under either in-tense attention or stress (Birnbaum 1993). The child needs to in-crease her efforts to focus.

Here is how the physiology of it works. Recall that pesky but use-ful synkinesis between *effort* to focus and convergence. The conver-gence is connected with effort, not results. The need for extra effort to focus at near against the sympathetic system drives the child's eyes to look too close. The result may be that he is looking too close when he is stressed, and things won't be clear because they are clear farther out than where he is looking (Birnbaum 1984, 1985). The sympathetic stress response also dilates the pupils, helping them to be set for flight or fight, not for test taking or reading, so he is even more hand-icapped visually (1993). This is why distance vision deteriorates after a hard day on the computer.

To visualize that mismatch between the two systems of focusing and converging, picture a string with two beads several centimeters apart. The string is held up to the nose and tied at the other end to a doorknob. Accommodative convergence (single vision) is resting on the closer bead, but focus (accommodation) is stuck out on the one a little farther away. This esophoric shift, one of the possible responses to near work stress, is one of the major observable factors in the onset or worsening of some kinds of myopia when it spreads to distance vision as well.

When this pattern spreads to distance, the complaints are of blurry vision because convergence of the two eyes lands closer than the object of regard, but the best solution is not more minus, which is usually given when doctors don't test the visual system function thoroughly and simply diagnose myopia.

Observation of patients doing vision therapy indicates that these patients increase the blur when they mistakenly try to focus their eyes more to clear the view. They need, instead, to relax the focus to see clearer. During procedures that use biofeedback by separating the views of the two eyes at distance and near with doubling glasses, both doctor and patient can see what is happening.

The esophoric child sees the image of the right eye on the right and the one from the left eye on the left, so instinctively she tries to converge her eyes more to get the overlapping images together. This is the opposite of the problem we saw with the child who is exophoric, going myopic. The esophoric child must learn to not only defocus (relax) the eyes, but also understand that spreading the eyes wider apart (diverging) will pull the images together. This is how the eyeballs are set up. Double vision, in which the image on the right is to the right and the left is to the left, is from overconverging. Counterintuitive as it seems, it is a fact that if learned helps train patients in a more successful use of their visual system.

Myopia reduction must be done gradually with training, though, because the patient needs to learn where the new "virtual image" is and how to align the eyes there and match his focus with his convergence. Minus lenses create a virtual image in space that is smaller and closer than the real objects of regard. If the mismatch between focusing and converging is not resolved, it will leave patients teetering between blurry and double.

There Are Several Other Visual or Life Habits That Help Create Nearsightedness

Tunneling from Emotional or Physiological Stress   Shutting down the periphery under stress leads to loss of awareness of where to focus and where to converge. This can cause myopia and lead to other warps in the accommodative/convergence system. Studies show that people do lose their peripheral (ambient) vision under stress or doing complex central tasks (Shipman in Francke 1988; Williams 1985). Also, sedentary near work reduces it (Trevarthen and Sperry 1973).

This is why children, without the basic visual skills needed to sustain focused effort at near, begin to close down the ambient system. If they are pressured for school success, near work becomes exhausting. If they do not avoid it, they must make an adaptation to allow continued effort. They give up their ability to refocus for distance, stop looking around, zero in at near, and are given minus lenses. They have lost the energy to use their vision for purposes other than burrowing into books or zoning out on television and computer screens. The minus lenses compound the reduction of periphery and increase the tension if they are worn for near work. These children gradually "tunnel" more and are eventually "lost in space."

One technique to use on tunneling children is to tap their occipital bone and say, "Vision happens back here. Be aware of the back of your head," or, "Be aware of the space behind you." Often they immediately get one or two more lines of acuity. A "blink and breathe" suggestion is another way to get them to relax and see more clearly. Experience has shown that how one perceives space—where one thinks objects are—has a large impact on how one's vision operates. If patients know where they are in space, they will have efficient vision. In therapy we tell patients that if they look where the virtual image of the object is located in the weaker lenses, it will be clear. This works. Learning to do that is what reducing myopia is all about. The minus prescription has trained the brain not to look far and wide, but to look at a closer, virtual image instead, compressing space. The more minus one wears, the more compressed space gets, the less volume one sees, and the sharper the flat outline world becomes.

Unfortunately, avoiding increases in minus or prescribing less are just the treatments that optometrists and ophthalmologists feel they cannot often do. Patients habituated to strong lenses want telescopic sight with sharp outlines every hour of every day, and they panic if they notice the fluctuations that occur in normal vision. They have lost the periphery, which makes them overly dependent on the sharpness of central sight. In many cases, it is the telescopic lenses that are the driving force for increasing myopia, because they gradually, imperceptibly cause the patient to ignore the warped periphery that nearsighted lenses cause and take away any chance that they will learn to relax focus at distance (Thomas 1992). Such a patient has lost the ability to use the signal of blur at distance to respond in a manner that clears the view. Since minus lenses cause some blur on the periphery, wearing them full time might cause elongation of the eye, which would mean more myopia (Crewther et al. 1984).

Blur at near does tend to increase myopia. It is an unconscious adaptation that happens very fast, as people take two weeks to "adjust" to their new, stronger glasses that are not so great at near, but really sharpen things up at distance. In a few weeks, near will be okay again, but far will slightly diminish. At their next yearly exam, they will "need" a stronger distance prescription again. In this way, the readaptive, progressive process goes on. I see it still going on in thirty-year-olds in graduate school who have never worn a lesser prescription for close work.

It is also increasingly clear that in children, full prescriptions for minus at distance are probably contraindicated on developmental grounds (Hung, Crawford, and Smith 1995; Smith 1994). These will interfere with normal visual development because there is no room for defocusing at distance to get a clearer view. Children have trouble learning to make distinctions between near and distance focusing when they are wearing full prescriptions.

Tunneling Is Aggravated by Learning to Read Up Close before Reading Far   After examining hundreds of children learning to read, it has been my clinical conclusion that if they could learn to read street signs, store fronts, license plates, and large flash cards across the room first, before they read books up close, they would not have to learn two things at once—how to read and how to focus on little print at near. They would not get confused about what their eyes should be doing to read street signs and eye charts at simulated faraway distances. Seeing far is different than seeing near. If kids read print at near first, they tend to think when seeing street signs, "Oh, it is print, I better focus to read." Yet that will not make the faraway print clear. If they read at far first, they would not tunnel because they would not be under stress and their eyes could remain aware of the periphery. This would go a long way to preventing myopia.

Print Size in the Early Grades Matters   This is one area that desperately needs research. What size print and what presentations should be made of reading materials at what distances for children in the early grades? Eye testing should never just assume the children are habitually working at fourteen- or sixteen-inch test distances (Ward 2006). They will look much closer to the target. Testing should never assume that just because they can see a letter for a second, they will be able to sustain focus for long periods of reading. Too many bright children are failing reading, and others are going myopic from adaptations to small print at close distances too early in their visual development.

The Right Kind of Bifocals Sometimes Help Tunneling   It is important that the prescription given for a reading bifocal does not cause blur at near, and that the bifocal type does not cause blur on the sides the way the progressive (no line bifocal does). There also must be a separate single vision reading prescription for the computer and homework. Small differences between distance and near prescriptions often work better than large ones unless there is a lot of esophoria (Friedhoffer and Warren 1988; Goss and Grosvenor 1990; Goss and Uyesugi 1995; Greenspan 1975). A good case has been made for a greater cut in minus or more plus in the bifocal as a result of the studies in near-work induced transient myopia (Rosenfield, Ciuffreda, and Novogrodsky 1992). There are many different choices in treatment with glasses. Your behavioral optometrist is the best practitioner I know to make those decisions for your child's specific visual needs.

Physiological or Induced Disparities between Eyes   Disparities between eyes can interfere with binocular vision and are often associated factors in the onset of myopia. For example, built-in size or color perception differences between the two eyes or minute amounts of metamorphopsia (degrading of a tiny central part of an image) in one eye interfere with balanced rivalry for cell connections in the visual brain (Zeki 1993). The more perfect eye has an advantage in the competition for brain connections during development, and it is often the overworked eye at near going myopic first. Patients are surprised that it's the good eye that is getting more nearsighted, faster.

When a child suppresses an eye on testing or says he usually uses only one eye, further testing is mandatory and training will be necessary to stabilize the system. If parents or doctors look for these things, their prevalence is not rare. If a binocular vision problem does not resolve quickly with training, it is likely that one of these disparities exists.

There are also *induced* disparities that result from the brain's attempt to stabilize vision. Many patients will try to salvage some distance and some near vision by adapting one eye for near and another for far, building in anisometropia (significant difference between prescriptions in the two eyes). This may begin when working distances at school desks are too close for the child to converge, so he picks one eye. I have seen this happen frequently, and especially with too early computer use.

Still other children will develop a kind of astigmatism (called "against the rule") in order to maintain a space where they are comfortable at near using both eyes, and still seeing far clearly (Birnbaum 1978; Nicholson and Garzia n.d.). In this type of astigmatism, the meridian going across the page horizontally is the more myopic or less hyperopic meridian. In other words, this horizontal meridian will facilitate easier focusing at near without effort because it is more nearsighted. That is what myopia does. It helps you see up close without too much effort. "Correcting" this fully with cylinder (astigmatism) lenses takes away this adaptation, locks in the astigmatism, and may drive the system to build in more astigmatism.

The rarer kind of astigmatism ("with the rule") that is not functioning to help the child read will, if it is a significant amount, need a prescription to help him see at near and far (Harvey, Dobson, and Miller 2006).

Vertical or Torsional Imbalances Interfering with Binocular Vision   These are due to pelvic, cervical spine, or cranial misalignments after auto accidents, birth trauma, head bumps with or without concussions, or falls. They often show up as a precipitating factor in vision problems if careful case histories are taken.

More data on post–auto accident vision problems need to be collected. Clinical experience indicates that sacro-occipital and cranial treatments with a qualified osteopath or chiropractor can often alleviate these problems, making vision therapy rapidly effective (Orfield 1994; Gilman and Bergstrand 1990).

Adults reducing myopia may have muscular or skeletal stresses locked into their postural systems that had repercussions for their visual development. Feldenkreis lessons (Heggie 1985), Alexander technique lessons (Huxley 1982), yoga (Agarwal 1986), tai chi, qigong, massage, and sacro/occipital or cranial treatments (see chapter five) may be suggested by the behavioral optometrist who treats myopia.

Other patients who have been doing bodywork, nutrition therapy, or stress management for other reasons often come in needing lenses reduced immediately. I have been seeing new patients like this for many years. It is interesting that Dr. William Bates (of the famous Bates method of better sight; Bates 1981), doing his type of vision therapy back in the 1930s, used "some kind of manipulations of the head, neck, spine, and pelvis in his treatment of those with defective vision" (Heggie 1985).

Clinical observation indicates that those who have no problems with nearsightedness are often naturally active, sit up straight, look up frequently, and move around a lot. Cultural lifestyles play a part, too (Carr and Francke 1976). Those who curl up on the couch with books, stay inside, and disappear from earth for hours at a time into their minds are more at risk. So are children addicted to computers and TV.

Poor Nutrition and Exercise Insufficiency Can Contribute to Myopia Nutrition and exercise allow focus shifts by creating the energy for them and the opportunity to move through space and look at many different distances. Deficiencies in these two areas stress the whole physiological system, so that it has to compensate. Such lacks are seen frequently in children going myopic or college students getting worse. Children or adult students who go myopic often take in fewer nutrients than those who do not, even though they may not be any smaller or thinner (Edwards, Leung, and Lee 1996). Often, they have a much higher percentage of refined carbohydrates in their diets (Lane 1981).

There is also a problem of chromium deficiency in many myopic children triggered by the extra sugar. The chromium is used up to metabolize a diet high in refined carbohydrates, and as a result, it is not available for helping the refocusing of the eyes' lenses causing a spasm in the ciliary (focusing) muscle. Pressures in the eye go up from constant focus at near, and the sclera (whites of the eye) stretches, enlarging the eyeball and leading to progressive myopia. The sclera that stretches with higher pressures stretches more in children who do not get enough calcium relative to phosphorus (found in red meat) in their diets, so calcium might be a good supplement to use if taken with magnesium to help absorption. Calcium must be there to keep the sclera strong and the eye from stretching (Lane 1982, 1994; Kavner 1985; Cooper, Yolton, Kaminski, McClain, and Yolton 1993).

Picky eaters, couch potatoes on junk food, bookworms who never go outdoors to walk and look far, those with ill health who spend sick days in front of TV, and video game addicts are the children and teens I see going myopic.

Many myopic children have several risk factors for their condition and may exhibit several specific functional syndromes as well. The result of all of these is a compromised, inefficient visual system, for which hunkering down into myopia and near focus is a good way to cope.

When your child is being tested for nearsighted lenses, tell your optometrist that you want the following tests done on that exam: near and far acuity without glasses as well as with the old glasses, randot stereopsis, the near and distance phorias and vergences, the gradient, the near point of convergence, negative relative accommodation and positive relative accommodation, cross cylinder tests, minus lens amplitudes (monocular and binocular), MEM retinoscopy, flipper facility, a careful refraction with binocular balance to the least minus for 20/30 (until they have to drive), binocular removal of cylinder for least amount necessary, and an ongoing case history relating to findings.

You will want a reading prescription and a pair of "house glasses" that are both less than the distance pair. The distance pair for school should probably be in a bifocal. The behavioral optometrist serving patients from that 25 to 30 percent of the population who are myopic (Sperduto, Seigel, Roberts, and Rowland 1983; Gwiazda et al. 2003) will know how to treat your child's specific type of myopia and visual syndromes.

A Case of Intermittent Esotropia Cured by Reducing Myopia   I had a patient who was a psychologist who conducted therapy across the table from her patients and liked to be able to look them in the eye. However, she was starting to see double, which meant her eye was starting to turn inward. She was wearing relatively strong minus lenses and was highly esophoric, at times esotropic. I told her that I would be able to stop the double vision if we could get her out of her minus lenses, or at least down to much less minus. She had acquired increasingly stronger minus prescriptions during high school, college, and her PhD program, likely as a result of too much visual stress with no separate reading glasses or good ergonomics for study.

This psychologist worked with me for a year on peripheral vision, focusing, relaxing, and controlled diverging and converging to get back to clear, single, binocular vision in a prescription that was just a fraction of what she had been wearing. The esophoria was gone. She backed out of her myopia one-half a diopter at a time by having three sets of glasses. She had one pair of glasses for her work with patients and around the house, reading glasses for all near work, which ended up being plus lenses after she had reduced her myopia, and distance glasses for driving and theater, which still had a little minus for the small amount of nearsightedness that was left. She never saw double again. I saw her for a one-month refresher course several years later and she was fine.

For years, optometrists have been doing studies of myopia control. It is important, because going myopic has its costs. It affects at least 25 percent of the adults who are then more at risk for retinal detachments, glaucoma, and myopic retinopathy (Sperduto, Seigel, Roberts, and Rowland 1983; Gwiazda et al. 2003).

The National Institutes of Health Comet myopia control clinical trial was a double blind, masked and matched study completed in four optometry school clinics. It used +2.00 progressive addition lenses (no-line bifocals) for the test group and plain distance prescriptions for the myopia control group. There was a small significant delay in myopic progression in the bifocal kids the first year of the study, but the protocol did not show enough help for myopia to "warrant a change in clinical practice," the authors concluded (Gwiazda et al. 2003).

The progressive addition bifocals allowed for the double-blind aspect of the study. It would be hard to tell who was wearing regular and who was wearing progressive lenses. I believe it would be hard for any study to produce positive results with all children getting the same +2.00 addition over their distance prescription. I also see a problem with no-line bifocals optically. They interfere with peripheral vision. The periphery is needed to help inform eye movements, get good depth perception and perspective, and prevent myopic progression.

MYOPIA AS AN IMBALANCE BETWEEN CENTRAL AND PERIPHERAL PROCESSING SYSTEMS, WHICH WE ALL NEED TO HAVE WORKING TOGETHER

So why would we want to go to this amount of trouble to keep our children from going nearsighted? The reason is that functional myopia is not just a successful adaptation to seeing up close when the child's system does not have the energy, skills, or calm to stay flexible. It is not just an elongation of eyeballs backward to get near focus clearer. This shift is based on a chemical signal from cells that are not getting clear vision at near or in the periphery (Norton and Seigwart 1995; Wiesel and Raviola 1979). It is not just a little spasm in the ciliary muscle that controls the focus of the eye's lens. It is all of the above, but it is more.

The way I and some of my colleagues see it, myopia is very much a shrinking of visual space, loss of periphery, loss of ambient vision (Gallop 1994 and 1996). Dr. Francke always said, and I learned from training out of it, that myopia causes perceptual mismatches between the mind's eye and the spacious real world. It leads to loss of coordination between peripheral and central vision Much more research on the ambient visual system as it relates to myopia is needed, but its significance to central vision has long been recognized by vision therapists and optometrists (Gallop 1996; MacDonald 1993; Marrone 1991) as well as scientists (Trevarthen, 1968; Goddard 1995). Its fibers course from the peripheral retina into postural centers in the brain, not into the centers for central vision. They feed information to the brain about space and affect balance, posture, and movement, as well as eye movements (Gallop 1996; Trevarthen 1968). Improving a patient's ability to use the peripheral system enhances sports skills, reduces stress, and, as clinical experience indicates, it can also help reduce myopia.

One role of the peripheral system is to inform the central system about location in space, thus controlling eye movements (Zeki 1993).

Movement through space involving balance is a major key to activating all these systems, because that is how all vision is learned and how the ambient system is turned on. Research on visual learning that underlies the visual-spatial-motor approach to therapy is relevant here.

Early Research on the Ambient System Is Relevant to Myopia Control

Colwyn B. Trevarthen and Roger Sperry at Harvard found that the ambient system maintains perceptual unity in human commissurotomy patients whose central system was split into two hemispheres of consciousness by that surgery. Trevarthen also researched the ambient visual system with his experiments on split-brain monkeys (1968). Sperry and Trevarthen discovered that this peripheral system is turned on by movement. When focus is held steady centrally, periphery (part of the ambient system in his model) fades out. There is, he said, a kind of "reciprocal inhibitory coupling" between the two systems that depends on movement.

Full-time near work, then, will dim down the awareness of periphery. We want a balance. Children cannot spend uninterrupted hours staring at a screen or a book and have that reciprocal visual processing automatically develop.

Modern children and adult patients, however, must literally be forced to do purposeful movement, such as walking, which has become unpleasant for them, maybe from the mesmerizing effects of sitting with screens. As Carla Shatz, a Berkeley neurobiologist put it, "The remodeling of connections is activity dependent," and "In a sense, then, cells that fire together, wire together"(1992).

Among those whose work begins with body reprogramming, the visual motor connection is also recognized. The Alexander Technique is a good method of getting in touch with the proper way to move that enhances vision. When I was doing vision training for myopia reduction I had dozens of Alexander lessons. There is an appendix in Aldous Huxley's book, *The Art of Seeing* (1982), which explains that a number of children going nearsighted who had lessons with Alexander for their head, neck, and torso balance in movement were cured of their beginning vision problem. Posture and movement count.

Jack Heggie, a Feldenkrais practitioner working with clients and other practitioners to teach methods of vision improvement, emphasizes that therapy for vision improvement must consider the "ongoing relationship between vision, kinesthesis and proprioception." Coordination as well as vision is radically enhanced when one does procedures that require total awareness of where each part of the body is located in space relative to everything else. This is because there is an "internal visual/kinesthetic map of the environment and we act on this map," Heggie explains (1985, 1993).

A simple experiment that I use to show my patients how motor activity enhances binocular vision is to stand on a minitrampoline (rebounder) and look at a stereo fly target wearing three-dimensional glasses. With some binocular alignment one will see the stereo fly's wings coming off the picture, but a minute or two after one begins jumping, the fly will get more and more three dimensional, to the point of having very large wings and a body that protrudes far off the stereo test plate—the "phenomenon of the huge fly."

"Use It or Lose It" Applies to Vision as Well as Muscles

"Use it or lose it" is the way body and brain work, patients are told up front. In truth they have lost the ability to see far and wide, because they have not looked, being too engrossed at near point or too lost in thought, which keeps the eyes focused at near, really. The "dark focus of accommodation" that occurs with thinking is about six feet in front of us. Patients discover this for themselves by watching the effects of outdoor walks with some peripheral awareness tasks.

Even a little walking practice each day helps, just as only 30 minutes in the gym four days a week strengthens muscles and cardiovascular fitness. Walking allows the peripheral "y cell" motion detectors in the retina to be stimulated, thus waking up the peripheral processing and forcing the patient to figure out what and where the apparent motion is. This stimulates other cells and pathways in the ambient system.

Training the brain is necessary because adjusting to stronger and stronger lenses is essentially programming the brain to see space differently. Retraining to weaker and weaker lenses requires relearning patterns of movement in relation to perceptions of space.

This concept is based on solid studies of the nervous system. We know that "eighty percent of the nerve endings in the muscles are connected directly via proprioception to the vestibular system, with motor nerves to and from the eyes" (Hannaford 1995). When visual/motor procedures with peripheral awareness feedback are used, the patient sees more "volume" of space out of "the sides of the eyes"—up and down, side to side, and out in front. As a result, the eyes can focus and converge more accurately at distance and near in each new reduced lens. Sports vision is enhanced by the same motor procedures, because they improve the patient's ability to move effectively through space in a totally aware state, seeing well far and wide on the x, y, and z axes.

"Visual learning is enhanced by doing," said the late, great Bruce Wolff of Ohio, who has influenced scores of other optometrists (1987). Many if not all behavioral optometrists use visual/motor therapy procedures (Francke 1988; Gallop 1995, 1996, 2002; MacDonald 1996; Orfield 1994; Padula 1988; Streff 1977, 2004). "Doing" with attention creates positive biochemistry for learning (Kasamatsu 1982, 1987).

Clinical experience and the research on visual learning in animals nothwithstanding, there is a major deficit in research to show how myopia reduction works. It does if the parents and the child believe that it will work and do the therapy. Many more people are interested in doing it than have the time and faith to see it through. Clinically, it is obvious that myopia is in part a serious imbalance between ambient and focal visual systems. Therefore, lifestyle needs to be changed to allow for the periphery to return. If it does, the payoff is fun, perspective, relaxation, visual beauty and joy for the rest of one's life.

Seeing through high minus lenses gives a flat, sharply outlined view with peripheral distortion. People who successfully reduce their lens power all report that the training has given them a broader, more three-dimensional view and a feeling of being wrapped all around in mellower, gently complex light. They are grateful patients. In 1994, one of my patients wrote me a letter to post on my bulletin board. Here is part of it:

> I am so excited and invigorated now that I can finally experience the world again—my old familiar world—without corrective lenses. The first week I could do this, and could see quite clearly, I would spontaneously break

into tears because I was so happy. The only "dark side" to this is that I am at times overwhelmingly angry with the unenlightened, uninformed optometrist who insisted . . . that I could do nothing to improve my vision.

In nine months, at age thirty, she trained her vision to see without lenses from a −2.75 to a plano in order to pass the Federal Aviation Administration eye exam for her pilot's license. One eye saw 20/20, the other 20/20 minus a few letters. The military doctor, having no knowledge of her myopia reduction efforts, told her it was obvious that she had always had great vision, but she probably should have reading glasses, because the stress of graduate school was causing her left eye to be a little less clear. To accomplish this makeover, she had come to the office almost every week, walked outside an hour a day, and most days completed half an hour of eye exercises. She wore reading glasses over contacts that were continually being reduced. The last I heard from her, she was teaching in a large university and still stable without lenses, but faithfully wearing her computer/reading glasses.

The bliss that young woman experienced when she got the full "volume" of space back after giving up her minus lenses is typical of patients who manage to reduce their minus lenses to low powers or nothing. It is very much like Oliver Sacks' story of "Stereo Sue" in the *New Yorker* (2006). The neurobiologist Dr. Sue Barry's descriptions of her joy at seeing snowflakes separated in space at different depths and her sense of being wrapped around in space is something I and some of my patients have experienced also. This woman, who eliminated her postsurgical vertical eye deviation with prism glasses and therapy with behavioral optometrist Dr. Theresa Ruggiero, wrote the following to Dr. Sacks: "I could see the space between each flake, and all the flakes together produced a beautiful three-dimensional dance. In the past I would have felt like I was looking in on the snowfall. But now, I felt myself within the snowfall, among the snowflakes. . . . I was overcome with a deep sense of joy" (Sacks 2006).

I had the same experience with snowflakes that year of vision training in Washington, D.C., out on the mall. I was never strabismic, nor did I have any eye surgery, as Dr. Barry had. I had handled my binocular problem and mild organic amblyopia by going nearsighted and wearing thicker and thicker minus lenses.

I felt the wonder and joy at the beauty of clear, single, binocular vision day after day when I had reduced my distance vision correction down to the last three quarters of a diopter. I was in binocular vision training with Dr. Amiel Francke in 1981. Stereopsis is reduced in strong glasses so, though the person is not strabismic, the thrill of new depth in lesser prescriptions is overwhelming. I can remember crying with joy that the three-dimensional spaces between birds flying in formation were visible to me, that spaces between flowers in a garden seemed to go back and back as if the garden were a forest home for fairies, and that there were long arching tunnels of space under the trees that overhung the streets in my neighborhood. There were layers upon layers of clouds below me when I flew in an airplane, and suddenly I was "wrapped in space" in the mellow light of a winter evening party.

I clearly did not have good binocular vision in my strong lenses, and maybe never had past babyhood. There are many childhood photographs of me squinting. It took vision therapy and a lot of bodywork to cut that lens power and teach me to have binocular vision. After that I wore very minimal lenses for theater and driving until six or seven years ago, when I totally gave up the last of my nearsightedness.

One gets a sense of being in the world, rather than looking into it, and seeing the spaces between even the tiniest things when myopic prescriptions are reduced to very minimal ones. The months I began to "see space," as I called it, was truly one of the most joyful times of my life. I believe it is well worth trying to stop a child from becoming myopic and resolving their binocular problems with vision therapy instead. The result may not be perfect 20/20 sight—though it might be—but that child will be better off by far in lenses of less power with good three-dimensional vision than what he will adapt into if nothing is done to stop him.

Well-known SUNY school of optometry professor and behavioral optometrist Dr. Arnold Sherman, who also has a private practice in New Jersey, wrote the following regarding the eye's penchant to continue transforming itself for easier close work: "When an adaptation is decompensated (by stronger minus lenses), a re-adaptation will occur in order to achieve steady state performance at near tasks, resulting in a further increase of myopia" (1993).

In other words, myopia is a tendency of the visual system to use eyeball changes to adapt to the strain of too much near focus. Dr. Sherman calls the continual prescribing of more minus without any help of vision exercises or reading glasses the "iatrogenic cause" (doctor-cause) of myopia.

The Main Point Is that Peripheral Vision Is Extremely Important

Based on what we know about the ambient visual system and visual motor learning from research over the last forty years, it makes sense that vision therapy for reprogramming a visual system to reduce myopia must involve the peripheral system with motor activities. We must apply what we know about binocular vision to developing therapy procedures.

When I began my practice, I realized that optometry equipment in darkened rooms coupled with the patient's tendency to overfocus at distance often leads to overprescribing for myopia. My exam room has two windows with room darkening shades, but it is never really dark. I want it that way because if a patient does not have good peripheral vision, the dark exacerbates his condition, and he will need a stronger prescription to see the chart. And increasing the prescription will further reduce his peripheral space world.

Weaker lenses need to be prescribed to work on the whole room view, not just the tiny letters on the bottom row of the chart. If I am worried about night driving and sight at a Red Sox game, the adult patient simply gets a stronger prescription for only that. I do not sell any of the many glasses I prescribe. I think of them as tools, and I want patients to have a full toolbox without wondering if I have a conflict of interest.

Most of the children who come in myopic have large pupils that are not very flexible. Bright light will, of course, constrict them, but attempted focusing often does not constrict them much, if at all. This is a sign of sympathetic nervous system outflow that is somewhat imbedded in their habitual work from day to day. Recall that the sympathetic nervous system is used for flight or fight and dilates the eyes. Near focus becomes difficult, so myopia solves that problem.

I talk to the child and the mother about the fact that any intense near work causes that sympathetic nervous system to kick in, even though fighting a bear or wildly riding a horse and hurling a javelin is not the kind of stress that is going on. That is the kind of stress that would "blow off steam" of the fight/flight system. Instead, stress at near taking tests is going on, but it kicks in the same system that was designed for racing around on horseback.

One high school patient, who was trying to prevent myopia because he was a good pitcher on his high school team and wanted to avoid myopic lenses, heard me mention riding horses for blowing off stress and reducing sympathetic outflow. He talked his parents into sending him for a month of the summer to a ranch in Jackson Hole to ride horses and thus improve his vision.

Unfortunately, our culture does not provide many opportunities for such adventures. The child needs small pupils and focused eyes up close, but the nervous system does not succeed in achieving that with intense near work. It instead produces big pupils and, as is discussed earlier in this chapter, the cycloplegic effects of stress on the focusing process. Therefore, we as parents have to do five things:

1. Give the child reading glasses and opportunities to look far to rest eyes while studying.
2. Give vision training to improve the flexibility of the focusing system, the eye teaming system, the tracking system, and the ambient (peripheral) vision system, so that the ambient and focal systems are more balanced.
3. Have the child do something every single day to reduce stress on his system, eat more nutritiously (especially by starting with a good protein breakfast with lots of calcium and a vitamin pill), and exercise.
4. Eliminate all unnecessary stresses for the child, because life alone will cause enough of them. Get him help to cope with extreme stress such as a death or divorce.
5. Be sure that the ergonomics of his workspace are adequate for good vision development and posture.

If your children are fortunate enough to have all of those things done for them consistently, all those healthy habits taught to them as part of daily living, and major stresses eliminated from their lives, they will most likely never go myopic while they are under your roof. If they live by those habits later on their own, they may never go myopic at all.

TREATMENTS THAT SUPPORT EYES AND BRAIN FOR LEARNING: SEVERAL ARE USED IN INNOVATIVE SCHOOLS

"The eyes and the body are one," said the famous optometrist. I had signed on for vision therapy, but I was also shipped off to a gentle method chiropractor and an Alexander Technique teacher to work on my posture to enhance the effects of the vision exercises and training glasses.

"Everything goes faster if the infrastructure supporting vision is in place," he said. He knew the best of the best practitioners to get that work done, and I saw with my own eyes its impact on my vision. That famous doctor was not minimizing the power of his amazing work with vision, which cured my severe nearsightedness and functional vision problems. Vision problems could throw the body off, as well as the other way around, he said. Other practitioners need to keep their eyes open and know when to refer to a behavioral optometrist. The eyes and the body are one.

Because pathways from the eyes are woven through the brain to connect with all the sensory and motor systems of the body, the first stop for a child who has a learning problem should be a behavioral (sometimes called "developmental") optometrist. Eighty percent of learning happens through the eyes, so a thorough visual evaluation has to be done.

Behavioral optometrists are also the best referral sources for other therapies that really work to support vision. They know the best of the best practitioners in various fields because they refer frequently and monitor results.

There are six therapies, one or more of which I sometimes recommend to get a patient's brain and body up to par for good vision development. Three of them are movement-oriented therapies, which is understandable because movement trains eyes and brain:

1. infant reflex integration
2. low-velocity, gentle chiropractic
3. educational kinesiology (including Brain Gym exercises)

The other three are nonmovement therapies that support vision and learning:

1. neurotherapy
2. syntonics (light sensitivity training)
3. homeopathy

All six therapies are methods of healing that I have personally experienced. I have also studied aspects of each to some extent in classes or workshops with the exception of neurotherapy. I want my readers to know why the overall health of a child affects vision, and how these ancillary therapies can help children regain natural abilities to enjoy learning. I wish every school could offer all of them. A couple of schools I know have several of these treatment modalities within their walls along with vision therapy, and those are discussed in this chapter.

Let's look at body learning and how it affects eye and brain learning first. I have been thinking about body movement and brain development for many years, since I read an article by Glenn Doman of the Institutes for the Achievement of Human Potential in Philadelphia, when I was expecting my first child in 1969. It described many kinds of movement and sensory activities needed to develop a baby's brain, especially creeping and crawling. I put it into practice as soon as my daughter was born.

There is a fascinating diary (Napear 1974) by the mother of a mentally challenged child with cerebral palsy—who had taken her child to Glenn Doman and Carl Delacato (Delacato 1961, 1970) at the Institutes in Philadelphia. No one expected this child ever to learn reading or walking. With movement therapy for her body, her brain was trained, and she learned all of those things and much more. The book was a day-to-day record of that mother's training at the Institutes and her experience carrying out her daughter's program. The child started very late, after she had turned three, but still the treatments were enormously successful. After being wheelchair bound, she learned to creep and walk with "patterning."

"Patterning" was a program developed by Glenn Doman, a physical therapist, and Carl Delacato, a PhD educator and reading specialist (1970) with help from Temple Fey, a neurosurgeon. It is a method of training the brain to move the body, by having therapists move the body to train the brain to do it. In other words, if a child is not learning to creep, which is essential for optimal brain development, that child can be moved in a creeping motion so that the brain can "get it" and then take over controlling the action.

This program was training Peggy Napear's daughter Jane by having helpers work long hours moving her body to creep and crawl in the ways it would have, if the brain had not been injured at birth. She learned to talk, read, write, do arithmetic, stand, and even walk with a limp. Many physical activities were used besides the patterning to train her brain to be a true vehicle through which she could express her mind. This was back when it was not generally known that we sprout new dendrites all the time, and that neuroplasticity of the brain is a significant fact useful for rehabilitation purposes (Goleman 1985; Stumbo 2006; Cool 1993).

Doman's methods are still being developed further at the Institutes in Philadelphia (Doman and Doman 2006). Part of that complex is the Evan Thomas Institute to train healthy children's parents to raise them with optimal development. It includes a private model school for children who live in the area.

Glenn Doman, Carl Delacato, and even earlier, optometrist Gerald Getman were probably the leaders of the pack in discovering how the body affects the brain, eyes, and nervous system, but hot on their heels came three other advanced therapies. First let's look at infant reflex work.

INFANT REFLEX INTEGRATION IS A MAJOR HELP FOR CHILDREN STRUGGLING WITH VISION AND LEARNING

My hope is that every parent and school will understand the power of infant reflexes (often called primitive and postural reflexes) for either aiding a child's development if these are well integrated, or arresting it, if not. These reflexes are why it is important not to induce a birth unless medically necessary, have a Caesarian unless medically necessary, put a child in a walker, or in any other way discourage movement on the floor. All of these normal processes are magnificently designed by the developing brain to create a healthy nervous system for the child through infant reflex action, movement, and later reflex integration.

A look at one primitive (infant) reflex will illustrate what can happen if a reflex is not allowed to do its proper job. Sally Goddard's book, *Reflexes, Learning, and Behavior: A Window Into the Child's Mind*, explains 15 major reflexes (2002). I have chosen to discuss the symmetrical tonic neck reflex, which is necessary to learn to creep. Therefore, it is highly significant for laying down basic visual motor experience that underlies vision skills for learning to read.

The symmetrical tonic neck reflex gets the baby onto his hands and knees for creeping. He doesn't have to think about it. It is a reflex that goes along with certain movements. It emerges at six to nine months of life and fades out at nine to eleven months. What happens in an ideal world is that when a six-month-old tucks his head down, the reflex causes the arms to bend and the legs to extend, putting his bottom up into the air. When the head is extended, it causes the legs to flex and the arms to straighten, sitting him up on his knees with support in front from extended arms. This helps develop his vision, especially "fixation skills at near and far," "the shifts between near and far," and "binocular vision," explains Goddard (2002).

These reflexes are automatic stimuli that develop in the normal nervous system and let the child start to move. When this unique, late-coming and then disappearing reflex works well, the child is blessed. If it has not developed properly or persists beyond its ideal time, problems often manifest with creeping. Later, if it is retained, it can cause the tendency to slump when sitting at a desk, an ape-like walk, clumsiness, difficulties with binocular vision and eye-hand coordination, and slowness at copying.

I can remember when my children were up on hands and knees, rocking back and forth, ready to take off on their first creep. I did not know then that their movements were probably the way the symmetrical tonic neck reflex is inhibited and the way the sacrum and the occipital bone start to function in synchronized fashion with breathing, to pump cerebral spinal fluid up from the sacrum to the area around the brain. Later, when the child stands and walks, he will need that pumping action geared to his breathing to overcome gravity so that spinal fluid can bathe his brain.

Goddard writes that children who "retain this reflex" have trouble creeping on hands and knees (2002, 22). Either they don't do it at all, or the timing is off. Creeping helps the child learn tracking for reading as he looks from hand to hand, and strengthens the hand muscles for printing. It helps with sensory integration that in turn helps the child develop depth perception, good balance, and spatial awareness. In 1987, researcher Pavlidis observed that a high percentage of children with reading difficulties omitted the stages of creeping and crawling (23). This has been verified over and over in my practice when I ask parents if their child ever crept or crawled.

Every school needs a reflex specialist. It is the fastest way I know to achieve the kind of things that Doman and Delacato, back in the 1960s and 1970s, took months to achieve. This is because the practitioners I know who do this work use a program that combines reflexes with applied kinesiology (a chiropractic muscle testing method) and Brain Gym exercises. This integrated approach was developed by Dr. Svetlana Masgutova, a Russian chiropractor with a PhD in developmental and educational psychology, who now runs a clinic and international training program in Warsaw, Poland. She teaches internationally, as do Sally Goddard Blythe and Peter Blythe, who run the Institute of Neuro-Physiological Psychology in England, and Catherina Johannesson Alvegard's group from Sweden.

All these pioneers in the field are developing a whole new paradigm for saving children's neurological abilities for visual processing, skilled movements, and school learning. These are treatments that are sweeping the globe right now. They are much needed, for there are so many children at risk, and yet we are always behind in what is being offered compared to what is known.

In Dr. Masgutova's clinic in Poland, which includes a summer and a winter camp for challenged children, miracles are happening with the reflex and kinesiology work. For example, she told us of a child with cerebral palsy who could not move because he had "motor development on a level of zero." Masgutova could tell, though, that he had intelligent eyes and he had sensations. When she pressed on certain reflex centers, he could come to his knees; when she pressed on certain vertebrae, he started to walk in a palsied walk. He was motivated. He "wanted to go out on the balcony and smell the roses, and he did" (Masgutova 2004).

She got into this work through Brain Gym when she heard a lecture in 1988 by neurobiologist Carla Hannaford, author of *Smart Moves* (1995). Musgatova told those of us at her February seminar in New Hampshire in 2004 that she was very skeptical at first of Brain Gym, developed by PhD reading specialist Paul Dennison in the early 1980s (Dennison and Dennison 1989) with help from a chiropractor, behavioral optometrist, and occupational therapist. Then, in 1989, there was a railroad catastrophe in Russia and Musgatova flew from Moscow to the Ural Mountains to volunteer as a rehab worker.

Musgatova's orientation had always been a listening style that was begun by Carl Rogers in the United States years ago. It could not work on those comatose children. They had burns on 60–80 percent of their bodies and had broken legs and arms. She decided to try "cross crawl" and "lazy eights" (two Brain Gym movements) by moving them in their comatose state.

To her surprise, "Death stopped occurring and recovery was 6 to 8 times higher than the medical statistics would have allowed." When the children were conscious, Masgutova and co-workers asked them to "imagine you are doing this movement." She was so impressed with the results that she did a 12-year study to see how and why Brain Gym exercises work. From that research, she realized that these movements "remind the body of primary motion patterns" of infant reflexes and lifelong reflexes. The principle she learned is that "when you activate de-

velopmental mechanisms from nature, you always have results"
(Masgutova 2004).

As she later studied more reflex work and used the Brain Gym
movements to stimulate healthy reflex activity or integration, she tried
them with many types of neurological problems. She reported that
they work with attention deficit and attention deficit hyperactivity disorders (ADD and ADHD), dyslexia, cerebral palsy, premature infants,
and children born with caesarian sections whose basic birth reflexes
did not get activated.

The exercises may also help the child who looks totally normal but
just can't read. There was a reading specialist named A. E. Tansley
whose book, *Reading and Remedial Reading* (1967), suggested to educators that "just because a child looks normal, do not assume that he or
she has the equipment to function well in the classroom" (Goddard
2002, 121). He had read the work of Carl Delacato (of the Doman-
Delacato program at the Institutes). Delacato had reported in 1963 that
the children he assessed at the Institutes with specific reading problems
were all children who had failed to do the normal "crawling on the stomach" and "creeping on hands and knees." They had also failed to pick a
dominant side of the brain.

I found that fascinating, because when I was running the vision clinic
at the Mather inner-city school in Boston, where only one-third of the
children were at or above the national average in reading scores, I talked
with the gym teacher to see if she ever did assessments about "cross
crawl movement." She told me that at least half of the children could not
creep or crawl when tested. I had hoped she would give me the names
so I could correlate them with what I knew about their vision and test
scores. It never worked out, but it would have been an excellent research project.

Two doctors in northern England, Peter Blythe and David McGlown,
developed a testing system for reading-disabled kids that included the
creeping and crawling assessment, visual–perceptual tests, visual motor
integration tests, and tests for laterality and emotional status. Each of
the items on an OBD (organic brain dysfunction) evaluation occurred
in patients with "a cluster of immature reflexes" (Goddard 2002, 122).
This complex of signs is called a neuro-developmental delay (NDD).
This means there are "measurable" signs of immaturity in the central

nervous system, as confirmed by a "cluster" of "abnormal primitive and postural reflexes in an individual above three and a half years of age" (123).

How Do All of the Reflex Discoveries Relate to Vision?

The reason this is all so significant for learning-related vision problems is that difficulties in the following areas accompany those abnormal reflexes: "automatic balance control, coordination, oculo-motor functioning and visual-perceptual difficulties." They can also create difficulty with cross laterality, or problems with auditory processing (Goddard 2002).

What behavioral optometrists see in children with visually related reading problems is a fair amount of poor coordination and balance problems, failure of crossing the midline, inability to do the simple task of hitting the opposite knee with an opposite hand and then crossing over again with the other hand to the other knee, and continuing this without getting mixed up and hitting the knee on the same side. We also see problems of making the lazy eight figure, even tracing it on a blackboard. It may also be impossible for the child to draw a horizontal diamond.

In addition, the top and bottom of the body is still overly connected; therefore, the child cannot walk with his toes out without having his arms twist out as well. He cannot walk with toes in without bending his hands around inward at the same time. Remember that the top and bottom of body need to be separable as well as work together. When eye tracking is tested with a child following a wand, his head goes with the eyes. If we hold his head, his mouth goes with the eyes. This is called "motor overflow" from an immature neurological system. All of the above problems interfere with ease and efficiency of vision for learning to read and doing schoolwork.

Research, too, supports the fact that there is a huge similarity of symptoms among dyslexic and dyspraxic children: 80 percent of each group shares the other group's symptoms of balance problems, spatial orientation, and motor skills (Goddard 2002, 123). Recall what the famous optometrist said: "The eyes and the body are one."

Early Motor Development Is Crucial for Vision and Reading

We now know that brain injuries can prevent the brain from doing the proper job of managing the primitive and postural reflex development and integration, and this can be treated successfully. Any child with a head trauma should have a workup for reflex problems, vision problems and cranial/sacral problems. Since the 1980s it has been clear that there are numerous possibilities for neuroplasticity in the brain. It can be trained, and new dendrites can form at any age (Goleman 1985; Zeki 1993). Through this training, many previously challenged children can start the normal process of development.

This whole field of brain training through body movement training seemed important to me, because of my own childhood struggles, being in casts and braces for years because of a belatedly discovered congenitally dislocated hip. I never crept and crawled until I got to an Alexander Technique teacher and a behavioral optometrist in my late 30s. I didn't take to reading until third grade, when my leg braces were finally off, and I learned to run, jump rope, skip, hop, and hang by my knees. I had always thought it was because Dick, Jane, and Spot were boring characters compared to Tom Sawyer, Robin Hood, Peter Pan, and Long John Silver with my Dad doing all the voices. Now I realize my body/brain system was not ready earlier to support the visual task of reading.

What I know for certain is that it is far more important for parents and schools to help their children with body/brain learning and vision development than sitting them down in front of a computer, which could be quite a negative influence on early vision and motor development. To illustrate what can be accomplished by combining vision therapy with Brain Gym and infant reflex work, I have included the case below.

The Case of Karen

Karen came to me at age four with her left eye crossed so badly that it looked almost into her nose. She had amblyopia in that eye, which means that eye could not see normally, no matter what prescription she was given. She was wearing very high plus (farsighted) glasses with a lot of astigmatism correction when she came in. The parents brought her to the optometry school clinic because they did not want her to have surgery.

Karen was so hyperactive and unmanageable that her father had simply given up, and her mother sat in my office in tears whenever they came. We talked about nutrition, food sensitivities, and brain allergies, but the habits of the family did not change very rapidly. The specific years I worked with her make me suspect now that she had been given the shots with thimerosal (mercury) preservative, but I was not aware at the time that shots even had thimerosal in them. It had been removed from all eye drops in the mid-1980s.

We tried to do some vision therapy in the college clinic setting, but the students could not handle her. I sent Karen out for work with Eliza Bergeson, the educational kinesiology expert whose report on Brain Gym appears in this chapter. After Karen had been seeing Ms. Bergeson and coming in for checkups with me and my students for some home patched activities for more than a year, we were able to reduce her prescription to one with very little of the old astigmatism correction. She still had to wear a lot of "plus power" because of her farsightedness and esotropia (turned-in eye).

Eliza Bergeson asked me to get back on the case with vision therapy, now that the child had some sense of calm direction, some ability to attend, converse, and take responsibility for doing what she agreed to do in a session. The two of us worked with her until she was eight, at which point her eyes were straight; they both saw equally well separately and even better together. Karen was wearing contact lenses of +3.00, with +1.00 near work glasses over them when she left the country. I heard from her mother later by an international long-distance phone call that the doctor we had sent her records to almost did not believe that she had ever had esotropia (a turned-in eye) and amblyopia (lazy eye).

With this case, I know behavioral optometry could not have done the whole job alone. Some good vision therapy doctors would have sent Karen out for surgery and done therapy before and after. But Karen was doing great with no surgery because of the added input of a gifted educational kinesiologist who was working with all the neurological error patterns that were operating across Karen's entire body system to make that strabismus useful to her. When those things were corrected and she was able to have proper fusion of the two eyes in vision therapy, her brain figured out that she could use both eyes focused together.

The result: Karen left the country at age eight with good vision in her farsighted contact lenses. She was not hyperactive any longer, attended to school learning, and was also an excellent student, her parents reported.

I tell all my parents of strabismic children, when we start vision therapy, that we are in this for the long haul and it will take time and may require some body work, too. There may be ups and downs, and one must continue with therapy for several years. I promise them, though, that if their child is normal, she will be very intelligent because of all the time that is lavished upon her with perception and motor activities to train eyes and brain.

"Eternal vigilance is the price of freedom" from strabismic vision development. It can often work a lot better if there is also an educational kinesiologist on the case.

GENTLE CHIROPRACTIC OR OSTEOPATHIC HELP IS SOMETHING PARENTS NEED TO SEEK OUT AND TEACHERS CAN SUGGEST IF THEY HAVE AN INJURED CHILD

Often children and adults with vision problems have visible faults in their musculoskeletal balance from old injuries, which means the nervous system and eyes are affected. If I have a child with vision and learning problems who also has balance problems, poor posture, one hip or shoulder higher than the other, or any history of falls or accidents, I work very hard to see that they go to one of the chiropractors in my area who uses gentle techniques appropriate for children, or to a cranial osteopath. Sometimes it takes the parents a long time to decide that they will try this ancillary therapy, but I have never had a parent who has regretted it.

One of the nonforce, gentle chiropractors to whom I refer and who is discussed in the next section is Dr. Lydia Knutson of Cambridge, Massachusetts, who is also trained in Brain Gym. She agreed to write an explanation for this book of the type of nonforce chiropractic treatment, and how it helps patients with vision and learning problems. Below is what Dr. Knutson has written for my readers.

Dr. Knutson's Report: Neurological Confusion and Injury Affecting Vision and Learning Can Be Treated Successfully with Gentle Chiropractic

A chiropractor is a natural ally for the child with developmental differences or delays in vision, motor coordination, balance, language acquisition, auditory skills, and learning. These abilities depend on the proper development and functioning of the nervous system. As chiropractors we view the nervous system as the key to understanding and improving human health and development.

Chiropractic is a discipline that uses noninvasive techniques to stimulate change in the nervous system. This unique perspective allows us to offer assistance in almost all cases of neurological confusion and injury, just the sort of assistance that might benefit a child with a learning disability.

Movement   Most of us assume we have a brain so we can think. But actually we have a brain so we can move. Movement is the basis upon which all other brain function relies. Exciting research in the last half century is beginning to reveal the complex and crucial relationship between movement, vision, language, emotions, memory, and other "higher" brain functions such as learning.

Higher brain functions are built upon more basic underlying motor patterns. Movement begins in utero with the development of primitive reflexes. The brain initiates these movements for its own development and cannot develop normally without them. This dependence on movement for brain development and function continues throughout life. The overwhelming importance of movement is evident from the amazing fact that 90 percent of the brain's capacity is spent in orienting and moving the body in its gravitational field.

The natural state of a child is one of constant movement, curiosity, and play. This movement is essential for normal brain development. Neurologists are finding that movement patterns, once sufficiently practiced and mastered, move to lower levels of the brain for connection to the whole body movement system, thus freeing up circuits for new learning. These circuits, first established to sequence actions, get reused later to help sequence, adjust, and time mental acts and thoughts. Motor development patterns such as rolling over, reaching for a desired object, hand grasping, or crawling seem to be crucial for the development of reading, writing, memory, and social interactions (Masgutova 2003).

For example, rerunning your movements in your mind is often enough to remember where you left your glasses. Walking into the study or *imagining* walking into the study to find them activates the same circuits in the brain for memory. Athletes, musicians, and dancers use this technique to mentally rehearse difficult maneuvers without exhausting the muscles involved. Even parts of the motor system, which for years were thought to have a specific and isolated "lower" motor function, are now being discovered to have broader participation in how we organize our world through thoughts and actions. These principles apply to emotions as well. Going through the motions of smiling even when you don't feel happy stimulates neurotransmitters in the limbic system and improves your mood (Ratey 2001).

In industrialized societies children often don't get the motor stimulation they need for proper development. Too much time in front of a TV or strapped into a car seat or stroller curtails a child's opportunities to physically explore his surroundings. Today's educational system further hampers this physical development by requiring hours of sitting in a classroom, now exacerbated by the alarming trend away from physical education classes and recess. Being physically involved in an activity makes us learn better and faster because more circuits are activated and harnessed for the learning process.

There are many, many factors that can interrupt the development of movement patterns: everything from lack of movement, inattentive caregivers, and dull surroundings to toxic exposure, poor nutrition, and physical injury. Physical injury is where the chiropractor can be most helpful. The lifestyle of a child is one of minor trauma, and these injuries often pass by unnoticed until a subsequent learning difficulty arises. Possible head trauma is especially important to investigate if a child develops visual learning difficulties or any kind of delay in the development of the visual system.

Chiropractic   Chiropractic looks to the nervous system as the basis for assisting human health and healing. If a child's system is struggling with

biomechanical inefficiencies due to injury, the circuitry in the brain becomes overloaded. Circuits are tied up dealing with input from the injury
leaving less available capacity for seeing, thinking, and learning.

In my practice, I use a combination of three well-established nonforce
chiropractic techniques: Bertram DeJarnette's sacro-occipital technique
(SOT), Arlen Fuhr's activator methods, and George Goodheart's applied
kinesiology (AK). Nonforce techniques tend to work from the "inside
out," gently encouraging more permanent change in the entire central
nervous system. I use these three techniques in a unique method developed by David Newton, DC, in Wellesley, Massachusetts. His method
seeks to restore stability to a musculoskeletal system that has become
unstable due to injury. This is different from the usual chiropractic approach, which uses manual manipulation to introduce movement into
joints that are restricted.

Based on my experience with Newton's method, I have come to view
biomechanical *injury*, in the most basic sense, as *confusion in the central
nervous system*. The brain constantly monitors the position and relationship of all bones and muscles in the body. In normal, healthy circumstances the brain restores these relationships after a fall or physical
strain, enabling the body to completely heal. Injury on the most profound
level happens when the brain becomes confused about what these
proper relational positions are and is unable to return the body to normal biomechanical functioning. This results in long-term, chronic biomechanical instability, such as that experienced by a person whose back
"goes out" periodically since a biking accident 20 years ago.

Musculoskeletal instability often presents as pain in adulthood but pain
is a less common complaint in childhood. Children usually appear to recover quickly from bumps or falls, and indeed usually they do! But sometimes, though the bruises heal perfectly, a child is left with a hidden biomechanical instability. When this happens some of the symptoms that can
ensue are emotional irritability and frustration, sensory integration problems, poor balance, poor immunity, neurological delays, learning disabilities, and visual problems.

The most basic positional relationship in the body seems to involve the
pelvis and the cranium. Destabilizing injury here appears to carry the
most confusion for the brain. Restoring stability to the cranium
and the pelvis can have wide-ranging effects throughout the nervous sys-

tem. In the case of the visual system, because the circuits used are so vast, confusion in motor networks can have deleterious effects on the ability to track, focus, visualize an image, coordinate the vestibular and visual systems, and coordinate the eye and hand, all of which are necessary for reading and writing.

The connection between pelvic and cranial instability on the one hand, and ensuing visual problems and developmental delays on the other, can be seen in the following stories of three of my chiropractic patients.

Case Number One   Dr. Orfield referred Daniel to me when he was seven years old. After a successful vision training program and corrective lenses, his acuity was up to normal, his reading up to grade level, and his tendency to let one eye drift was gone. But in addition to these visual difficulties, Daniel had poor balance and poorly developed gross motor skills, which made running slow and difficult. Coordination between the eye and hand for both gross motor (throwing and catching a ball) and fine motor activities were noticeably worse than his classmates' abilities. In fact, Daniel explained that writing made his hands "tired, then they hurt a little and begin to sweat." Dr. Orfield felt that the key to resolving his remaining visual motor problems would be found in resolving his physical problems.

During our first meeting, Daniel did most of the talking. He was confident, charming, and verbally advanced, easily able to pinpoint his difficulties. In addition to his colorful description of his sweaty hands, he said he couldn't hop on his left leg (it had always been weaker), and the left side of his neck hurt when he built Lego structures—something he did for hours a day. His mother commented that he couldn't stand up straight.

Upon examination, I found injury to the pelvis, more pronounced on the left side, and instability in the upper neck and cranium. Over a period of three months, he came in for a total of nine treatments. At each visit, he reported to me the changes he had noticed since the last appointment. After the first visit, he happily said his neck no longer hurt so he was spending even more time making Lego structures! After several more visits, he reported being able to run faster in gym class and his mother said he was standing up straighter.

The big change came after we completed stabilizing his pelvis. The very next visit, he came bounding into the office saying, "Look! I can hop on my left leg!" proceeding to hop, hop, hop around the office on his left leg. The next week, his parents had a conference with a reading teacher who knew him very well. For the first time, he received glowing reviews: his reading had soared in the last few weeks. At the last visit, he said he was now playing basketball with his dad and making almost every shot. He had figured out how to throw a ball straight!

Daniel's mother had always noticed that he had difficulty standing straight, and indeed, when I first examined him his right shoulder was higher than his left, the right side of his pelvis lower than the left and in between, his spine curved back and forth. But neither Daniel nor his parents had any memory of what injury might have compromised his musculoskeletal system.

Many injuries, long forgotten, can have profound effects later on in a child's life. Whether the injury is remembered or not, any obvious uneven morphological development, or difficulty with balance or coordination, is a sure sign of musculoskeletal injury (barring other, more serious medical conditions).

The following story of Leah involves a child whose primary complaint was headaches. Children should not be in chronic physical pain. Intervention at an early age can save a lifetime of accumulated physical complaints.

Case Number Two   Several years ago, Diana brought in her six-year-old daughter Leah. Leah had been complaining of frontal headaches for the last seven months. All pertinent medical tests had been done and the conclusion reached was that she was making it up. Laura was convinced she was really having headaches and insisted they had started shortly after Leah had had six dental fillings over a five-week period. She had nearly given up mentioning the dentist because she had been routinely told there was no causal relationship to the headaches.

During our first meeting, Leah said almost nothing. Her mother said Leah had a language delay and rarely spoke, relying on her twin sister to speak for her. Diana didn't have many specifics about the headaches except that Leah often furrowed her brows, spontaneously wincing and grabbing her forehead. She was easily distracted and sometimes spacey.

I asked Leah to write some letters on a page, as part of a brain, hand, and eye, dominance assessment (Hannaford 1997). She refused to write letters or draw a picture, so I drew a circle with a smile in it. She finished the picture with eyes and ears and then drew another face. This was an angry face with slits for eyes and a frown.

After this, I was quite sure she wasn't making up the headaches. During my exam I found several bones in her head that had been injured at some point. Given her more long-term difficulties with language development, I suspected that the dentist had exacerbated an underlying older injury and I assured her mother that repeated trips to the dentist over a short period of time could easily have set in motion her current complaints. At some point Leah had also sustained an injury to the pelvis.

We began treatment and her system responded very quickly. After some cranial and pelvic stabilization, she began to talk. And talk. And talk. She became uncorked! Her mother said she spoke more in that first week than she had in her whole life. Her socialization skills rapidly advanced. Comments and stories poured out of her, talking and laughing about all kinds of things. She was now able to talk about how she felt, something she had never done.

She said she still had headaches. After some advanced cranial treatments, her headaches finally resolved. As soon as we started this advanced work, she began to draw huge, daring pictures in bright colors. Her teachers noticed remarkable changes in all of her abilities. Leah is now 10, and I have seen her three times in the succeeding years, each time after a blow to the head caused the headaches to return. With these subsequent injuries, just a few visits were needed for her body to fully recover.

Chiropractors routinely cure headaches and resolve musculoskeletal complaints. The more interesting questions raised in these stories are, why did a child suddenly begin to hop on a weak leg or throw a ball straight, or suddenly begin to tell stories and draw colorful pictures? Why is the pelvis so important? Why would stabilizing it make such a difference? Some possible answers are suggested by the concept of the "dynamic" brain.

Dennison's Dynamic Brain   One of the most innovative thinkers on the topic of learning and development is Paul Dennison, PhD, reading specialist and founder and developer of Brain Gym and the international organization of Educational Kinesiology. Following on the groundbreaking work of Paul MacLean's "triune" brain, Dennison developed the concept of the "dynamic brain" (Dennison 2004). In the 1960s, MacLean proposed an evolutionary map of brain development with three main parts. At the bottom is the brain stem or reptilian brain with command centers for basic functioning: respiration, sleep, temperature regulation, and automatic movements. In the middle is the midbrain including the limbic system, where we have co-ordination of movement, memory, emotions, and the beginnings of the apparatus necessary for social interaction. At the top are the left and right hemispheres of the neocortex, where "higher" brain functions occur: reason, inner dialogue, abstract thinking, planning, and the fine-tuning of "lower" functions.

Dennison's dynamic brain also has three main parts. He calls these "dimensions" of brain function. These dimensions include emotions, associations, muscle checks, and movements that correspond to the three levels of the triune brain. Dennison found through this work with children and adults that learning gaps and difficulties are more easily resolved and integrated into the vast neural network of the fully functioning dynamic brain if the neurological confusion can be associated with a "dimension" of function including emotions, associations, and movements.

As with MacLean, at the bottom of Dennison's map is the brain stem or "old brain," the first to develop in utero and during infancy. This he calls the "focus" dimension. The question that is explored during this time is "Where am I and am I safe?" A loving, nurturing environment full of interesting physical stimulation will encourage an infant to explore the boundaries between herself and her surroundings. These neural networks, forged by movement patterns explored in a safe and comfortable environment, set up a solid base for the next step toward growth and the development of the other dimensions. The most basic default mode of the brain is survival. Fear of injury (and worse) is our most trusted emotion to keep us out of harm's way. It is also primary: If we do not feel safe, it is difficult for the brain to move on to less essential topics, such as reading, writing, and consideration for a neighbor.

The "centering" dimension asks the question, "Where is it and who are you?" The toddler begins to explore the differences between themselves and others. This dimension correlates with MacLean's midbrain, our emotional brain. This developmental stage should not be hurried. Establishing emotional connection to people and objects paves the way for the natural development of social community and joyful cooperation. Generosity, sharing, and compassion for others are natural human responses, but only if the child has the time and environment to establish the neural networks that allow these emotions to develop.

Dennison's third dimension is "laterality" and corresponds to MacLean's neocortex or "new brain." This is what we most closely associate with our distinctive human abilities. It is the ability to ask the question "What or why is this?" and our ability to speak, think, self-reflect, wonder, and imagine. Most learning difficulties and disabilities are first noted in this context, when Johnny can't read. This dimension continues to develop throughout life and may result in what we call wisdom.

The Triune Chiropractic Model   When I first began my chiropractic practice, I set out to see if I could find a relationship between the three-part model of the brain and the musculoskeletal system. What I have found is a similar model of hierarchical ordering within the neuromusculoskeletal system.

Focus Dimension: Pelvis   Injury to the pelvis seems to trigger a struggle in the "old" or reptilian brain, the part of the brain that corresponds to fear and asks the question, "Where am I and am I safe?" Since the default mode of the brain is survival, if the brain is in fear mode and does not perceive that the body is safe, many circuits that should be used for new learning are locked up processing a barrage of proprioceptive information coming from the injury. This vigilant monitoring takes its toll. Injury of any kind is a distraction for the brain, but I have found that injury to the pelvis seems to tie up the most circuits. Certainly vision, language, and speech are not found in the brainstem. But over and over again I find that if there is injury to the pelvis, stabilizing it can open surprising and exciting doors for development and learning.

Case Number Three   Sam was almost four when he first came to my office. He had the diagnosis of PDD–NOS (pervasive developmental disorder–not otherwise specified); that is, he was somewhere on the autism spectrum. He was about a year behind in speech and fine and gross motor skills. He was visual and very good at puzzles but had trouble listening and was easily distracted. He had a mild congenital left-sided hemiparesis with low muscle tone. Both his pelvis and cranium were unstable.

After the first visit he went home and asked to ride his tricycle for the first time. After the next several visits he continued to make progress in his physical confidence and overall coordination. For the first time he was able to take off his own clothes. He was also making up new stories instead of repeating ones he had memorized.

His parents reported that he seemed more discombobulated than usual, as if his head was full of new thoughts, which were overwhelming him. Within a couple months he had learned to swing on a swing set and was out of diapers. I saw Sam again recently after a bad fall. His developmental progress in the last two years has been amazing. He is now almost six, riding a bike, and reading fluently. The largest part of this is due to his cheerful optimism and his remarkable parents' continuing ability to spend hours a day with him. But it does seem that stabilizing his musculoskeletal system was an important step for this further dramatic development.

Centering Dimension: Midline Cranium and Sacrum The centering dimension or the "emotional" brain seems to correspond to midline bones such as the sacrum and some midline cranial bones. With Leah (the child with headaches) several of these bones in her cranium were under stress. The early injury to her head may have played some part in the "angry" face drawing, her slowed socialization skills, and her inability to communicate how she felt.

Another dramatic example of the possible relationship of the emotional brain to certain cranial bones was demonstrated with an adult patient of mine who came in one day saying she had been having anxiety attacks for the last week. I found nothing wrong with the pelvis, but a midline cranial bone was out of place. We adjusted it and the panic *immediately* went away.

Laterality Dimension: Extremities The arms and legs seem to correspond to Dennison's laterality dimension. They are the icing on top of the cake. When a child bangs an arm, or even breaks it, it is a painful and inconvenient injury but it doesn't usually interfere with normal brain development and if it heals completely is soon forgotten. However, chronic pain in an extremity is often an indication of a more central and important injury. Back pain is rarely a child's presenting complaint. More common are ankle, knee, and hip complaints (such are those described in Daniel's case). Stabilizing underlying injury to the pelvis, spine, or cranium will often resolve the complaint in the leg or arm.

Most children with learning disabilities who come out of my office even greatly improved still have ongoing brain integration challenges. But once the musculoskeletal structure is stable and more basic neural circuits freed up, the doors for new and exciting avenues for development become more and more of a possibility.

Lydia Knutson, DC
February 2006

BRAIN GYM AND EDUCATIONAL KINESIOLOGY PREPARE THE BRAIN AND NERVOUS SYSTEM FOR SCHOOL LEARNING: THERE ARE CLASSES IN EDUCATIONAL KINESIOLOGY FOR TEACHERS, AND TEACHERS ARE USING IT HERE AND ABROAD

The Brain Gym approach for neurological rehabilitation through body movements mentioned earlier in this chapter is discussed below by Eliza Bergeson, the practitioner who comanaged the case of Karen with me. She works part time near Lebanon, New Hampshire, and part time in Lexington, Massachusetts. Since 1989, she has been a licensed Brain Gym consultant through the Educational Kinesiology Foundation, founded by Paul Dennison, but she has also had extensive training in infant reflex integration with the Svetlana Masgutova approach.

I have had the pleasure and benefit of learning from this brilliant teacher and sharing patients like Karen with her. Bergeson agreed to write this report including an interesting case of a child whose reading was helped by using reflexes and Brain Gym motor work. The child was not a patient of mine but had glasses from another optometrist.

Eliza Bergeson's Report: Brain Gym and Reading

Move It or Lose It! Child's play is serious business. For the first seven years of life, children explore their environment, developing their ability to respond to life's experiences. This exploration is physical, repetitive, and challenging, and it ensures survival and safety in a rough-and-tumble world. Given the option, children love to roll, wiggle, jump, run, skip, spin, hang up-side down, swing, wrestle, shout, sing, and laugh. These activities develop dependable reflexive responses, laying the groundwork for coordination, balance, flexibility, sensory integration, and core muscle strength.

In this way, children are well prepared for their next "jobs": developing cognitive abilities, refining sensory abilities, and widening social skills between the ages of seven and fourteen. Movement stimulates the development of neural pathways in our brain as well as the body. If we wish to stay cognitively fit, physically active, and creative throughout our lives, we need to move. But we seem to have forgotten this fact, wooed away from physical activity by our romance with cars, television, and computers. We sit and sit and sit!

In recent years, scientists have been able to verify the brain's need for physical activity through high-tech imaging systems. "It has come as a big surprise in neuroscience that physical activity is a big promoter for keeping our brains healthy and adaptive," says Dr. John Ratey, clinical associate professor of psychiatry at Harvard Medical School (2001).

The Brain Gym Difference   Developmental specialists have long understood the body and brain's need for physical activity. Over the last half a century, they have explored ways to maximize learning and performance potential. Educator Paul E. Dennison, PhD, a pioneer in applied brain research, developed a sequence of twenty-six Brain Gym movement activities that strengthen the skills of focus, organization, and communication needed for academic success. They naturally address developmental deficits by strengthening innate movement patterns and restoring muscle coordination for both eyes and the entire body. They can also be used to target specific gaps in a child's movement vocabulary.

These simple movements, taught in Brain Gym 101, are easy to incorporate into school or work settings and can be performed either in groups or individually. The Brain Gym International (the Educational Kinesiology Foundation) now offers a comprehensive training program consisting of more than sixty courses that are taught in about eighty countries.

In the purest sense, education means to draw out (from the Latin *educare*). Brain Gym sessions are organized around each person's goals with the radical understanding that each person knows, on some level, exactly what they need to achieve their goal. They are motivated to learn and grow because the agenda at hand is their very own agenda. Innate brilliance cannot resist appearing in these circumstances.

We learn best when we are allowed to follow our own interests and inclinations. Our concentration, memory, vision, listening, organization, and coordination grow as we actively pursue our passions in life. The

Brain Gym activities make it possible for us to follow these main interests with gusto.

Each one of us knows exactly what we need to enhance our experience in the classroom and in life. This may sound like an outrageous claim, but, like other mammals, we humans are born with the ability recognize when we need to stretch, move, look in the distance, rest, drink, or eat. Our innate *self-response-ability* allows us to reduce internal stress and restore equanimity before any imbalance becomes chronic. However, in our current culture of nonstop activity, we are losing the ability to monitor our wellbeing. Brain Gym reconnects learners with their ability to notice how stress affects their bodies and provides simple tools to alleviate undue strain.

From a Brain Gym point of view, communication within the brain and throughout the body increases when stimulated by three distinct patterns of movement in three "dimensions" of experience:

1. The **focus dimension** coordinates the brain stem and frontal lobes with forward and backward movement. Basic safety, place recognition, and the ability to alternate between focused attention and perspective are hallmarks of this dimension.
2. The **centering dimension** coordinates the midbrain and cerebral cortex with up-and-down movement. When all elements of this dimension are in harmony, children are free to acquire a sense of connection, a sense of belonging and being loved, and the ability to organize themselves for play.
3. The **laterality dimension** coordinates the left and right cerebral hemispheres with side-to-side movement. This dimension supports the cultivation of the communication and cognitive skills needed for academics.

Reading and writing are laterality dimension skills that develop naturally and easily when the focus and centering dimensions are fully integrated. Too often, we try to put the cart before the horse, pushing many children to read before they are physically and emotionally ready, which results in stress and confusion. For these children, physical and emotional safety, loving connection, and unlimited play are prerequisite to the full flowering of academic skills.

Brain Gym in Action   Many of the children and adults referred to my
kinesiology practice for challenges of learning, coordination, or vision are
missing a significant portion of their movement vocabulary, skipped during those first seven years or lost through shock or trauma later on. They
face learning, coordination, or vision challenges as a direct result of these
movement vocabulary gaps. As a kinesiologist, I am able to identify the
gaps and support them in restoring full, unbridled pleasure in whole-body
movement. Brain Gym, or Educational Kinesiology, provides an elegant
framework for these changes to take place, opening the door to pleasur-
able, successful, lifelong learning.

Quite often parents of young clients initially arrive at my office exhausted and frustrated by their efforts to locate appropriate support services for their children. They hand me the results of extensive testing with
multiple diagnoses and are often relieved when we put these findings
aside to focus on their child's strengths, abilities, and interests. Brain Gym
is unusual in the world of learning-enhancement programs, in that there
is no diagnosis or treatment plan per se. Brain Gym practitioners base
each session around the client's goals and interests, and all positive change
evolves from that process.

I have never met a human being who didn't enjoy a playful, self-moti-
vating challenge. My clients play their way to integration; they catch, juggle, balance on large therapy balls, balance beams, dance, draw, sing. Together, we have a great time exploring the Brain Gym activities and infant
reflexes.

Below is a case illustrating what this work can do for a child having
trouble learning to read.

Case Number One   Last year, eight-year-old Jenny arrived in my office
full of fire and enthusiasm. She proudly proclaimed, "I can snowboard, I
can rollerblade, I can ride a bike, and I can play soccer, but," she said hanging her head, "I can't read."

Jenny had been referred to me by her chiropractor, Dr. Lydia Knutson,
with the following notes summarizing her challenges:

> History of musculoskeletal problems from age 2: scoliosis and internally ro-
> tated femurs. As a little child her hips and legs 'hurt.' Had worn corrective
> shoes until recently which solved the problem of hurting legs. Scoliosis was
> improving with age. More recently, she had been getting aches in mid-back

after picking up heavy things, repeated bending over, and most notably after gym class. She also suffered from frequent bouts of insuppressible hiccoughs. Came with a diagnosis of non-verbal learning disability, dyslexia, and ADD.

All her pain disappeared after stabilizing pelvis, jaw, and cranium. Hiccoughs also disappeared. Now when she gets them, she knows it's time to come back for an appointment!

Jenny was having difficulty reading because her eye muscles were weak and not teaming or tracking smoothly together. She had started wearing glasses at age five for astigmatism and farsightedness and was prone to frequent injury. I found her overall muscle tone low, and her movement was awkward and ungainly. She tired easily and had limited endurance for sustained physical activity.

Yet Jenny approached her personal goals and the Brain Gym activities with characteristic zeal. She chose to master advanced balancing feats. She learned to throw, catch, juggle, do hand stands, turn elegant cartwheels, and run quickly without getting out of breath. Occasionally she returned to the chiropractor to bring her structure into alignment with her new prowess. At times, she collapsed in discouragement and rage about her physical limitations.

As Jenny focused on her goals, I helped her to strengthen her core muscles, coordinate her eyes with the movement of her head, shoulders, and hips, and integrate postural reflexes. As Jenny's neck muscles were particularly weak, we began working in the focus dimension so that she could move her head easily and freely without injury. Three months into our sessions together our work all came together. Jenny bounded into my office and trumpeted, "I can read, and I am halfway through my first Judy Blume book!"

Over the next eight months, we continued meeting on a twice-monthly schedule and balanced thirteen infant reflexes from the focus and centering dimensions. Jenny's eye coordination and overall muscle tone improved dramatically. Incidents of sprains and strained muscles diminished. Jenny plowed through the Judy Blume books. She began to take pleasure in math and found new, positive ways to express herself and to make friends. Jenny's self-confidence sparkled and she had growing appreciation of herself as the captain of her ship.

Jenny's story is not unusual. Children who have difficulty visually focusing for reading and writing or attending to academic work often have weak core muscles and poor coordination and posture compounded by low self-esteem and social difficulties. When these deficits are addressed, learning competence increases. We naturally learn, thrive, and grow if we follow the magnificent protocol hardwired into our brains and physiology.
Eliza Bergeson
Licensed Brain Gym Consultant
April 20, 2006

NEUROTHERAPY: GOING DIRECTLY TO THE BRAIN FOR CHANGE IS BEING DONE IN SOME SCHOOLS

Dr. Jolene Ross of the Advanced Neurotherapy Clinic in Wellesley, Massachusetts, believes neurotherapy is one of the most useful treatments for an ADHD child. She sees ADHD as the result of a child's self-treatment for slow brain waves. The excessive movement is a way for the body/brain complex to speed up the wave patterns. Neurotherapy can do this also, and then the body's hyperactivity can slow down.

In general the slow waves (low frequency) are not as useful as the higher ones. They "disrupt the ability to coordinate across cortex and have been correlated with symptoms such as attention deficit," says Ross (2006). Sudden spikes or episodic bursts are not normal either, but they could be averaged out of the picture in a data analysis. This is why computer electroencephalogram (EEG) specialist Jim Caunt does a very individualized analysis of the details of the EEGs done at the Ross clinic.

Neurotherapy does not involve moving the body at all. It is strictly neurofeedback for brain wave patterns. It helps to make these patterns optimal rather than inefficient, and creates connections that are needed but may never have developed properly or may have been hurt by injury to the brain. Injuries can be as small as a painful head bump or whiplash, or as serious as a severe concussion from a car accident or a fall, a birth injury, anesthesia, or a stroke. They can also be damage from toxic chemicals or oxygen deprivation. Neurotherapy may improve coordination and control of movement and reduce muscle spasticity, but it cannot cure total paralysis. What it does best is rehab circuits in the brain for more efficient thinking and emotional processing.

Neurotherapy is relatively new on the scene of brain rehabilitation and training. The *Scientific American Mind* magazine for February/March, 2006 ran a story called "Train Your Brain," by Ulrich Kraft. It described a German clinic, the Institute of Medical Psychology and Behavioral Neurobiology at the University of Tuebingen, which is using neurotherapy to effectively work on many disabilities. Neurotherapy is also called EEG biofeedback because it frequently bases its protocols on what is happening on an EEG for a particular patient.

The real father of neurotherapy, and perhaps the most famous researcher in this country, is Barry Sterman, PhD, now an emeritus professor at UCLA. He began in the 1960s working with cats' brain waves. He found that the cats he had trained (by giving rewards of snacks) to have more of the relaxed and awake brain waves, called sensorimotor rhythm (SMR), were more resistant to toxic fumes that the military was finding in rocket fuel.

Dr. Ross is one of the PhD psychologists who has studied and worked with Dr. Sterman recently. Her clinic treatments are tailored very precisely to individual brain wave connections across cortex and to imbalances between the two sides of the brain, or the front and back of the brain. She also works on shortening amplitudes of waves that are too long. This kind of treatment works well with head injuries, attention disorders, autism, learning difficulties, attachment disorder, and many other neurologically based conditions that she and Jim Caunt see in their clinic.

Neurotherapy in the Schools?   All of these problems impact the resources of schools. Some advanced educational thinkers believe neurotherapy should be in the schools, and it is in a few notable ones. I had my first look at neurotherapy when I visited the New Visions School in Minneapolis, Minnesota, in 2000. It is a public charter school dedicated to serving learning disabled (LD) children. The founders had rehabbed an old warehouse building with bright paint and wonderful facilities for indoor large motor activities, as well as classrooms and therapy rooms for all the support services they had.

New Visions was founded in 1983 by Bob and Kathy DeBoer, whose daughter Jesse had suffered fetal distress syndrome and oxygen deprivation at birth. She had been rehabilitated to normal. They had worked with physical therapist Art Sandler, who knew of the neuroplasticity concepts and believed that with the right efforts, alternative pathways could be developed in the brain.

Jesse was "patterned" in the Doman/Delacato manner, like the young girl in the *Brain Child* book (Napear 1974). The kinds of programs that worked for their daughter are provided in the school. There were behavioral optometry exams and vision therapy by Dr. Janyce M. Moroz, as well as occupational therapy, physical therapy, sensory integration treatments, light therapy (not syntonics), and neurotherapy.

Bob DeBoer allowed me to be hooked up to their neurotherapy computer and electrodes. I had to keep a "PacMan" image moving across the screen with its mouth open to swallow up little blobs. If it did keep moving, my brainwaves were good. If it stalled, there was a glitch. There was no input of energy into my brain but a lot of chances for biofeedback. I remember doing fine. The PacMan moved and gobbled globs efficiently, I thought.

I did not consider trying neurotharapy extensively for myself then. However, I was considerably intrigued. There had been an interesting article in *Psychology Today* in the May/June 1998 issue titled, "Wired for Miracles? Neurofeedback Therapy" by Jim Robbins. He had friends whose child was saved from epilepsy by the new brain feedback, and he tried it himself out of curiosity and as a result, reaped the benefit that he felt much more productive early in the mornings.

The Robbins article reported that neurofeedback had been used successfully with alcoholism to stop cravings, migraine headaches, insomnia, Tourettes, chronic pain, and hyperactivity. Schools in Yonkers, New York, had used it to save 20 students from needing special education classes for a district savings of $500,000. In a center in Colorado Springs neurofeedback was being used successfully for clearing the symptoms of head injury. A New York City psychiatrist was using it for posttraumatic stress disorder (Robbins 1998).

Laurence M. Hirshberg, PhD, and clinical assistant professor of psychiatry and human behavior at Brown University Medical School, has become one of the major East Coast experts on EEG neurofeedback.

He is the director of clinics in Boston, Lawrence, Springfield, and Worcester, Massachusetts. *The Brown University Child & Adolescent Psychopharmacology Update* of February 2005 reviewed his research paper, interviewing Hirshberg and second author Sufen Chiu of the University of California at Davis. Hirshberg, Chiu, and Frazier wrote about how EEG biofeedback (called EBF) is a solid alternative or ancillary treatment to drugs for children's attention and behavior problems.

Hirshberg reported that 70–80 percent of participants (children and adults) benefitted from EBF in studies on ADHD with around the same extent of effect as stimulants for ADHD symptoms. The authors suggest that EBF "be considered by clinicians and parents as a first-line treatment for ADHD when parents or patients prefer not to use medication, and as an option in cases when significant side effects or insufficient improvement occurs with medication" (Hirshberg, Chiu, and Frazier 2005). The authors also review many of the other things that can be treated with neurotherapy such as epilepsy, migraines, alcoholic cravings, seizure disorders, reading disabilities, autism spectrum, and reactive attachment disorder.

This new therapy was something I planned to watch and wait on, but when two patients were helped a great deal in 2004, I decided it was time to learn more about this treatment for the brain. It has taken off as a sometimes medically covered therapy when combined with psychotherapy, and has become vastly more complicated than the simple kind I had observed at the New Visions School in the summer of 2000.

One of my patients went to see psychotherapist Jeffrey Bradley of Milton, Massachusetts, to work on her attention problems and especially her difficulties sleeping, which she had experienced since she was a baby. While she did the whole 40 visits with good effect on her schoolwork, her sleep problems disappeared after two visits. I asked Bradley how this could happen. He said that he achieved a calming overall influence with points on the central motor cortex.

There are points all over the skull on which electrodes can be placed for various purposes. Remember, this is not an input therapy. No one will receive zaps of energy or electricity or anything else. The electrodes are strictly for biofeedback purposes, to record what happens in the brain, and then "teach the brain to regulate itself better by giving it rewards if it calms down or perks up" as the situation requires, says Bradley. The brain is rewarded by sight and sound (Bradley 2006).

He explained that he usually sees three types of patients. First is the "overaroused" patient, second is the "underaroused" patient, and third is the "unstable, disregulated" patient. His protocol uses a "decision tree model," which is followed as long as improvements are made. If there are not major improvements, the patient must get an EEG. Overarousal calls for beginning to train the right-sided brain wave patterns. For the under-aroused, he begins on the left.

For hyperactive kids, he will start on the right side and "see if they need to move to train in the back or front of the brain" (Bradley 2006). Sensory integration issues are also connected with the back of the brain, he says, which would be the occipital cortex, where vision is processed. The problem delivering these therapies has been cost, but we saw how much money neurotherapy saved for a school system with treatment for just 20 kids.

Psychologist Ross decided after years of doing talk therapy that she could improve people's lives more by going directly to their brains. She has seen even things like attachment disorder from early trauma trained away with neurotherapy. It is most effective, says Ross, for very serious head injury cases ("the more serious, the more dramatic the results"), autistic children, and those without full-blown autism but still on the autism spectrum with ADHD, PDD–NOS, Asperger, and so on. It also works for anxiety disorders, obsessive compulsive disorders (OCD), and children adopted from other countries who have had a lot of early trauma or neglect prior to their adoption. I believe this treatment will be expanding rapidly because it works (Ross 2006).

Dr. Ross also believes it can help with eating disorders, especially in those kids who had such a rocky birth that they really will not eat much. Dr. Ross does recommend chlorella and sea vegetables to detox from heavy metal poisoning along with the neurotherapy to rehab the brain of a mercury-sensitive child. She tells her parents that the child may not have any more flu shots with thimerosal (there are some without it but you have to ask for those) to avoid further disruption of the brain.

In the fall of 2005, I finally booked myself into Ross's clinic to experience advanced neurotherapy for myself. The intake interview with Ross covers all possible threats to one's brain. I had had a few minor head bumps and a couple of whiplashes as an adult and loads of poisonous anesthesia (the old ether kind) as a child; I had spent years in leg braces during crucial development times and was a relatively slow reader for someone with my level of education.

I also had suffered severe headaches since I was in my twenties (possibly since the first whiplash), and they were becoming worse, rather than better, with age. I had cut their frequency by eliminating all trigger foods, but they were still severe, not helped by any over-the-counter medications. I decided there might be a glitch somewhere that could be fixed if this neurotherapy really worked to cure headaches, as Ross had told me. Sure enough, after about 16 of the 40 visits, the headaches were almost totally eliminated. The few I had were much milder and easily stopped with homeopathic remedies. Previously, I had had to tough it out for 24 hours almost every week.

As a behavioral optometrist I have cured a lot of other people's headaches with glasses and therapy, and I do believe I have the correct glasses and I have done my therapy. Neurofeedback did something different for me. If this freedom from headaches continues, it is well worth every penny I spent for this part of my education. I was at that time working on this book and noticed that my typing was a little more accurate, but I did not think that had anything to do with the brain training, until I learned months later, talking to Jim Caunt, that people can sometimes improve motor skills with the training.

I think that the serious problems that Dr. Ross sees every day are likely well served by a dose of neurotherapy after two other problems are cleared. First, a child should be seen by a chiropractor or cranial osteopath to evaluate the infrastructure of the body and circulation to the head to be sure it is not interfering with brain action. Second, a behavioral optometry eye exam must be done to be sure vision in current glasses or problems like intermittent double vision are not interfering with a balanced brain. Because neurotherapy utilizes a computer screen at a distance of about six feet, eyestrain could interfere with processing if vision is not optimal.

At my therapy sessions, I was hooked up to receptors of brain wave patterns. I would view a television screen with a problem on it. The problem was a blank screen with one little square of a famous painting. For children, other kinds of pictures are utilized. If I wanted to see the rest of the painting by adding one little square at a time, I had to sustain brainwaves that the computer would recognize as the good ones and then reward me with a pleasant sound and another square of the picture. I could also be hooked up for reading, and if I read efficiently, the soft bongs would keep coming for a rhythmic reward of sound. If I started to go to sleep as I once did when I was reading a dull article, there would be no rewarding sound. A good book kept the bongs coming.

Another method of training that one of my therapists developed was to let me watch the screen showing my brain wave patterns. There were four going on at once, so if I could get all the green bars to light up at once, then I would hear that very nice bong. This was more motivating for me than the pictures because I could see exactly what was happening before I even got a bong. I could see when my brain waves stayed in the prescribed template, which was altered to make it harder every week based on last week's learning. I could also see when they overshot the limits and became too long.

The "magnitudes go down, when the brain is engaged" says Caunt. If one is "not paying attention, the magnitudes go up" (2006). Evidently, with children who have slow waves interfering with reading, there is another problem. If the waves are too slow, one's brain dumps working memory during processing. If these are momentary glitches of slowness, the individual has to build in a compensation strategy called "procedural memory," not as efficient as direct processing.

One of Dr. Ross's therapists mentioned to me that keeping one's blood sugar at a normal level rather than letting it drop too low by skipping healthy meals made for much better brain wave responses. That is more proof of the need for adequate nutrition every day, especially for children at risk.

SYNTONICS: COLORED LIGHT THERAPY TO BALANCE THE AUTONOMIC NERVOUS SYSTEM AND ENHANCE PERIPHERAL VISION

Syntonics is the process of delivering a steady or gently blinking, colored light stimulation to the eyes for 10 to 20 minutes of therapy time. My introduction to this treatment modality was at the national Syntonic Optometry Conference for 1992, held that year in Boston. I was struck by a story that someone told of a child in vision therapy using some syntonics procedures. The little boy started crying in the waiting room when he saw his mother come to pick him up after his vision therapy and syntonics session. The doctor was called out to see what was the matter.

"Was it something that happened in the therapy session?" the mother wanted to know.

The little boy said, "Now I can see my mama's whole face."

Before that he could only see one of her eyes or her mouth, or nose, or a part of her hair or cheek. He was crying because he could see how beautiful she was with her eyes and nose, mouth and chin, forehead and hair, all visible at the same time. It was the light stimulation that had awakened his peripheral retina and related pathways into the brain and balanced the autonomic nervous system, allowing him to see more than the tiny little circle that he had always thought was the way everyone sees.

This functional field constriction is not uncommon, I learned. Dr. Ray Gottlieb and Dr. Larry Wallace reviewed the syntonics literature and wrote, "Studies since 1927 report between 9–20 percent of unselected school children have fields of less than 15 degrees in diameter. Some children lose all but the central 1 or 2 degrees of vision" (Gottlieb and Wallace 2001, 32).

I immediately purchased, while it was still on the drawing board, Dr. Jacob Lieberman's "light sensitivity trainer." There are a number of machines that do syntonics work, but this one appealed to me. When I finally received the device, which I still have and use in my office, I kept it at home and worked with it a little myself. A friend who had the field tester that is often used with syntonics did a color field on me. My fields were quite large from all the peripheral awareness training I had previously done to reduce my myopia. She told me, however, to sit with purple light every night for 10 minutes, and then blue for another ten. This went on for a few months. Then I lost interest in pursuing my own treatment in the press of time for my practice, research, and clinical teaching.

Without any more vision therapy, I realized around that time that I really did not need my distance glasses very often at all. I had stopped wearing my very low-powered contact lenses (1/4 and 1/2 diopter). My glasses had very low-powered lenses (1/8th of a diopter on one eye and only ⅓ on the other). I used them for driving and theater. Several years later, an ophthalmologist treating a corneal abrasion in my eye said that I was farsighted now at distance and I should stop wearing those minus lenses. I had done no therapy to complete this process of total myopia cure. Looking back, I suspect it was the syntonics machine. I had not had my vision checked after those "treatments."

After a syntonics conference in 1997 in D.C., my old optometrist, Amiel Francke, began using light therapy with all of his patients. He lectured on the subject of syntonic home therapy in 2003 at the Syntonic Optometry Conference, reporting that almost all of his patients reduced their myopia and gained many other benefits by using a take-home machine developed by Dr. Stanley Levine (Francke 2003).

So what is this syntonics treatment? How does it work and what does it work on? The most interesting book on the subject that I have seen is *Light: Medicine of the Future* by Jacob Liberman, OD, PhD (1991). It usefully discusses the history of the field's development, talks about treatment, speculates about why it is important in our frenetic culture—which requires late nights and days of artificial light—to treat with light. It is well accepted that patients with seasonal affective disorder (SAD) are helped with full-spectrum light indoors during the winter months (Gottlieb and Wallace 2001 36). Patients of mine with special needs at Harvard have been able to arrange for full-spectrum light in their carrels in the library.

Other light treatments are less well known, but light researchers are now talking about the two different types of lighting needs—those for seeing, and those for managing circadian rhythms, which have to do with sleep and alertness cycles (Boyce, Hunter, and Howlet 2003).

Syntonics works with specific wavelengths of colored light that influence the autonomic nervous system. Before the discovery of penicillin in the mid-1900s, those who worked with light therapy thought it truly would be the medicine of the future. A doctor born in India in 1873, named Dinshah P. Ghadiali, used it on various parts of the body, calling this treatment the "spectrochrome" system. At least one American surgeon, Dr. Kate Baldwin, used his methods for decades with success and lectured on it to her Pennsylvania Medical Society in 1926. Light therapy of various kinds has long been used in treating tuberculosis (Liberman 1991).

Harry Riley Spitler, PhD, a physician and an optometrist, worked with colored light in the 1920s. His book, *The Syntonic Principle: Its Relation to Health and Ocular Problems* (1941) is still a classic for understanding the principles of light therapy. He realized, after doing experiments in altering the color of light rabbits lived under, that without full-spectrum daylight they were getting sick in various ways. Could humans get well, then, if the light we lived beneath was more full spectrum? Or could we deliver light through the eyes (instead of the body sections outlined by Ghadiali) with specific wavelengths (colors) to cure different problems? He decided we could and developed machines to do that and a theory to explain it (Spitler 1941).

One reason light delivered through the eyes can have far-reaching effects in the body and nervous system is that we have a pineal gland that responds to light and, with the pituitary gland, regulates many hormonal systems of the body, keeping us in synch with planetary time, the seasons, and much more. We also have an optic nerve, which may respond to different frequencies of light, and blood vessels on the surface of the retina that pick up light frequencies. This is medium-frequency medicine, which many believe to be the light of the future. For now, optometrists who use syntonics know that it speeds up therapy when combined with traditional vision therapy and lens training (Gottlieb and Wallace 2001; Getzell 2006).

Researchers at Harvard Medical School and Brigham and Women's Hospital sleep medicine department have determined that blue light can reset one's biological rhythms and allow one to work or study at night. Night workers have done this with white "light boxes" but, according to this latest research, blue light is more effective.

Steven Lockley and colleagues Charles Czeisler of Harvard and neurologist George Brainard of Thomas Jefferson University in Philadelphia studied blind subjects as well. They found that the blue light helped them set their biological clocks so they would not toss and turn at night, lacking the normal visual turnoff into sleep in the dark. Their light detector system is separate from the visual system, and if this is still intact, the blue light works (Cromie 2006). One part of that system is a particular type of photoreceptor cell in the retina, which was discovered in mammals in 2002. It is not a seeing cell, but is sensitive to levels of light and dark, and so is part of the circadian system (AOA *NEWS*, 2002).

One of my colleagues, a truly exceptional behavioral optometrist and frequent lecturer from Evanston, Illinois, Dr. Jeffrey Getzell, has used light therapy with almost all of his vision training patients for nine years. They all purchase the small Levine machine with glass filters. It is the same lamp with filters that I often sell at cost to patients who appear to need a swift opening up of their peripheral vision. It is especially effective with children.

Dr. Getzell explains, "Syntonics uses phototherapy to balance the autonomic nervous system, sympathetic and parasympathetic. Imbalances may show up in the behavior of a person in certain ways: sleep patterns, energy patterns, and visual patterns." He does not use syntonics unless there is a visual problem that he can measure. The visual problems that can be treated with syntonics include "binocular vision dysfunctions" and "reduced peripheral awareness." Some patients notice a difference "after just one treatment," Getzell says (2006).

There are major benefits of syntonics treatment that Dr. Getzell and other behavioral optometrists see. First, "Within a week, it will increase the field of view, the peripheral awareness of that patient," Dr. Getzell says, "if they do three sessions minimum and better yet every day with their home machine." He sees it also as causing "an immediate increase in the ability to take in new information in a more organized manner and then respond more effectively." It also can "improve performance" in other activities and "make patients more available to the benefits of vision therapy activities." Getzell believes it is the fast track to helping the brain and visual system grasp a more three-dimensional space world (Getzell 2006).

Dr. Getzell told me of one very badly behaved little boy who always "tackled little girls." After syntonics treatment, he stopped the tackling and was able to focus on his schoolwork and vision therapy activities. Another case was a psychologist who told Dr. Getzell that it "reduced her anxiety" and she was "no longer bumping into things" now that her functional field had been enlarged (Getzell 2006).

As is discussed in chapter four, stress is a big factor in the development of vision problems, because of the imbalances it creates between the sympathetic and parasympathetic nervous systems. Stress can also constrict functional color fields, which is different from the absolute field loss indicating major brain or visual system damage. Color fields can be opened up with colored light stimulation, and this improves overall peripheral awareness, but that is not the only good result from syntonics treatment.

Studies have been done by Kaplan, Liberman, and Ingersoll that "all showed that relatively short-term syntonic treatment can significantly improve visual skills, peripheral vision, memory, behavior, mood, general performance and academic achievement" (Gottlieb and Wallace 2001, 33).

There are, as explained by Gottlieb and Wallace, four major syndromes affecting vision that syntonics can treat with specific colors, in some cases, better than any other system. These include chronic syndrome (80 percent of patients, including LD kids and those with long-term thinking and movement problems), emotional fatigue syndrome (often seen in children with many of the symptoms of those who need vision therapy), acute syndrome (head injury and inflammation), and lazy eye syndrome (amblyopia/strabismus). There are protocols of the appropriate blue/green, yellow/green, indigo/red, red/orange, and so on, for all of these different visual syndromes that have been worked out by optometrists for decades. Blue green is often used in the cases of head injury.

These problems may be occurring partly because we live in artificial light that does not have all the proper wavelengths for our brains. Full spectrum light, which feeds all the colors into the eyes, is necessary for healthful learning. When my children and I were patients of Dr. Francke in Washington, D.C., he suggested I read John Ott's book, *Health and Light* (1973) and later, *Light, Radiation and You* (1982) and obtain full spectrum lights for at least part of my house. I only had fixtures for them in the kitchen and the bathroom. It seemed that in the winter or on rainy days, the children tended to gather around the kitchen table or spend a lot of time playing in the bathroom.

Years later a study was done in California that showed that classrooms without windows did not facilitate learning as well as rooms with sunlight coming through windows (Eklund, Boyce, and Simpson 2000). Gottlieb and Wallace cite this study as reported by *The Washington Post* news service. The students scored "as much as 25 percent higher on standardized tests than other artificially lit students in the same districts" (Gottlieb and Wallace 2001, 33). This is just one study; others might be different, but it makes sense to let children have windows for light and gazing far to rest their eyes. My adult patients in little computer cubicles would all vote for windows.

Light is a powerful force for training and healing vision. We know that movement in the light is necessary for babies and animals to learn to see (Hein 1972). We also know that colored light can help a child see a broader, wider world and be a better learner. A head injury patient can improve in visual areas with syntonics, and, in some cases, a myopic patient can see clearer with less lens power. Having a syntonics practitioner in a school setting is valuable if it is done along with vision therapy, as in the Ingersoll school in Michigan (see chapter three).

HOMEOPATHY: GENTLE TREATMENT FOR CHILDREN WITH LEARNING AND BEHAVIOR PROBLEMS

The concept of homeopathic treatment with gentle remedies that work with the body's own energy has always appealed to me rather than strong medications that have side effects, especially for children and sensitive adults. I have used it myself to prevent and cure flu and colds, cure traveler's diarrhea, heal pain from a bad fall, and feel better in times of stress. Use of this over-the-counter healing modality is wonderful for parents to help maintain their children's health.

However, there is another use for homeopathy, which is vastly more important for children with hyperactivity, behavior problems, autism, developmental delay, emotional trauma, or chronic illness such as asthma, repeated ear infections, and allergies, all of which interfere with learning. This use for homeopathy is quite complex and needs a trained homeopath to be maximally effective.

In addition to using it over the counter myself, I have been treated several times by homeopath Begabati Lennihan, and so have most members of my family. She is the head of the Teleosis School of Homeopathy in Boston, with classes at the Massachusetts College of Pharmacy. Lennihan agreed to write out for my readers her take on the importance of homeopathy for children with learning issues.

Begabati Lennihan's Report

Homeopathy is a form of natural medicine developed by a German physician two hundred years ago. It is now a well-established and accepted part of the health care system in many countries around the world, including the United Kingdom, France, Germany, India, and much of South America. It works with the body's own healing energy, like acupuncture, yet it is a form of healing that children actually enjoy. No shots, no needles, no unpleasant-tasting medicine—homeopathic remedies look and taste like tiny sugar pills. If the tiny amount of sugar is an issue, a pellet can be dissolved in water and given by the teaspoonful.

In my own practice, I have many kids who love their remedies and know how to ask for them by name, even some as young as four years old. I have two-year-old patients who, when they feel sick, toddle over to the cupboard where their remedy is stored and pat the door to get their mom's attention. I even have a baby in my practice who gets visibly excited when his mom opens the remedy tube. He seems to know that his teething pain is about to go away!

Homeopathy can be used for a wide variety of conditions: energetic (whether hyperactivity or chronic fatigue), behavioral (such as oppositional defiance disorder), mental (problems with memory and concentration), and emotional (separation anxiety, depression, panic disorder). It covers a wide variety of physical conditions, both acute (such as colds, coughs, diarrhea, teething, cuts and bruises, burns, and insect bites) and chronic (asthma, fibromyalgia, and diabetes, to name just a few).

Your doctor may try to tell you that homeopathy is unproven. That just means that he or she is unfamiliar with the research. Most research on homeopathy has been conducted overseas, because the American government does not provide research money for it, and American drug companies cannot make a profit on it. One of the few studies published in the United States in Pediatrics (Jacobs et al. 1994) documented the effectiveness of homeopathy in treating childhood diarrhea. A meta-analysis (summary) of over a hundred studies on homeopathy has shown it was effective in a wide variety of conditions (Linde et al. 1997) The research is well summarized in Dr. Bill Gray's *Homeopathy: Science or Myth?* (2000) and in Dana Ullman's *Homeopathic Family Medicine* (2002).[1]

I have seen amazing changes in children in my practice and I feel fortunate to have had the opportunity to work on them, because in many cases they would otherwise be on drugs indefinitely. Homeopathy is deeply healing, so that once the condition is reversed, the patient no longer needs the medicine. Also, instead of having side effects, the remedies often have side benefits.

Children treated with homeopathy for a chronic condition like learning or behavior problems often have the side benefit that they get fewer colds and ear infections. I have children in my practice from other countries who were brought up entirely on homeopathic medicines and have never had antibiotics or other drugs. The parents often tell me that their child is the only one in the class who never gets sick.

Homeopathy works by strengthening your child's underlying constitution. The homeopath must match your child to a particular individualized homeopathic remedy by observing your child and asking many, many questions about your child's nature and temperament, behavior, health history, even preferences in food and clothing. Some of the most common remedy types are described in Catherine Coulter's *Homeopathic Sketches of Children's Types* (2001) and Paul Herscu's *The Homeopathic Treatment of Children* (1991).

The causation is also important if known; I have treated children who were "never well since" (to use the homeopathic term) a birth trauma that left them oxygen-deprived, or since a traumatic breakup of their parents' marriage. Homeopathy can even treat emotional trauma that the child received in utero. A baby in the womb is swimming in a warm bath of the mother's emotional state; if the mother has a severe shock, such as the baby's father dying suddenly, the baby will be born needing the same grief remedy that the mother needed and may have lifelong symptoms from this unresolved grief.

Homeopaths also glean clues by carefully observing a child. The initial information gathering is likely to last an hour or two and may involve a written intake as well as interviewing the parents and the child. A homeopathic interview is easy, maybe even fun compared to other health care appointments your child has had. Usually, there is no physical examination, and the homeopath can learn a lot just by watching your child play.

Just to share one example among many children I have treated, four-year-old Pia was brought to me for "selective mutism." She refused to speak except at home, and then only when she was alone with her parents. Clearly her problem was emotional; there was nothing wrong with her vocal cords. Pia was growing up in the shadow of an older sister who was fully autistic, who could not speak a single word, and whose uncontrollable behavior was a constant preoccupation for the parents. I sensed that Pia's problem was feeling abandoned and neglected, plus jealous of the older sister who got all the attention. Apparently, she figured out that refusing to speak would get her a lot of special attention. The two beleaguered parents were involved in an endless round of appointments and specialists for both daughters.

Pia received the remedy Pulsatilla, perhaps homeopathy's top remedy for children. Not only can it help heal sniffles and tummy aches, measles and chickenpox, it also releases the jealousy of sibling rivalry and calms the terror of separation anxiety. However, it will not treat all children with these conditions; it must match their specific symptoms. I did not give Pia a remedy for mutism. I gave her a remedy for feeling abandoned, neglected, and jealous, which she had chosen to express through her refusal to speak.

Pia's parents reported clear progress throughout the next few months in everything but her speech. She lost her extreme indecisiveness and was able to tell them what she wanted to eat or wear. Her sibling rivalry lost its steam; she no longer pushed her sister aside to be the first into the car or house. But she still stubbornly refused to speak. I advised her parents not to make a big deal of it, to give her as little attention as possible for it. Then on her fifth birthday she announced, "I'm a big girl now and I'm going to talk to *everybody!*" which she proceeded to do!

To learn more about how homeopathy can help children with learning or behavioral problems, I highly recommend books by Dr. Robert Ullman and Dr. Judyth Reichenberg-Ullman: *Ritalin-Free Kids* (1996), *Rage-Free Kids* (1999), and *A Drug-Free Approach to Asperger Syndrome and Autism* (this last with Dr. Ian Luepker; 2005). The dramatic story of an autistic child's complete cure with homeopathy is recounted in my favorite introductory book on homeopathy, Amy Lansky's *Impossible Cure* (2003).

Just one caution, however: These books are meant to inspire you to find a professional homeopath for your child, not to guide you in treating your child at home. Treating your child with a homeopathic remedy from the health food store is great for teething or diarrhea, but it is simply not possible for long-term problems. Not only is it not likely to work, it can even muddle the situation so that later a professional homeopath may have a harder time treating your child.

Finding a good homeopath can be a challenge, as there are not enough trained homeopaths in this country, and most are concentrated on the two coasts. It is best to find someone who can see your child in person at least the first time rather than working over the phone. The effectiveness of the homeopath will depend mostly on her or his training and experience, as well as on the ability to form a positive relationship with both parents and child. For major medical conditions, I recommend a homeopath who is also a licensed health care provider (some homeopaths are also physicians, naturopaths, nurse practitioners, etc.). But for a physically healthy child whose problems are behavioral, a medically licensed individual is not necessary.

The best way to find a good homeopath is by word of mouth, since you want someone who has both good results and good rapport with patients. If there is a small independent health food store nearby, where the owner knows all the practitioners in the community, that could be a good place to start. Or ask another alternative practitioner such as your behavioral optometrist, chiropractor, or acupuncturist. Otherwise, try a website such as the National Center for Homeopathy at www.homeopathic.org, which lists most of the homeopaths in the country. If you cannot find a local homeopath, you can consult with the Reichenberg-Ullmans by phone as described on their website, www.healthyhomeopathy.com.

If you do not get good results with one homeopath, try another one. Don't say "homeopathy doesn't work"; it just means that one particular remedy from one particular homeopath does not work. Your homeopath should be someone who you like and respect, whose remedies work for your child (at least after a couple of tries), and who is available to answer your questions by phone in a timely manner. (Most homeopaths do charge for phone call time.)

Homeopathic treatment for your child will probably take some extra effort in terms of finding the right practitioner, but the results are likely to be life-transforming for your child. While the initial consult may cost several hundred dollars, the overall cost of treatment is remarkably inexpensive given the benefits. The remedies themselves are inexpensive, and the consults with the homeopath will become shorter and more infrequent as your child gets better and better. I encourage you to educate yourself, to read one or more of the books recommended above, and to embark on a journey of homeopathic care for your child.

Begabati Lennihan, RN, CCH

January 2006

Vision Problems

The therapies described in this chapter are in no way meant to take the place of a thorough behavioral/developmental vision assessment and vision treatment if needed. Vision therapy always works at the level of effort put into it (Maino 2005). It may be supplemented and enhanced in its effects by utilizing one or more of the above systems of healing. As Dr. Amiel Francke explains it, the "infrastructure" of health and a balanced body is essential for vision at its best.

In my personal experience, vision therapy has been an extremely powerful tool for accomplishing radical change in visual competence and even thought processes, study skills, and so on. It is brain training. I tell the story of my myopia cure in chapter four. Chapter three discusses vision therapy for learning problems in the children behavioral optometrists treat.

The power of vision therapy comes from the fact that the eyes are connected to all parts of the brain, and through those connections, to movement, thought, emotions, and skill with hands and feet. However, sometimes these other parts of the human body/brain complex need extra help before, during, or after the relearning of vision. When that happens, I call on one of my "big six" supplementary treatment modalities to get that patient well.

Case of a Teenager with a Childhood History of Head Trauma: Combining Vision Therapy, Neurotherapy, Gentle Chiropractic, Primitive Reflex Integration, Brain Gym, Syntonics, and Homeopathy

My first patient who did neurotherapy was a high school student (we'll call him Simon) who had trouble sustaining focus on reading for more than 20 minutes at a time. He was a very popular B student, but he could not complete all his reading assignments in a tough suburban high school. He had loving parents doing everything they could to help him. He had even done some vision therapy as a child in another town. He needed more, so we did vision therapy (including some home syntonics treatments) for a whole year, but at the first visit I was sure he had sustained a head injury and would need more support than just my vision work. As is typical of head trauma, this boy's peripheral vision was very poor, which is unusual for a normal farsighted young person. It was a red flag for me. There were also problems tracking across the midline smoothly. I knew he needed to see Dr. Lydia Knutson, the chiropractor with the Edu-K background. She would find the injury and fix it.

After his first visit to her, the memory of the injury came back. An accident had caused a severe head bang when he was four. He had hit the right side of his head and his low back, and Dr. Knutson found injuries to both the right side of the cranium and to his pelvis, which she could fix. Knutson and I were able to coordinate efforts to synchronize his neuromuscular "foundation" with tracking across the midline, shifting gaze from near to far, and seeing the periphery.

This boy also did a full treatment of 40 visits of EEG neurofeedback work with Dr. Ross simultaneously with vision therapy and chiropractic. There were major changes for the better on his follow-up "brain map" after 30 neurotherapy sessions. His mother felt neurofeedback played a big part in his being able to read faster and longer, do math easier, and have hope for getting through the work in college.

Following the neurotherapy he was sent to Eliza Bergeson (the Brain Gym educational kinesiologist who wrote the Brain Gym section of this chapter). She identified the reflexes needing integration to facilitate better reading, and which Brain Gym exercises were needed to sustain them. Dr. Knutson continued to monitor this with adjustments so that his structure could handle the new shifts Bergeson was fostering. Besides the vision therapy and syntonics, all of his ancillary treatments interacted with vision and other workings of the brain. He even took homeopathic allergy remedies for his summer allergies so that his eyes were not bothered by symptoms.

The results of all these treatments and the vision therapy were quite spectacular. Simon could finally accept glasses with enough plus to make him comfortable for his reading and also process visual information rapidly and efficiently. Simon got straight As his last year in high school and really enjoyed the reading. He is off to a demanding university now, very happy and doing excellent work.

All his treatments worked together to help this young man become what he was meant to be. I don't think we could have tossed out any of them and gotten equal results. Without all four of us delving more deeply into perfecting his system, he might have always been a hard-working B student who was popular with friends, but had some reading problems. The head injury could have gone untreated and unremembered for the rest of his life.

This is the problem with a lot of head injuries, says Dr. Irwin Suchoff, retired behavioral optometrist who formerly ran the SUNY College of Optometry head injury unit (Suchoff 2006). Many people who do okay in life after a head trauma are handicapped in relation to what they were or might have been, but no one is thinking that this is something that needs fixing. It does, and it can be fixed for new and higher function, but courts and insurance companies believe there is nothing to treat. The severe cases are the only ones that insurance covers and doctors think of treating. It is important to remember, though, how a few well-managed, paid-out-of-pocket therapies can improve a person's life.

A problem of reading efficiency is one of the major symptoms of post–head trauma vision syndrome or other threats to the brain, such as toxic chemicals or oxygen deprivation. This is because peripheral awareness, tracking, focusing ability, and the convergence system are diminished. The complication with Simon was that adaptations to what is called "post-trauma vision syndrome" had been made and locked in for thirteen years. Instead of the usual post-trauma convergence insufficiency along with his focusing deficiencies, he was over-converging because of his excess effort to focus. Remember that synkinesis between focusing and converging muscles explained in chapter four?

Simon needed to wear stronger plus glasses because of his farsightedness, focusing problem, and overconvergence. Before all his therapies, he could not release that locked-in focus to wear more helpful glasses without feeling that he was getting a headache, but he couldn't read for more than 20 minutes without a stronger prescription. So he was stuck. He needed these various therapies to get his very bright brain

and visual system back to how it would have functioned without the disruption of the early post-trauma vision syndrome.

Schools Should Have at Least Some of These Services and Vision Therapy within Their Walls if We Are to Upgrade the Skills of Children Who Come with Compromised Systems for Learning

Each principal needs a list of outside resources to give to parents with
insurance or for those who are able to afford them. Which outside referrals schools should pay for are local issues. Eye exams and vision therapy are absolutely essential within the walls of any school with children
who are learning disabled. (Recall from chapter three that 34 of 37 children tested visually for an individual education plan evaluation had vision problems.)

Light therapy (syntonics) could be a routine part of vision therapy in
the schools. While chiropractic, cranial osteopathy, and homeopathy
might have to be on a referral basis, teachers should be allowed to train
in and use Brain Gym in the classroom, and someone should be trained
in each school to do primitive reflex work. Neurotherapy has been successful in the few schools I know that have provided it. The more people who know how to actually shift learning capability to higher levels,
the better for all of our children and all of our schools.

NOTE

1. Both books are available from Homeopathic Educational Services at
www.homeopathic.com, which has extensive information on homeopathic research
right on the website.

6

TEACHERS ARE THE FIRST LINE OF DEFENSE AGAINST VISION-RELATED LEARNING PROBLEMS

"I am holding strong for kindergarten for these kids," says Sandy Christison, probably one of the most loving and skilled kindergarten teachers in Massachusetts. "We are being told to do many things that are not appropriate for kindergarten." She is facing the challenge of preparing her students for what promises to be a highly pressured first grade. By third grade, her students will face the challenge of being evaluated by statewide, high-stakes testing. The knowledge is there for the asking now on how children's brains develop best—through graceful and loving days, with positive self images, calm freedom to be curious and move, and absence of pressure (Pearce 2003; Schore 1994; Pert 1997).

All of this wisdom is not, and in some cases cannot be, applied. Many children are on the autism spectrum. Many are stressed in single-parent families financially on the edge. Many are fearful, often abused. Numbers of them have asthma. Others are medicated for attention deficit and attention deficit hyperactivity disorders (ADD and ADHD). Very few are eating a healthy diet. They come to school with society's failure in their brains and small bodies and with eager hope in their faces. How can we keep from snuffing out the light in their eyes?

Christison teaches in an inner-city school where, because of Head-start cutbacks, fewer and fewer children have had preschool experiences. Reading now is required to be taught in kindergarten in most schools to prepare for first grade testing. Many children, however, are not ready visually, physically, mentally, or emotionally to tackle small printed words. At least, they are not ready for words in books or worksheets close to their eyes. They have not had the home experiences that ready eyes for looking up close at print, ready fingers for holding pencils, ready bodies to sit still at a desk, and ready brains to learn phonics and to visually process those small black letters.

However, with third-grade high-stakes tests looming ahead and less and less money available for teaching, the push is on to start earlier and earlier to teach children to read. This is being done even if it means that large numbers will be declared learning disabled, simply because they are not ready.

When Christison and I were working in the Mather school in Boston, I helped her set up a small area in her room for children to become more visually aware. It included a 2-x-4 walking rail and a hanging ball used for exercises with a stiff, cardboard bat with different colored stripes. The exercises helped children learn tracking, the difference between right and left, and eye/hand coordination. There was a blackboard for drawing lazy eights, a minitrampoline for kids to jump on while teachers coached them on their ability to do cross/crawl patterns with arms and legs, a box of beanbags for tossing into a bucket, a red and green eye chart, and red and green glasses for children to wear while teachers checked to see if they were suppressing an eye. She had her aide work with the children, one at a time, on these basic visual/motor activities to ready them for learning.

Christison also worked hard at using large print on her writing board for "circle time," so the children could easily focus on the board. She made very large letters for the wallboards and good-sized letters for the tables, so her students would have ways to learn the alphabet at distance before they learned it on a worksheet. They could make words at their desks with large letters without stressing their eyes. This helped her students, and they tested better than I ever expected on the Developmental Eye Movement Test (a visual tracking test that is normed for six-through 13-year-olds) at the end of that kindergarten year, when most had turned six.

Any preschool or kindergarten teacher should have the freedom to help children get ready to read who are not ready in visual/motor ways yet. Everything in learning is based on movement, and we need to structure our learning so that children gain what they have missed by being cooped up in apartments with TVs blaring and no chance to develop eye/ hand coordination, eye/foot coordination, brain and body, eyes and brain, through all the "smart moves" (Hannaford 1995) that we now know create good brains for children through movement in space. For more discussion, see chapters 3, 4, and 5.

As a behavioral optometrist, I have a fantasy school in mind, where all children receive needed catch-up work to ready their eyes, such as vision therapy, before they have to perceive small print. In a school eye clinic, low-powered reading glasses would be available. My utopia also includes basic Brain Gym[1] exercises in the classroom at the start of each day and frequent trips for children "to be in nature" doing large muscle activities (Louv 2005; Louv 2006).

A lot of natural light would be available in each room (Heschong, Wright, and Okura 2002). All children would get a healthy school breakfast. The desks would be at the right height so that the child would not strain his eyes by focusing too close (Harmon 1958). The desktops would have a slant board provided to place written pages parallel to a child's face with a very slight down gaze. The child's head would not hang down over a flat surface a few inches from the book. He would play required sports or take yoga, movement, or martial arts classes after school for an hour. He would laugh and play at two recesses during the day on a safe and imaginative playground.

In this fantasy school there would be visual readiness work before learning to read, and learning to read would begin with very large letters at a distance. Then when all the words in a story were learned, the story would be read up close. By then, when much of the vocabulary would already be mastered by sight, learning to focus at near would not frustrate learning to read. The child would already know how to read.

None of these reforms would compromise anyone's teaching style, and they would not be expensive to implement. They would help immeasurably in preparing our children's brains and visual systems for learning. Schools want their children to succeed. It would be good for society to help that happen by providing what it takes in money and systems to avoid snuffing out the light and joy of learning in so many children's lives.

Many times I have cooperated with schools to do special things for individual children. They are very willing to do this. Together, teachers and I have arranged for larger print on written material for several children. Some teachers have arranged for children to sit closer to the blackboard and to the teacher's desk. Sometimes a teacher has agreed to keep the children's glasses in her desk and dole them out when it is time for close written work or reading. Others have been happy to give more time on tests or less homework for a period while the eye training was going on. Several have taken patches off and on during the day on a timed schedule.

All of this is extra work for the teacher, some of which would be eliminated in the ideal school of my fantasy, because every child would have the basic support needed for good visual learning from a clinic in the school and appropriate programs for vision development. This chapter is designed to help teachers identify visual problems in children and figure out how they can help and what help can be requested from the family, the school, and other sources.

Teachers can help students enormously by recognizing and referring the specific visual problems of their students. Eighty percent of all learning that takes place in school is visually transmitted. If children's vision problems can be resolved, they can concentrate better, read better, write more neatly, remember longer, and have more eagerness to learn, because their vision will support these tasks and activities. Many teachers know these things already. Behavioral optometrists get referrals from occupational therapists in the schools and from a number of teachers who also have great eyes for spotting kids who are visually floundering. It would be more efficient, of course, if there were a vision clinic in each school.

If teachers were to have a short manual telling them all the things they could do for their students' vision, it should be one that states how talented teachers are, how much they care, and how much they already have to do for each of their children to make up for what the world and the family has not done. Here are the categories of specific information that I think teachers might find helpful on their desktops to aid in increasing their children's ability to learn and pay attention.

1. A checklist of symptoms and signs of vision problems that interfere with learning, as well as explanations of what these signs reveal about vision difficulties that a child may be experiencing.
2. Specific guidelines about school desks and glasses, "working distances," and light that contribute to vision problems related to learning.
3. The factors that interfere with referring students for or obtaining outside help.
4. Some incredibly useful ideas, called the Snapp method, for what to do about teaching reading when the children's eyes are not ready yet. The Snapp method is used only by those who trained with Snapp in Mississippi or Texas. It is not generally known, but it should be taught across the country.

To this end, I have consulted not only my own teaching background and teacher friends, but a researcher in education, who is specifically interested in the visual process of learning. She is Betty Ward, PhD, an educator from Texas who wrote a dissertation that determined the actual longest distance from eye to desk students in grades one and two (ages six through nine) have when working at a best-fit desk and chair (Ward 1989).

In her discussions with vision care professionals, she explained that vision examinations arbitrarily use a near-viewing distance that is appropriate for older students or adults.

This is "partly because such information was not available to them since measurements had never been made of the longest distance available to these young students when working at their desks." Ward suggests that "problems of learning in the classroom can be caused by a student who is not at the proper visual development state for what he is being expected to do, and cannot sustain proper body posture because of the desk and seat constraints that cause lots of stress on students' visual systems" (Ward 2006).

If the student is too small for the desk height and does not have enough distance from eye to page for focusing and convergence ability, he will be less able to learn. That is just a fact, and Ward told the world that this was a very common problem by actually measuring the distances available.

Dr. Ward, with years of experience in special education for both physically handicapped and learning-disabled children, all levels of music teaching, Montessori teaching, and elementary school teaching, is also well informed on visual stress and learning. Her understanding across disciplines is quite rare. Her dissertation was so relevant to behavioral optometry that it was placed in the Skeffington Memorial Library and archives in Santa Ana, California, as a research resource for optometrists by the late Dr. Gerald N. Getman, a major researcher on the connection between vision and learning in children.

My experience as a former high school teacher, a parent, and an eye doctor is that teachers are astute observers and are on the frontline for identifying problems that truly can ruin a child's learning life if not identified. Many wish for more information about what symptoms of the eyes mean and what they can do to help. Based on my research (Orfield 2001), I would say teachers should refer any child who is not working at grade level or "up to his potential" for a comprehensive functional vision exam. These are the kids in dire need of those full functional vision examinations described in chapters one and three. Screenings will not identify the problems. The quickie health clinic exam will probably not do that either.

Even if near vision is tested, it is likely to be done at distances that are not comparable to what the child faces sitting at his school desk, especially if he is small. Ward mentioned that there are also problems with the thickness of the child's thighs under the desktop. If the desk needs to be higher for larger legs, the desk height might be too high for the child's eyes to be comfortable. It could put the child's armpits at desk height, which interferes with writing and focusing. Elbows need to be able to clear the desktop as recommended by optometrists Francke and Kaplan (1978). Behavioral optometrists know that reading glasses of low plus power can often help a child be more comfortable with these excessively near distances in school.

Referral for the right kind of visual evaluation is a good first step when children are struggling. The National Parent Teacher Association (PTA) now has guidelines for the kind of complete learning-related vision exam that children need (National PTA Resolution 1999). With a developmental/behavioral optometrist, appropriate tests will all be done, glasses will not be given unless needed, surgery will not be ordered if there are better alternatives with training, and, if surgery is necessary for crossed or walled eyes, the pre- and post-training will get done as well.

Most behavioral optometrists are also licensed to treat eye infections, so they can become a child's regular eye doctor. They are all optometrists, with doctoral degrees as any other optometrist. What distinguishes them is that they have had hundreds of hours of postdoctoral training on vision therapy, the management of binocular vision problems, and pediatric vision development. They are usually members or fellows of the College of Optometrists in Vision Development, which is a certifying body for this specialty.

Another diagnostic step is for schools to send out lists to parents at the beginning of the year for them to observe possible visual problems while children do their homework. Schools might be wise to get some of the PAVE (Parents Active in Vision Education) sheets and pass them around to all parents and teachers. Often teachers or parents may observe behaviors in the student that are similar to some on these lists, but they are not aware that they indicate the student has visual problems. By third grade the children should see a checklist themselves for self-diagnosis. Most younger children with vision problems have no idea that the way they see is not the way everyone sees. If they have problems like those on the checklist, they think it is just the way eyes work.

There is a pamphlet from the Optometric Extension Program called "Do You Have a Vision Problem?" which could help older students self-diagnose a learning-related vision problem. We know that third graders do show awareness and often complain that their eyes hurt or that things are blurry when they read (Vaughn, Maples, and Hoenes 2006).

Below is a comprehensive checklist for teachers. I have organized it the way Ward did for teachers, but I have added diagnoses that optometrists suspect when they hear these visual complaints. The Optometric Extension Program also has put out a useful teacher's checklist, available at www.oep.org/educator.htm. The College of Optometrists in Vision Development[2] short list is in chapter three. The following is a sign and symptom guide that is a composite of a lot of lists that Ward put together, and that I added to from the other sources, including the PAVE[3] list.

CHILDREN'S VISION PROBLEMS: A DESKTOP GUIDE FOR TEACHERS

Teacher and Parent Check List

Appearance of the Eyes: What to Look For

1. One eye or alternate eyes turning in or out at any time (esotropia or exotropia, which means eyes crossed or turned out; strabismus is the medical term for these problems).
2. Reddened eyes (allergy, infection, or not enough sleep, rubbing eyes from blurry sight).
3. Watering eyes (allergies, continual eyestrain, or infection).
4. Encrusted eyelids (infection of lash follicles likely).
5. Frequent sties (behavioral optometrists can treat these, and often they are signs of visual stress in the system, so likely other problems with functional vision will show up).
6. Pupils are different sizes (referral to eye care provider necessary; it could be serious, or not).
7. Eyes that involuntarily move constantly (this might be a condition called nystagmus. Behavioral optometrists can treat, and refer if need be to a neurologist or neuro-ophthalmologist).
8. Drooping eyelids (this could be a serious problem. A talk with a parent would establish whether this has existed since birth and has already been discussed with the pediatrician, if it is a new, sudden onset condition, or if the child is tired and fighting off desire for sleep).

Signs of Near Vision Problems: Most Need Referrals to a Behavioral Optometrist

1. Frowning or scowling while reading or writing (focusing or converging problems).
2. Thrusting head forward or tilting to one side (neck problems that advanced chiropractic or osteopathic evaluation could help, visual problems like blur at near from any kind of refractive problem, focusing problem, or convergence problem).

3. Covering or closing one eye habitually, sometimes just by holding arm over it to rest head (likely being done to avoid diplopia [double vision], which the child does not know is abnormal, so may not mention).

4. Unusual fatigue after completing a visual task (likely needs reading glasses or vision therapy for focusing, but could be insufficient sleep, poor nutrition, or all of the above).

5. Holds reading materials at an unusual angle (attempt to block out one eye or an astigmatism that is not corrected).

6. Turning head so as to use one eye only (avoiding double vision, trouble focusing with two eyes and has discovered that one eye is easier, sight problem that has allowed one eye to see better at near).

7. Bending over to see material (trying to get face parallel to the material to avoid constant shifts in focus as he reads down the page, since he has no way to prop the material up parallel to his face, possibly needs glasses for near).

8. Constantly shifting position (fatigue of focus and convergence, responding to intermittent blur or intermittent doubling, trouble crossing the midline).

9. Easily distracted (too many problems to list, but could be poor peripheral awareness or focus fatigue).

10. Holds reading material closer than normal (trouble focusing or converging, needs to use just one eye rather than try to use both, print too small for his abilities, needs glasses for better clarity).

11. Writing is unusually large (possible trouble focusing or needs glasses, poor assessment of size and space, may have minus glasses for distance, which minify everything).

12. Writing is unusually small (may have plus glasses that magnify things so he does not realize he is writing so small, poor peripheral vision, perceptual problems).

13. Difficulty copying letters and/or numerals from textbook to paper (poor saccadic ability, trouble shifting focus, poor eye/hand coordination, poor visual memory, poor spatial awareness).

14. Difficulty copying letters and/or numerals from chalkboard (or overhead) to paper (focusing or convergence problems, eye hand coordination, poor spatial awareness).

15. Difficulty completing assignment in allotted time (possibly doing auditory learning rather than visual learning, any functional vision problem, poor auditory visual integration).

16. Leaves out parts of assignment put on top, side, or bottom of chalk board (poor peripheral awareness, poor tracking ability, fatigue of focus, refractive error, rarely visual field loss.).

17. Difficulty completing or reading dittoed materials (poor focus, needs reading glasses).

18. Difficulty completing or reading xeroxed materials (poor focus, needs reading glasses).

19. Unduly sensitive to light (possible vitamin deficiency, trouble converging eyes).

20. Begins writing in center of paper or does not use complete line for writing (visual motor integration, eye/hand coordination, peripheral awareness problem, laterality and directionality problem).

21. Unable to distinguish colors (hereditary color deficiency likely if a boy).

22. Tends to reverse letters and words or confuse letters and numbers with similar shapes (laterality/directionality problems, form perception, visual memory, and span of recognition difficulties).

23. Frequent or constant loss of place in a sentence or on a page (poor eye movement control, convergence problems, or lack of peripheral awareness).

24. Poor spacing in writing (eye/hand coordination, eye movement control, convergence problems, focusing, clarity of sight).

25. Cannot read for long periods without tiring; reading worsens as time span increases (poorly sustained focusing, convergence problems, or eye movements poorly controlled, taking a lot of effort).

Problems at Distance (But Not Necessarily from Nearsightedness)

1. Squinting or scowling while reading from board (poor clarity from nearsightedness, astigmatism, or significant farsightedness, or poor eye teaming at distance, poor eye movement control).

2. Thrusting head forward or moving forward (lacks clarity of sight, or glasses are not best Rx—they have cut down on peripheral vision).

3. Falling more frequently than other students (poor clarity of sight, poor peripheral awareness, needs visual motor development, gross motor development).

4. Difficulty locating wall clock from 20 feet (clarity problem, near-sightedness or farsightedness, focusing problem at distance after doing near work, peripheral awareness).

5. Unable to tell time when the hands are on any of the two-digit numbers (clarity of sight problem, may need glasses).

6. Fails to see distant objects readily visible to others (clarity of sight problem, may need glasses).

7. Unable to accurately estimate locations of objects, hence, frequently runs into things (laterality and directionality, poor peripheral awareness, poor visual motor integration).

8. Walks with extreme caution, watching feet while moving (eyes guiding movement) looking closely or feeling with the foot for a step up or down or for small obstructions (poor sight, poor depth perception, poor peripheral awareness, poor eye teaming coordination).

Peripheral Vision

1. Startles when approached from side; note which side or both (poor peripheral awareness, or in rare cases visual field loss).

2. Frequently loses objects outside of central line of vision (poor peripheral awareness, or possible field loss).

3. Bumps into objects on either side (poor peripheral awareness, and also poor gross motor and visual motor coordination).

4. Turns head while traveling (poor peripheral awareness, possible neck misalignment aggravated by gait mechanism).

5. Begins writing in center of page or does not use complete line for writing (eye-hand coordination, poor visual spatial organization, directionality, poor peripheral awareness).

Complaints Associated with Using Eyes

1. Headache (visual focus or convergence problems, insufficient daily protein intake, astigmatism, farsightedness).
2. Nausea or dizziness following close work (poor near alignment and focus, farsighted, allergies).
3. Blurring of vision at any time (might need glasses for nearsightedness, farsightedness, large amounts of astigmatism or poor focusing ability. Or child has insufficient sleep or convergence problems that are not quite causing double, just fuzzy vision).
4. Words or lines run together (convergence problem, visual motor problem).

Child Complaints in General

1. Pain in forehead or temples (focusing problems, convergence problems, stress, constant or persistent could be serious medical problem).
2. Definite dislike of reading or other close work (general binocular vision disorder that could include deficiency in many skills, farsightedness, or large amounts of astigmatism).
3. Stomach aches (could be a medical condition, but might have to do with visual stress of having to use eyes up close when not ready yet developmentally).

Symptoms Based on Appearance of Child

1. Watering of eyes while reading (usually convergence problem).
2. Lids often red (allergies, infection in lash follicles, other infection, rubbing).
3. One eye tends to turn inward or outward when tired (intermittent strabismus, which takes effort to control eye alignment; that effort is not possible when child is tired).
4. Frowning or wrinkling of forehead (trying to focus or converge using forehead muscles where eye muscles are not working well).
5. Excessive blinking (trying to clear distance vision, or perhaps dryness of eyes from allergy medication).

Visual Behavior

1. Rubs eyes frequently (experiencing blurry vision and visual stress from any number of problems with vision development, allergies).
2. Tries to brush away blur (needs glasses or has allergies or both).
3. Sees the blackboard with difficulty (nearsighted, very farsighted, has astigmatism compromising clarity of sight, or double vision).
4. Holds the book close to eyes (either using just one eye because of a convergence problem, poor clarity farther away from nearsightedness or farsightedness, or having trouble focusing so trying to get near distance magnification; children do not push their arms away if they are farsighted, usually, the way adults do in their 40s).
5. Sits with poor posture while reading (primitive or postural reflex that failed to integrate, possible chiropractic problem, Brain Gym needed, vision poor in various ways, or glasses too strong).
6. Inattention and symptoms of fatigue while reading (convergence problems, focusing problems, farsightedness, poor nutrition, lack of sleep).
7. Stumbles or trips over objects (poor visual motor or gross motor development, poor peripheral awareness, or unclear sight).
8. Squints or shades one eye with hat or hand in bright light (convergence problem or poor nutrition).
9. Continually tries different positions and angles during close work (lack of stability in focusing or convergence system, poor clarity, sensitive to light system in room in relation to his desk).
10. Shuts or covers one eye while reading (avoiding double vision or making it less difficult to focus by allowing just one eye to do it without having to converge both eyes together).
11. Frequently moves book closer or further from eyes while reading (trying to vary distance of focus because focusing/convergence system is unstable).
12. Eye appears to wander during close work or far focusing or fatigue (child has an intermittent strabismus; one eye goes out or in when he is too tired to focus on close work or chalkboard because both eyes are not very stable together).

THE PROBLEMS OF DESKS, GLASSES, AND WORKING DISTANCES

At one time, I had a child in private vision therapy who kept standing up to read at school. The teacher did not understand why and insisted that he sit down. She called me to see if I could explain why that might be happening. Once the teacher understood the reason, she and the school were very accommodating. The reason was this: If the child stood up when reading at his desk, he could be farther from the print, and not have to focus so hard to see it.

Although the child had reading glasses, they needed a particular working distance, what we call "the Harmon distance," which is the number of inches from middle knuckle to elbow. Kids his age usually need about an 11-inch (based on testing I have done) working distance, but sometimes the desk to eye distance is not enough. It can be only six inches, or as many as 16, Ward reports from her research. This can create serious eyestrain for many children. Harmon's adjustable desks and chairs are not available anymore. The Michigan schools run by optometrists tried to get them made, but could not find anyone to do it.

Darell Boyd Harmon, PhD, was a true genius in his understanding of vision and posture. He came up with the idea for a "coordinated classroom" where desks, chair sizes, lighting, and distances from the chalkboard were all selected to enhance vision. He was able to look at someone's back as they walked and know the prescription of their glasses. I heard that story from three different optometrists who knew the doctor, and saw him deducing prescriptions from posture.

Harmon was concerned with posture because bad posture threatens good vision. Also, minus lenses (used for nearsightedness) alter posture as they get stronger. In fact, if the posture is not good, the muscles in the neck cannot efficiently help the convergence process of the eyes. Children then, with hunched posture and inefficient neck muscles (sternocleidomastoid muscles are the main ones) must overfocus to converge, which drives them into myopia.

When nearsighted glasses are worn, the neck pokes forward even more. The ears are no longer over the center of the shoulder. Computer work is now ruining many people's good vision, in part because we all tend to hunch at the computer.

Dr. Ward's solution to inappropriate desk heights was to make writing boards from stiff, corrugated cardboard with flat surfaces on both sides. The children put these boards on their laps and leaned them up against the desktops. Large rubber bands were placed around them to hold the paper in place. This would allow the proper working distance for deskwork, on a parallel slant to their faces. If reading material and writing material is parallel to the face it is more efficient to read, because the focusing does not have to shift with each line down the page. This may be necessary because so many children are visually stressed, and desk heights do not help, Very few have near (reading and writing) glasses, and if they do, they often are embarrassed to wear them.

Many kids will get up on their knees to get more distance from the paper at the desk. I can certainly remember doing that a lot as a child, but I never imagined why. It is really instinctive, similar to the way adults in their 40s extend their arms out farther, holding the print away in order to see it. This desk distance problem makes for a lot of eyestrain for kids. It is a good reason to see a behavioral optometrist for preventive medicine—reading glasses for classwork and homework.

Preventive glasses work to help relax the eyes for reading and can even help prevent nearsightedness if kids will wear them. My own children wore theirs sporadically at school and with constant reminders at home. One of them, who was farsighted, did wear her glasses all the time at school. They were executive bifocals from our Dr. Francke in D.C. There was no prescription on top, but a reading prescription on the bottom half. She told me once that the reason she wore them all the time in school was that "the noise doesn't bother me when I have my glasses on."

The problem with glasses is that often children do not want to wear them for social reasons. The styles are better now. There were times, in the Boston school where I worked, when children begged us for glasses because they were hoping to be magically made smarter. The principal would get on the PA system and tell the children that anyone who had reading glasses from Dr. Orfield should wear them for the testing. There were other times when we heard they never brought their glasses to school but did homework with them. Sometimes the teachers kept them in school and brought them out of their desks for testing. Scores did go up on the children who received glasses (see chapter three).

Recently, a lovely little girl who is farsighted, and needs a lot of vision therapy, was tested for reading skills at her school. She did all right on most tests, but her comprehension was a total failure. I asked if she had her reading glasses on and she said no. If a child is struggling to focus, there is not enough energy left over for processing the reading. She also was not wearing them in school. I am sure, as cute as they were, kids teased her. Sometimes the teasing is out of jealousy from children who cannot see well and wish they had glasses. Other times, it is just meanness. Teachers can help immeasurably if they can create an environment where teasing kids with glasses is unacceptable so that no one would dream of doing anything of the sort.

WHAT DO TEACHERS NEED TO KNOW ABOUT GLASSES TO HELP THEIR STUDENTS?

How can a teacher know when it is crucial for a child to have glasses on and when does it not matter? Below are my simple rules. At the end of these, there is a quick method that teachers can use to know what kind of prescription is in their students' glasses.

1. Distance glasses. For most children with small amounts of myopia (nearsightedness needing a minus lens), they do better up close without their distance glasses. For children who are farsighted enough to need distance glasses or bifocals, they need their glasses to do close work. For children with a lot of astigmatism, it might be useful to have the glasses for near vision. For just a little astigmatism, it is okay if they don't want to wear them for up-close work. If they cannot see the blackboard, they may be motivated to put them on for distance.

2. Nearpoint reading glasses. These should always be worn during tests and close work at the desk but not for other activities. Sometimes a reading bifocal is prescribed to let a child see far with a little bit of a nearsighted minus lens on the top, and then a plus reading prescription to help control myopia on the bottom. Those glasses should be worn for close work if they are set so the child is really looking through the bottom half. Some children bend over

and look through the top at their books. It would be easier, then, for them to read if they took the glasses off for tests.

3. When not to worry about glasses. The child should never be made to wear distance lenses for test taking unless they are for extreme prescriptions, and are needed to see up close as well as far. There is even an association for the prevention of myopia that suggests that myopia (minus) lenses should be withheld from children, except in dire cases. Of course, if the test is written up on the chalkboard, and the child must copy the questions, distance glasses would be necessary. This is why I prescribe bifocals for school.

4. The problem of nearsightedness (blurry vision at far). Myopia in the early grades is mostly "school myopia" from near work eyestrain. Reading glasses can prevent a great deal of nearsightedness if they are used. If not, eyes under stress will have to adapt and become the kind of eye lenses that a person needs to see up close. If that adaptation is made, the eyes lose their flexibility and clear sight at distance. The glasses given for distance will make them worse again if they are worn for near. Most doctors tell the children with early myopic prescriptions to take them off to read.

BECAUSE MANY CHILDREN DO NOT REALLY KNOW OR DO NOT TELL TEACHERS WHEN THEY ARE SUPPOSED TO WEAR GLASSES, HOW CAN A TEACHER KNOW WHAT THE GLASSES ARE FOR?

Here is a quick trick. If the lens prescription is plus, assume it is for seeing well at near distance. If minus, assume it is for far distance. So how will you know if it is plus or minus? You hold the glasses up about six inches from your eyes, and look through one lens at a vertical object, like a doorframe. Keep looking and move the lens side to side. Notice if the motion of the object goes with (in the same direction as) your motion of the lens or against (opposite) it.

If the lens is a plus lens for reading, the image will move opposite your motion. If the lens is a minus lens for far, the object will be moving with yours. If the target seems crooked, at a diagonal, it is an astigmatism lens. (Astigmatism is a condition in which the optics of the eye are not the same all the way around the eyeball.) After you have checked horizontally on a vertical doorframe, move the glasses up and down vertically while viewing a horizontal line, such as the top of the door frame. The glasses are held horizontal at all times as if on a face. If the motion is different from when you went side to side on the side of the doorframe, there is definitely astigmatism. If the image moves horizontally in same way it moved vertically (whether with or against your movements), there is likely little or no astigmatic correction in that lens. With astigmatism, there will be diagonal-looking doorframes or differences in the speed and/or direction of the motion with vertical and horizontal targets.

When a plus (against your motion) lens is detected, make certain that the student wears the glasses for near work. If a minus (with your motion) lens is detected and the child is not close enough to the board to see without them, make sure he wears the glasses for work at a distance. Let the child decide if he needs the glasses to see clearly at near if they show an astigmatism correction.

THE PROBLEMS OF REFERRING FOR OUTSIDE HELP

Most schools employ occupational therapists now. They and the teachers are reluctant to refer for vision analysis because it is assumed that the analysis is related to learning accommodations, and parents can then try to get the schools to pay for it. Of course, it has to do with the child learning! Although my dream is that there should be a vision clinic in every school, or at least one for a group of schools to share, the parents are responsible for making sure their children are visually ready to learn. That concept is currently not a paid-for benefit of public education, even though not being visually ready to learn is probably the number one roadblock to education that schools have to face. It is also one that is much more fixable than all the other problems children might have.

As educators and practitioners we cannot go into the homes, we cannot control what the child eats, we cannot limit his hours of TV, we cannot insist that parents provide the best environment for learning in the home, we cannot make sure that mothers eat properly and stay calm during pregnancy, and we cannot force the child to get a comprehensive eye exam with treatments of special reading glasses and vision therapy when needed. The one thing we can do is refer a child to a behavioral optometrist with the stipulation that the parent is responsible for this cost, unless the school district is already on board with covering vision therapy and outside referrals, as they did in Kansas (Sullivan 2001).

The other problem of referrals is that teachers may get the parents to take the child for an exam, but it will not necessarily include the 21 points and more required by behavioral optometry's functional vision evaluations. The child may come back and tell the teacher that he does not need glasses and his eyes are fine, because someone just checked for distance acuity, refractive error, and eye health. He was a little far-sighted, but he is thought to be young enough to focus on his own. No one checked that he is so stressed out that his focusing mechanism and his ability to sustain convergence is not anywhere near what the demands of school require. With the right exam, he would likely have reading glasses and/or vision therapy and be on his way to school success (Cook 1992).

If there is a way for teachers to obtain a list of optometrists in their area who do thorough pediatric exams of the sort requested by the National PTA and outlined by the American Optometric Association, it would be very helpful to their students. This can be done by logging onto the website www.optometrists.org and adding a forward slash symbol and your own state. Another option is to log onto www.oep.org and click on the "find a doctor" link. Parents need to recognize that in this less-than-perfect world, vision exams will not be paid for by the schools. Schools should not pressure the teacher not to refer because her superiors do not want any hassles with parents over who pays what bills for treatments outside the school doors.

IDEAS FOR TEACHING READING WHEN CHILDREN ARE NOT READY TO READ VISUALLY

When I first heard of the Snapp method developed by the late Ed Snapp of Mississippi, I knew that it was the way to teach reading to save the eyes. It would end the visual struggles for these beautiful children who are trying so hard against huge odds because of their underdeveloped visual systems.

Snapp, a physical therapist who founded a clinic in Columbus, Mississippi, developed his methods working with physically handicapped children and quickly realized they could apply to visually delayed kids and even kids without disabilities. He taught his instructional approaches in Texas and Missisippi at special seminars for educators and physical therapists.

Dr. Betty Ward used his methods for many years in her own teaching in Texas. The method covers processing of visual input, movement, kinesthetic input, and verbal comprehension. The skills must be learned at a level of automaticity (being "subjugated," Snapp called it) before the next stage is tackled. Dr. Ward said she usually had a group of delayed children for only one year, but in that time nearly all of them were ready to sit at a desk and read after learning with this method.

Snapp maintains that by presenting the instructional material at the proper developmental level for the student, not only the material but also the perceptual stage will be mastered. The ultimate goal of mastering visual perception is achieved simultaneously with learning to read. By being able to rapidly perceive the whole gestalt of a word or word phrase, the student also develops speed and fluency in reading.

The secret to enabling rapid perception is having the visual target at a far point (about 20 feet), so near focus or convergence is not required. The visual target is a 12- x 18-inch card. The card is held upside down facing the teacher, and the back facing the student. It is then rapidly rotated on a horizontal axis to face the student right-side up. By having to perceive the rapidly "snapped" (rotated) target in 1/3 of a second, the reading then becomes an efficient visual process rather than one that has the student whispering to himself in order to understand what he is reading.

Snapp's "foolproof" method is also used: The teacher tells the student what is on the card, and tells the student to say it when he sees it. If nothing is seen, the student does not respond. With practice, he will see the things on the cards more quickly.

Try it. Write a word in large print on a stiff paper and hold it upside down at a distance with the blank side toward the child. Then spin it in almost a full rotation around. The word will appear right side up toward the student, and then the card will spin back to the blank side toward the student. The blank side first gives the child a place to focus his eyes with expectation. There is a kind of optical illusion created by the spinning card, so that the word hangs in space for about 1/3 of a second for the child to see what is on the card in large thick black letters,

There are five stages of development learned in the Snapp method. The teacher always starts at the most basic level with the children.

"There are no assumptions that a kid has truly mastered any level," says Ward. There are adults with PhDs who cannot see in a flash the cards snapped at the more advanced stages. Mastery has to be at an automatic level at each stage before the student goes on to the next. Below are examples of how reading is taught using the Snapp developmental stages.

First Stage: Recognition of Absence or Presence of Illumination versus Darkness, So That It Is Easier to Distinguish Black Print on a White Page

Why should this learning be needed? Ed Snapp explains that because we live in a light bubble with no real darkness for children from the moment of birth on, children cannot fully develop that contrast sensitivity between darkness and dim light. It is difficult for a child to experience true darkness. Lights are on long after they go to sleep at night; they may have nightlights, and even the moonlight from the window provides some illumination, as well as streetlights and city lights. Failure to experience true darkness can mean they just don't develop a visual system that is able to pick up the contrast of black letters on a white page very efficiently when they are learning to read. Contrast sensitivity is one of the things that many behavioral optometrists and sports optometrists evaluate.

The Snapp contrast sensitivity program can be done in a classroom with the children sitting in a circle with crossed legs, Some will need cushions for straighter backs. Ideally, the students would be in a totally darkened room with a low wattage bulb in a lamp with no shade to provide intermittent illumination. The room is darkened so that it initially appears to be without light. A lamp without a shade or cover is placed in the middle of the circle with each child about six feet from the light.

Usually a silent switch is used, so no auditory clue for off and on is perceived. The students look straight ahead while in each position. They turn their bodies to the left or the right, to get the light stimulation on their peripheral retina, and finally they face the light source. At each of these positions, the light is switched on for three seconds and off for four seconds. The purpose of the three positions is to stimulate the peripheral vision with the light flashed on each side and central vision with the light in front.

Ward used to do this in the classroom, but she has also recommended that parents do it in the home every night when the child is going to bed. She told me the case of a ten-year-old child who had not learned to read at all or write her name (composed of three letters). The mother worked with her daughter every night, flashing her room light off and on as she lay in bed on first one side, then the other, then on her back. The lights were on for three seconds and off for four seconds. In about two weeks, the child was writing her name everywhere. She had had no additional instruction on writing her name. Snapp felt this was the result of her mastering that first stage of light and dark perception, so she could move on.

Optometrists would note that she was probably at last able to perceive the contrast of the print on the paper, and her pupils were stimulated to react to light, which helped them react to near focus tasks as well. It also likely woke up her peripheral awareness so that she could see the whole page and the whole word at once. Chapter five features a discussion of syntonics treatment with some data on how many children have very narrow peripheral vision.

Dr. Ward's experience reminded me of something I read years ago in a Glenn Doman article about how best to help a baby develop. One of the exercises was to flash that room light off and on for several times every night when the baby is ready for bed. I did it for months with my kids, but I never was clever enough to turn them on alternate sides and their backs to stimulate awareness of peripheral versus central vision. This light exercise was to help the pupils react. The old Bates exercise of "sunning" was used for the same purpose. With eyes closed, the patient faces the sun and turns his head from side to side, first stimulating the contraction of the pupil on one side, then on the other. Pupils must contract in near focus as well as in bright light.

Second Stage: Perception of a Single Fact Using a Solid Color Target at Far Distance

The teacher holds at chest level the large 12- x 18-inch card, which is covered on one side by a single color, tint, or shade. With the color side toward her, she tells the student the precise name of the color (one of 68 named colors in the Crayola box) and tells him to say it when he sees it. She turns the card very rapidly, in just a snap. If the student sees it, he says the name she gave. If not, he doesn't. The plan for what to say when the color is seen is an integral, necessary part of the procedure.

After giving the instruction, the card is rotated very rapidly, making sure that the axis of rotation is the center of the visual target and that the arms do not move the card axis either up or down. It is the precise positioning of the card, while it is rotated, that allows the student to see the optical illusion of the card. The entire target appears to be suspended in the air for a moment, preventing any blurring that might be caused by an up or down movement.

Ward emphasizes that in order for this "snapping" to be done well and easily, it required practice in front of a mirror. Use of the mirror allows the teacher to monitor the position of the card remaining steady as it is snapped. (By "snapping" the card, she means it is turned rapidly for about one-third of a second, and then back.)

After a session, cards that were not perceived are put aside and reintroduced at the next session. There are no "wrong answers," just the fact of whether the child can see it or not. If he can, he says the name. He is learning rapid visual processing. The next day, he is shown some of the cards he saw and some that he did not see, as well as a few new ones.

Third Stage: Silhouetted Objects Familiar to the Student

The third stage is silhouetted pictures. However, if a child cannot do this stage, he will need to stay in the one-fact (color) stage longer to learn to perceive faster. Ward explained that Snapp requires that each of the stages be imbedded before the child can move on to the next stage.

An optometric tool called a tachistoscope can flash words, shapes, or letters, at much less than 1/10th of a second, and some people can see them easily; others cannot. It would be quite wonderful if all children learned this rapid seeing before they learned reading.

Dr. Ward describes the method this way: "A large, blackened in silhouette of a single object is drawn on a stimulus 'card' (about 11- x 14-inch or 12- x 18-inch). The object must be familiar to the students." Silhouettes would be things like a table, chair, pumpkin, car, basket, sock, shoe, boot, tree, bell, truck, ship, plane, and so on. "The 'foolproof' teaching/learning method is used. The backside of the card is in position and facing the student, and just before snapping the card, state: When you see this, say, _____. When these are seen 100 percent consistently, you may then proceed to the next developmental level. But, if the student is consistently less than 100 percent successful, then he needs to go back to the lower level and do some more work." His visual perception is still too slow for perceiving shapes rapidly, which means it is too slow for efficient reading and writing.

Fourth Stage: Make Yours Like Mine

This stage involves prewriting with big, round writing instruments short enough to be held entirely in the palm and rectangular paper. The paper is placed on a writing surface held in the lap while the student sits with crossed legs on the floor or on a cushion if needed for good posture, and the target presentation is at far point.

This stage is to teach the perception and recognition of both the directionality of strokes later used to write letters and the position of the stroke within a defined space, such as left side, upper right corner, bottom central, etc. Below is what Dr. Ward told me when she described this stage. It seems totally ingenious to me, and I cannot believe it is not generally being done.

A Snapp card of a single stroke forms part of a printed letter. For example, it could be a straight line that is diagonal, leaning toward right or left like the forward or backward slash used with computer addresses. Or it could be a curve up or down as when drawing a cup. The strokes are not named, but presented with the statement: "Make yours like mine." The target stroke must be very wide and very black. I use a wire pen and India ink. When drawing the curved stroke, be sure that the stroke is the same width throughout its length.

The student is sitting tailor fashion on the floor, and has a writing surface and paper that is the same size as the Snapp background card for the stroke being "snapped." The writing surface can be lap desks or turned over lunch trays so there is no lip on the side used to write. These are placed in the student laps as they sit on the floor. This allows the greatest distance between the eyes and the writing surface, and allows the writing to be controlled by the shoulder rather than the hand, elbow or wrist.

Each stroke is replicated by the student using a short, blunt crayon or chalk, which works well enclosed in small hands and provides a broad stroke, easily seen. The Snapp strokes are presented in all different places on the card (top, bottom, left, right, middle). The student's job is to "make yours like mine," which also means to mark it on the paper so that the stroke has the same spatial relationship to the outline of the paper as the target has to the edges of the card. (Ward 2006)

Many children do not know how to line up their work on their papers to match something on the blackboard or the book. This spatial skill needs to be learned if they have not had an excellent visual background before they come to school.

The printed word is built up as follows, Ward explains: "Once the single stroke is mastered, it is followed by a series of 2 strokes. Once these are mastered 3 such forms are presented. Only when 3 forms are mastered is a simple letter presented. Then a simple word. Note, please that is only after repeated 100 percent success over several days that the student is advanced to the next level" (Ward 2006).

Those strokes need to be made with movement from the shoulder, which relaxes the hand. Because of the fortunate seating on the floor with lap desks, "It is almost impossible to have the movement centered at just the wrist, elbow or heel of the hand," explains Ward (2006). Naturally this is not learned at home if children have begun life on computers instead of learning to use their arms and hands to write. Those who might someday want to be surgeons or have some other career that requires delicate eye/hand tasks are shortchanged mightily if this process cannot happen.

Occupational therapists to whom I have taught vision assessment are very concerned about the fact that hands and arms are not developing the way they should, and they say that this is new. It was not this way 15 years ago, they assure me. By the way, the computer mouse does not cut it for eye/hand coordination. Also creeping on hands and knees is necessary for hand strength. Children in walkers do not get enough of that.

Fifth Stage: Comprehension; From Heard and Spoken to Reading and Writing

Reading at far distance is only done after some work on aural understanding of sentences is completed successfully. Betty Ward explains, "Since language is heard, spoken, written, and read, comprehension is first mastered using auditory input which requires a verbal response. This matches the development of a child's use of language" (2006).

As parents we use "the one word presentation which the child repeats (echoes) after us." Then, Ward says,

> We begin to use a more complete but short sentence. In the picture books we point to an object, and tell the child what it is. Then we advance to stating to him as we point to the object, "Tell me what this is" or "Show me the—." Only after that do we advance to pointing to the object and asking him, "What is this?" Snapp uses this same developmental sequence to build comprehension skills. He starts with the echo stage of a one-fact sentence. (2006)

For example, in the echo stage, the teacher says, "Say what I say. This is a tree." The next stage is "fill in the blanks." The teacher says, "This is a—." Finally, the teacher says, "This is a tree. Tell me what this is." The student has to say, "This is a tree." When that stage is mastered, a question is introduced. "What is this?" asks the teacher. The child has to respond with a complete sentence: "This is a tree."

At the next stage, sentences with first two and then three or more nouns are used. Then adjectives with more questions are added. These are all done with pictures on the Snapp cards and auditory responses.

Then reading cards with single words such as "under" are explained and then flashed at a distance from the children. Sometimes the distance is across the room, sometimes it is better for the group to be at a middle distance. The same foolproof process goes forward. Then two-word phrases such as, "When you see this, say 'the boy' or 'the tree,'" and then whole sentences are used: "The boy is under the tree." This is all happening at distance so that the child does not have to focus or converge his immature eyes. Yet he is being forced to see this in a flash, in a snap. He will learn to grab visual information quickly this way. If he sees it, he says it. If he does not see it, he cannot say it.

Once a good primer vocabulary is learned by sight with speed at distance, the words are placed on the floor, with the child standing up looking at them. This is intermediate distance. It was very successful for a seven-year-old boy, who did not know how to read and did not even want to hold a book. Ward told me that after learning the words on cards on the floor while standing up, the child asked to have the book from which the words and sentences had been taken. He could read. His aversion to books was over.

Obviously the child who comes to school with a lot of experience hearing his parents read to him will likely not need this kind of preparation. This sounds a little like learning a foreign language. However, it is a way of teaching rapid visual processing along with reading. I see the Snapp program as ideal for children who are not ready to read when they have to learn to do it, as in Ms. Christison's kindergarten in that inner-city school.

However, Ward reminded me that we should make no assumptions. She told me of a fourth-grade boy who entered her class with poor reading comprehension. She said that he had normal conversational language and was not a poor reader except that he could not answer questions about what he had read. After two weeks of Snapp's verbal comprehension work, he knew what was expected and was above grade level on comprehension.

Ward told me that Ed Snapp felt that if his program were used in regular—not just remedial—classes, there would be very few reading failures, if any. A successful regular teacher switched to using this program for one year and told Dr. Ward it was her best year yet for percentages of students learning well.

What I want readers to take from this method is that it helps develop rapid perception without the interference of having to focus the eyes up close. It teaches all the underlying skills of reading and writing in a fun and painless manner when children are not yet ready to tackle small print. It could lead to more students being visual learners, rather than slower processors or auditory learners, compensating for poor visual development.

I believe that if the working distance is changed to be across the room at first, then across the table, or at arm's length with a child seated on the floor until third grade, a lot of children who otherwise struggle with reading and writing because of their vision would learn without a problem. In my utopian school there are large boards across the room to project flashed words in large print for a third of a second, then sentences, and whole primer books. In the meantime, the Snapp method should succeed where close-up worksheets and small print books can drive some children away from reading. This does not have to go on for long. Children's neurological visual development should reach the ability to read up close if the right preparation is given by about age eight or nine.

NOTICING VISUAL PROBLEMS IN KIDS: TWO STORIES

Two stories illustrate the problem of seeing up close for kids who are farsighted. Ward tells of a student in the first grade, who was always "in trouble" for keeping one arm out in front of him to maintain his space from the student in front by touching that student's back. When he failed the school eye screening, he got glasses for farsightedness and he never had to use his arm again to keep his spacing.

Another student, a retainee in grade two, wrote large and thick letters, which he traced repeatedly until they were very big and black. The psychologist referred to this activity as "perseveration," until the boy got glasses for farsightedness. He never darkened his pencil strokes again.

Many adults who are poor spellers cannot see words flashed across the room, though their vision tests at 20/20. They were never trained to see the whole gestalt of a word and relied on phonics, which in the English language is not always reliable.

There are some games that optometrists use to help students bring these visual abilities up to par. In my office I use a tachistoscope, a machine that flashes one, two, and three words, or a series of numbers on the wall, or even pitcher's grips on baseballs. My training patients of all ages have different levels of trouble seeing these things in a flash. Some who have other vision problems do not have any problem at all on the fastest settings. My slowest flash is a tenth of a second. Everyone can become faster with training. Athletes especially like to train this way to speed up visual processing time.

ED SNAPP'S MATH FACTS

There is a Snapp series for math facts, too. It begins at the echo level. First, it is hands-on with large black circular objects, such as coffee can lids. The child places these on the floor and is told, "Make yours like mine." The teacher flashes a drawing of objects in a particular pattern at distance. Then it progresses to Snapp cards, on which solid circles are drawn in the middle of the card. Again, it is done by saying, for example, "When you see this, say three." There is no chance for confusion and mistakes regarding quantity, no guessing, and no programming brain patterns with error. If you see it, you know it.

Then the round circles are put on opposite sides of the card in groups. The child has to say the total quantity if he sees it. "When you see this, say three." Eventually, after a few cards, one of the children recognizes that he is seeing two groups of quantities, one on the right and one on the left. This is how adding is introduced. The student will say, "Three. One and two are three." This presentation of arithmetic facts goes on to subtraction, multiplication, and division. It is all with rapid seeing and complete saying.

In vision therapy terms, we would call this training for rapid visual processing, and it carries over to mental processing. Some older children, who have not had this training, may not be able to do this and will have to use subvocalization to get auditory and kinesthetic help with processing. Phonics is very helpful in cases of specific reading disability (true dyslexia), but it does slow reading speed.

OPTOMETRISTS' SCHOOLS IN MICHIGAN WANT RAPID SEEING FOR NEW READERS

Optometrists sometimes try to train children early to be visually dominant so they can learn rapid reading. Dr. Steve Ingersoll, who founded those Michigan charter schools (see chapter three), believes that children do not need to use nonvisual crutches if their vision is trained properly at first. It is very hard, though, to break those habits, if they are developed as part of a child's survival pattern in school. It appears to me that the Snapp method may go a long way to helping develop the visual sense for reading readiness in children who must learn to read before their eyes and brains are ready.

BRAIN GYM CAN HELP

It also helps if children are taught Brain Gym exercises to do each day at the beginning of class (as discussed in chapter five). These can be learned in weekend seminars for teachers given by Brain Gym International (Educational Kinesiology Foundation). It is much better to learn it in person, but there are many good books available. Sharon Promislow, in her book *Making the Brain Body Connection* (1999), is a nice read for teachers and parents interested in this modality of treatment for learning delays discussed in chapter five.

ONE SCHOOL SYSTEM'S PROGRAM

As I said in the beginning of the chapter, I have a dream, a vision really, about how every school should have the facilities for the vision development of children who come to school without their learning systems in place. Even in the best of home worlds there will be kids who fall and hurt themselves, who have head bumps, who are in car accidents, who have sports injuries to the head. These all affect vision and visual processing if they are not treated with osteopathic or chiropractic treatment, Brain Gym, primitive reflex work, and/or vision therapy (Cohen and Rein 1992). There is one school system now in Massachusetts, Framingham Public Schools, that has installed a vision clinic, run by an optometry school. The school nurse who set this up, Kathy Majzoub, was kind enough to write up her description of what they did and how they did it. Below is that big piece of good news that might help others create a new vision for their own schools.

FRAMINGHAM PUBLIC SCHOOLS / NEW ENGLAND EYE INSTITUTE VISION CENTER IN FRAMINGHAM, MASSACHUSETTS

The Framingham School Health Vision Initiative began in 2002 as a response to the belief that good vision is critical to the wellbeing of children and that many children were not being served by current practice. It was felt that the state's mandated school vision screening protocol was inadequate and that an alarming number of children were unable to access vision care when a referral from the school nurse was made.

Obstacles to vision services include lack of insurance, lack of resources, and in some cases, parents who are unable to respond to the needs of their children. To achieve the goal of assuring optimal vision for all of their students, thereby supporting health and learning, school nurses in Framingham, Massachusetts, developed a new screening protocol, an expansion of the Massachusetts vision screening protocol. A major focus of this new protocol is to assess functional and near vision, aspects of vision that are critical for accessing education. At the same time, discussions were initiated with administrators and clinicians from the New England Eye Institute, the clinical arm of the New England College of Optometry, regarding the possibility of creating a school-based vision center to serve the children of Framingham.

It was postulated that having vision specialists on site would not only assist in the educational mission of the schools, but would also provide an exciting opportunity to share knowledge and strategies regarding the important links between pediatric vision, education, athletics, and other childhood activities with teachers, nurses, therapists, administrators, and special educators in the Framingham Public Schools.

With the support and approval of the director of School Health Services, school superintendent, and the Framingham School Committee, an agreement was entered into in the spring of 2004 to collaborate with the New England Eye Institute and create a school-based vision center to be located in the Fuller Middle School—the Framingham Public Schools/ New England Eye Institute (FPS/NEEI) Vision Center. The principal of the Fuller Middle School embraced the opportunity to house the center in his school and supervised the renovations needed to accommodate two exam rooms, a waiting room, and an area for vision therapy. The space required for the center is approximately 1,300 square feet. Renovation of this previously vacant room was the responsibility of the Framingham School Department. Optometric equipment was provided and installed by the New England Eye Institute. The institute is responsible for direct costs and bills third-party payment programs for services. The vision center became fully operational in the fall of 2004.

The vision center is directed by an attending optometrist and serves as a clinical site for residents of the New England College of Optometry. Care is provided to children and school employees two days a week. Services include comprehensive vision exams, vision therapy, and optical services. The vision center accepts most insurance plans. If the child has no insurance and the family cannot pay, the vision center offers a sliding fee schedule. A local health care foundation has provided a grant to pay for the eyeglasses of children who have no family resources. A trilingual administrative assistant is on site during hours of operation.

In its second year of practice, this vertically integrated, school-based vision program has been a successful model in addressing many of the challenges previously described. Screening and referral procedures are as follows:

1. Students in preschool, kindergarten, and grades 1, 3, 5, 7, 9, and 11 are screened by the school nurse or trained designee, using the Framingham vision screening protocol. In a system of 8,500 students, this translates to approximately 5,000 children. There are over a hundred volunteer vision screeners to assist in the screenings. These are parents who have been recruited from the community.

2. Students being evaluated for special education services, initially, or during the three-year reevaluation, are screened by the school nurse.

3. Self-, teacher-, therapist-, or parent-referred students are screened by the school nurse.

4. Children who are new to the Framingham school system are screened by the school nurse.

5. Parents/guardians of students referred for an eye exam as a result of the screening are notified by mail. Information about the FPS/ NEEI Vision Center is included with the screening report with a re-

quest that the child have a comprehensive eye exam. The school nurse acts as a case manager in communicating with the parent to ensure that the child is examined by an eye doctor if a referral has been made.

6. If so selected by the parent/guardian, referred children undergo a comprehensive vision exam at the FPS/NEEI Vision Center. If it is determined that the child would benefit from vision therapy, the service is provided on site. Glasses may be selected and purchased at the vision center.

7. Findings and interventions are communicated directly to the school nurse by the examining optometrist so that they can be included in the student's health record and are available if needed.

Having a well-established, school-based vision center offers numerous opportunities for further study as it provides tremendous opportunity to work closely with students, families, school nurses, educators, and other specialists to assess outcomes of vision interventions on a pediatric population. These outcomes will range from practice issues such as access to care, lapsed time from referral to care, and sensitivity and reliability of vision screening protocols to clinical outcomes such as physical, academic, and emotional progress following the provision of vision care. Of course the most important accomplishment of this school-based model is that all children who need help with their vision will be given the highest quality of care regardless of their diagnosis or personal circumstances.

Kathy Majzoub, RN
February 5, 2006

If teachers and parents can work together to make sure each child is visually ready to learn, there will be much less school failure, and many fewer learning-disabled children. Children with vision that supports learning are fortunate children. A teacher with a class of visually competent children is a fortunate teacher. The parents of children who are visually ready to learn will enjoy their children more and experience less stress over homework and school success. A child with good vision is a happier, healthier child, one who can learn lessons efficiently and have time left over for long, golden afternoons of creative play.

NOTES

1. Brain Gym is a nonprofit educational organization based in Ventura, California, that was founded on the work of Paul Dennison. Address for Brain Gym International is P.O. Box 3393, Ventura, California 93006-3395. There is more on Brain Gym in chapter five.

2. COVD can be contacted at their Inernational office, 243 North Lindbergh Blvd. #310, St. Louis, Mo. 63141-7657.

3. PAVE can be contacted at 960 Chesapeake Drive, Ste. 105, San Diego, California 92123.

THE SEVEN HOME HABITS
FOR RAISING A
VISUALLY SUCCESSFUL CHILD

I would wager the farm, if I had one, on the premise that if your normal child is well developed visually, he will be curious, intelligent, coordinated, interesting, creative, and competent to do whatever he is meant to do in this life. If his vision is shortchanged somehow in the ongoing rush of days, he might still have all those wonderful qualities, but will have to work tremendously hard to maintain them. My hope for the generations of children growing up now and those soon to be born is that they will develop their vision in a home that practices these seven home habits as part of daily life. Here they are:

1. Reduce overall stress starting in pregnancy and continuing forever.
2. Provide a lot of gross motor activity, starting with creeping and crawling and later outdoors and in nature.
3. Provide three-dimensional fine motor activities as soon as your baby sits up.
4. Allow no television until age four; hold off on computers at home until age nine or ten, and substitute with time spent reading aloud every day and time in nature.

5. Make excellent nutrition your daily fare for good health and protection from environmental toxicity.
6. Keep your child's body aligned properly for good posture and movement.
7. Have family activities serve to build a space world for a child's mind and imagination, distance vision, perspective, memory, and perception.

If we can think as a society about how to help families maintain these habits, we will not need high-stakes testing or other worrisome measures to keep kids from slipping through the cracks. In an age of pressures in both home and school, with both parents working outside the home or a single parent doing it all, this is not a simple proposition. When teachers are of necessity teaching for "the big test," all these developmental processes may be left to luck. The seven habits take planning because they are no longer, or never were, part of daily routines practiced by our culture.

Many young parents with school-age children now have to do catch-up treatments after their children are already in school. Before the age of television and computer games, when more people lived with freedom to be outdoors safely, when more mothers were home with their preschoolers, when children learned to do chores around the house or farm, many of the developmental activities were commonly part of daily home routines. They are not that common in our current timeframe.

For that reason, I have tried to think of ways to give children these experiences that create vision and develop visual systems that can withstand and efficiently minimize stress. These ways seem reasonably available to working parents if they keep a checklist and plan time and money for them. Good day care can provide some, but one needs to be vigilant about seeing what is provided and making up for what is not.

Time for other things like TV watching every night and weekend may have to go. Money for advertised toys, such as plastic toy kitchens and other frivolous consuming, may have to go. It is important to get the basics done and have good long visits to the free library and the free park with children every week if all else fails. Here is what is known about the hows and whys of each of the seven home habits.

REDUCE OVERALL STRESS AND ENTRAIN THE CHILD'S "HEART BRAIN" WITH HEALTHY RHYTHMS

If you cannot remember what stress has to do with vision, please go back to chapter four and read about stress and its complicated effects on vision.

Babies entrain to the biorhythms of the mother long before they are born. Parts of these rhythms are from her organs, including her heart. This does not mean the beat of the heart in the baby will equal that of the slower mother's beat. It means something much more complicated. It relates to coherence of electromagnetic energy and to the nerve signals from heart to brain. The heart sends many nerve pathways to the brain that carry information about what is going on at heart level. We know now that if the mother is calm, loved, feeling protected, and happy, the baby will have greater cell growth in the frontal brain. If the mother is under threat, worried, or scared, the baby's hindbrain, the part used for survival, will be more prominently stimulated for growth (Pearce 2003). Good frontal brains are better for vision and learning.

We also know now that the heart is, as Carla Hannaford (2002), Candace Pert (1997), and the HeartMath researchers in California say, "a little brain."[1] It has cells in it that are nerve cells called multi-functional sensory neurites, and others that remember. It sends information to the brain via its own hormones and nerve impulses. It also receives from and gives information to the amygdala (the emotion center in the brain) and the prefrontal cortex and base of the frontal lobe, where thinking and motor planning are processed. The heart also has direct links to the thalamus, where it influences hormones throughout the body.

The heart has the same neurotransmitters as the brain, explains Candace Pert in her book, *Molecules of Emotion* (1997). It also has two hormones of its own that we have known about since the 1980s. One is called atrial natriuretic factor, which affects many organs, the emotional regions of the brain, and even affects learning and memory. The heart is significantly affected by feelings, as the poets have known for centuries, and the scientists have just recently discovered (Cantin and Genest 1986).

Evidently, the heart is not just a pump, as the old-time cardiologists used to say, or the people who designed a mechanical heart that never kept anyone alive for more than a few days. The heart's electromagnetic field is 60 Hz greater than that produced by the brain. The heart vibrations bathe the baby before and after birth in love or fear. Parents need to be aware of this. The baby's intelligence will not start when he is given a new computer at age two, but rather with the rhythms and sounds he feels and hears before he is even born. These can set up a coherent energy field in his heart and brain or an incoherent one. Coherence is good.

If a mother has no way to get out of a long-term stressful situation during a pregnancy, she may help protect her child from the physiological impact of those stress emotions by using the FreezeFrame biofeedback system available from the HeartMath Institute in Boulder Creek, California. There is only a simple finger monitor and a computer screen that will show you your heart beat pattern. If it can become more coherent, in spite of stressful experiences, that is good for the baby. Also, older children who are stressed out can use it. It is one computer game that I would recommend, but check with your own health care practitioner.

What kind of plan can we have then, for making sure our older children's little brains in their hearts and their big brains in the heads are well synchronized, and feeling hale and hearty? They need to be in "flow" as former University of Chicago psychology professor and department chairman Mihaly Csikszentimihalyi wrote in his book, *Flow: The Psychology of Optimal Experience* (1990).

WHAT IS FLOW? AND ONCE WE UNDERSTAND IT A LITTLE, HOW DO WE GIVE IT TO OUR KIDS?

> In our studies, we found that every flow activity, whether it involved competition, chance, or any other dimension of experience, had this in common: It provided a sense of discovery, a creative feeling of transporting the person into a new reality. It pushed the person to higher levels of performance, and led to previously undreamed of states of consciousness. (Csikszentimihalyi 1990, 74)

Flow reduces stress and saves "a great deal of psychic energy" for the brain and heart. It is likely what the children in the Cheshire schools' experimental groups experienced that reduced the prevalence of school myopia (see chapter four). Teenagers who easily achieve flow, which is the fun and creativite factor that we all want for our children at any age, had the following five components in their relationships to their parents. These were discovered in a study of teenagers done at the University of Chicago by Kevin Rathunde, part of the "flow team" there (Csikszentimihalyi 1990, 88):

1. Clarity: They knew what was expected by parents in terms of goals, and they got feedback.
2. Centering: The parents were centered in the present feelings and actions of their children, not concerned about things such as what college their child might enter in the future or what career he might have.
3. Choice: The children had choices but knew they had to face the consequences of their choices if they violated rules.
4. Commitment: This was the trust in his parents that the child had which allowed him to get involved in what he cared about without maintaining defenses.
5. Challenge: The parents were at work to provide "opportunities for action" that were of greater and greater complexity for their children.

Csikszentimihalyi explains why these family habits allow for more flow. It sounds like there is a real stress-reduction factor in the five Cs. "In less well-ordered families, a great deal of energy is expended in constant negotiations and strife and in the children's attempts to protect their fragile selves from being overwhelmed by other people's goals" (Csikszentimihalyi 1990, 89).

Although the book is quite interesting, it may be easier to pick up the Simon and Schuster Audio Program with interview questions and excerpts from the book. It is a two-tape package, which I found riveting. The humanity and wisdom of the author shines through his words (Csikszentimihalyi 1994).

Flow, as he explains on the tape, is a way of approaching one's whole life, even the little tasks, even a job, even a problem. We simply have to know with clarity what the goal is and what each step is in order to get there, so that the feedback about whether or not we completed the right steps is immediate and we can monitor our progress.

The challenges cannot be too difficult. A smart goal for me would not be teaching calculus. Doing an excellent eye exam or vision therapy program is very manageable for me, challenging enough to be interesting, and filled with specific steps. It keeps my attention, my thoughts on the diagnosis emerging, the treatment process, and the patient's well-being. I forget other problems when I am working with a patient. I am in control of what I am doing, and feeling that what I am doing is a good service. Time flies, and I am always going over the allowed exam time and having fun. I am grateful every day for finding so much fun in my work. Many other people would not have this much fun doing the same work. It is important that children know they have choices early on about their short-term, little goals, so that they learn how to make choices when they get to long-term goals.

It would be good if we could facilitate that for all of the children coming up in this new generation. It would eliminate huge stresses if they all could find a line of work that gives an easy path to flow. Too many colleges now are channeling students into something that may have a lot of status, but is boring for that individual, and while some are able to make the job work with flow, too many are wondering why they got that MBA or law degree when they would really like to be teaching teenagers, joining the Peace Corps, founding a dance company, saving the environment, or coaching tennis.

One thing that is very hard for parents, I know from experience, is to find a balance between setting some reasonable goals and expectations of children, and not putting pressure on them for success in terms of society's rewards, like earning As. I thought my children's father and I had not put pressure on for grades, but I was told later that yes, we had, in loads of subtle ways.

It might be easier to drop our own deep and worried interest about grades and long-term outcomes if we go with the flow and know that a child in flow is a happy and creative child who is building structures for the mind that will serve his creativity and happiness for a lifetime. If schools would follow Harvard's Ellen J. Langer's advice in her book, *The Power of Mindful Learning*, we parents would have less to worry about (1997). "Mindfulness" is more like play than work. It allows children to step back and imagine possibilities, try on ideas, and see several ways to solve a problem. It fosters creativity and relating knowledge to experience and one's internal ways of seeing things. It is not the cut-to-the-chase, linear, just-the-facts approach that successful students can master and still miss out on the fun of learning. Mindful learning is also a de-stressor. Trying to remember facts and formulas under pressure on weekly tests sets some children's brains into a tizzy with stress hormones and keeps their eyes from focusing well up close for the task at hand.

Dr. Christine Meloni, a professor emeritus in languages from George Washington University, told me recently about a type of language training that was developed by a Jesuit priest, Fr. Charles Curran, in the 1970s. It is important because it speaks to the necessity of reducing pressure in our schools and families so that children will be able to learn more. And, incidentally, they will have less chance of visual difficulties. He called his method "community language learning." The idea was that students would not be able to learn a language if they were afraid to make a mistake.

Fr. Curran put the students all in a circle, stood behind them and tried to make them feel calm and comfortable. They would each get a chance to say something in English that they wanted to say in the new language and then he would tell them how and write it on the board. The odd part of it was that after a while no one was even thinking about the English, but easily remembering the words that kept appearing on the board. What he had done was break down what language teachers call the "affective filter" against the new language. This is a filter caused by fear of failure and the resulting inability to relax. If that filter is high, the individual cannot learn a language because he is too scared. Language teachers need to get that filter down low. Perhaps "high-stakes tests" are not the way to coax a child to learn more of anything.

Another stress that we need to inoculate our children against is the penchant many adults have for not living in the present, not "being here now." Instead, we are ruminating over the past and worrying about the future. We are in our heads and not in the world, not in our child's world on a golden afternoon with the sounds of summer around us.

One of the things that eastern thought has brought to this western type-A world is the idea that we need to stop what Joseph Chilton Pearce (1981) calls "roofbrain chatter" and calm our thoughts to calm our hearts. Meditation is one solution, being in nature is another, and enjoying the beauty of everyday views with open, curious eyes is a third.

Journalist and nature advocate Richard Louv (2006) reports that researchers at the University of Illinois showed that "children as young as five showed significant reduction in symptoms of attention deficit disorder when they engaged with nature." Even greenery that was out the window helps, but kids do better in the midst of it.

"Sixth grade kids in environment based programs improved their math and science scores 27 percent," he reports (2006). A walk is a whole different thing when we are looking and seeing than when we are lost in thought, worry, problems, and remembrances. It is easier to do a vision walk in nature than on a busy sidewalk. We all know this, but now there is a book that gathers all the evidence for us: *Last Child in the Woods: Saving Our Children from Nature Deficit Disorder* (Louv 2005).

Weekends in nature or trips to the local arboretum or botanical garden are food for the pregnant woman's heart and the baby's soul. A toddler can enjoy butterflies in a backyard garden for a whole morning, whereas he would get cranky in a playroom filled with plastic toys and no one to play with him. It is the "frequencies" given off by nature that we need to make time for in our children's lives. And let us not forget the frequencies of holding them close to our loving hearts.

HOW TO PROVIDE THE NECESSITIES OF GROSS MOTOR DEVELOPMENT

Movement builds intelligence and vision. Years ago my family's behavioral optometrist, Dr. Amiel Francke, convinced me that what children need to develop their vision is movement in light, preferably outdoor light. This idea was well substantiated by research of Austen Reisan at the University of Chicago in the 1950s (Reisan 1961) and Alan Hein at MIT (Hein 1972) in the late 1960s on visual learning in cats. Their articles were reprinted in Francke's text for behavioral optometrists (Francke 1988).

Of course, cats are not kids, but Hein's animal studies were suggested by observations Helmholz made in 1867 about how human adults learn visual skills—specifically, how they adapt to the distortion of prism glasses (Helmholz 1867). If they could watch their hands to get feedback about their gross errors in grabbing for objects, they could adapt to the prisms and connect with the objects. If they could not see their hands, they could not learn where things were. Hein retested the hypothesis again with adult subjects. Indeed, they could not learn to adapt to the prisms if anyone else guided their hands, even if they could see them.

In a later study on a proprioceptive chain of connections from eye to foot, Roll and Roll (1988) emphasize the relationship of eyes and body movement in the development of human spatial perception. The proprioceptive system is the sensory system involved in processing information from muscles, tendons, and joints. They stated: "In conclusion, we suggest that the muscular proprioceptive chain linking eye to foot may be of major importance in the inter-relating of body space with extrapersonal space."

The principle that "the body and eyes are one" is one of Francke's epigrams. The concept is applied in a great many visual therapy procedures for reprogramming the visual system. Procedures give definite visual/motor feedback, linking movement and perception, and so new ways in vision are easily learned.

So what can we do, then, to develop good vision in our children? For starters, let us take a look at their environment to be sure there is plenty of movement in the light and other important things for growing brains and eyes.

Four experts and their books on movement that I put faith in are the late Dr. G. N. Getman, with the optometric classic, *How to Develop Your Child's Intelligence* (1962); Glenn Doman with his book *How to Teach Your Baby to Be Physically Superb: Birth to Six* (1988); Carla Hannaford, with her book *Smart Moves: Why Learning Is Not All in Your Head* (2005), and Roxanne Small, using Ed Snapp's methods in her book, *Building Babies Better: Developing a Solid Foundation for Your Child* (2005). All of these books are available online.

Doman says, "All kids given the chance love to be physically superb" (1988, 3) and then presents joyous photographs of small children climbing ropes, babies sprinting down crawling tracks on their bellies, and toddlers doing balance routines, all with faces of natural eagerness and delight. How are they learning to do these things? When the book was written, they were at a school that was part of the Institutes for the Achievement of Human Potential in Philadelphia, called the Evan Thomas Institute. At this institute's school for training normal kids to be supernormal kids, two-year-olds can swing hand to hand across a horizontal ladder six feet from the ground, three-year-olds can learn to do one-handed cartwheels, four-year-olds run three miles nonstop around the campus, five-year-olds swing from trapeze to trapeze, and six-year-olds can climb tall trees.

Doman believes that it is possible for all kids to be physically superb. He believes this is their birthright. Why should we care about the development of athletic prowess in infants and toddlers, one might ask? Wouldn't it just be better to count on early computer games to build brains?

Doman's answer is this: Every part of the brain is developed with the different levels of physical activity that he has outlined in that book. He takes the child through stages of brain development from medulla and cord to pons, to midbrain, to initial cortex, to early cortex, to primitive cortex, and to sophisticated cortex in every category of sensory, motor, and intellectual development. This includes vision development.

"Inextricably tied to human *mobility* and *manual* function is human *intelligence*," he explains (Doman 1988). That is the reason we should care. We should also care because this is how vision is learned.

Mobility and manual intelligence are two of Howard Gardner's six kinds of human intelligence (Gardner 1983). We should not sacrifice these on the altars of computer games. Carla Hannaford reminds us that movement and hand action train our brain for creativity and cognitive function, as well (Hannaford 2005). Behavioral optometrists remind us all "the eyes and the body are one." A well-developed body is healthy, and its eyes and brain have had sufficient practice in all the natural developmental steps of seeing distance and space.

One simple example of how the eyes develop and maintain themselves with gross motor activity in space is the focusing system. It does not get much practice in sedentary children. They come into my office with very poor focusing abilities on testing and complaints about not seeing clearly at near and switching to far. Even after middle-age sight sets in, by doing physical activity in space so that constant adjustments of the focus of the eyes is demanded, patients can maintain more flexible vision.

Naturally, the vast majority of us will not have kids at the Evan Thomas Institute model school or the better-baby parent-training program they also run. We need quick plans that we can fit into our lives to help our kids grow strong and physically coordinated and get those eyes working at various distances.

Don't the schools and the preschools do it all, one might ask? No. Very few of Doman's challenging tasks for preschoolers' body and brain development are done in day care or preschool. These facilities don't have the one-on-one helpers to make sure such exercises are safe for kids in groups. Some schools like the Waldorf schools do try to help with gross motor development. Some dedicated physical education teachers try, in their 40 minutes two times a week with a whole group of children, to do many things that are excellent and not on this list. However, physical education is being cut out of the schools' budgets these days, under the ridiculous illusion that it has nothing to do with brain development or learning or vision.

Following is what I suggest as the best activities for busy parents who both work. We need to make a checklist for a child's motor development, and instead of sitting with them in front of the TV, do some of these things every weekend and some evenings each week.

Parent's Checklist for Gross Motor Activities

Infants

1. Put them on a slippery gymnastics mat, playpen mattress, or slippery, laminated wall board panel (Dr. Ward's suggestion) on the floor and get down with them, cheering them on during their early weeks (as early as five or six weeks old), helping them try to dig their toes in and move. Let their feet be bare, the house warm, and the clothes minimal. Do this every night and have the babysitter do it also two times a day, at least. Read Roxanne Small's book, mentioned earlier, for all the many things you can do during that baby's "tummy time."

2. Do not borrow or buy a walker or bounce-up seat. It is bad for your child's development of brain and body and eyes. It circumvents the normal progression of body/brain development. Allow lots of crawling and creeping floor time, and if they do not creep normally, take them to someone who does infant reflex work (see chapter five).
3. Take them to baby movement classes or baby swimming classes—often offered at a YMCA—once a week, or take them swimming regularly until they learn.

Toddlers

1. Take them to a good playground every nice day that you can spare the time—at least two times a week—and, holding their hands, have them balance on the curbs that enclose the playground, hold them up to grip the overhead bars, help them to climb on the stone animals or the ladder to the small slide. Help them hang onto an overhead ladder while you hold them. Get them to walk as much as you can.
2. If you have a woods near your home, go there when you can, and they will want to walk.
3. Work on swimming or toddler gym activities from a YMCA course or a book.

Three-Year-Olds   Get a seven-foot 2-x-4 and store it under your couch to take out for evening balance fun. Don't raise it up. Keep it flat on the floor for safety. It stimulates peripheral awareness for balance, while the child fixates on a central target in front.

The centers for balance in the brain are connected to pathways from the peripheral retina. Hold up objects on the sides as your child walks the plank and fixates a target straight ahead. Ask him if he can see them out of the sides of his eyes. This stimulates processing in the peripheral retina pathways. Peripheral retina vision, the more global kind of vision, is thought to have a special pathway from the visual cortex in the brain up to centers where one processes location. Central, detailed vision is done with fixations of the fovea, the central part of the retina, and is connected with speech and language centers in the brain. Learning the coordinated use of both kinds of visual processing is necessary for good vision and good reading.

These pathways through the brain are sometimes referred to as the magno (global) and the parvo (detail) pathways. Disabled readers are thought to have poorly developed magnocellular pathways. (Brannan, Solan Ficarra, and Ong 1998). Vision therapy (Solan, Shelley-Tremblay, Ficarra, Silverman, and Larson 2003) and appropriate children's learning activities can improve their function, and sometimes blue filters have helped. (Solan, Brannnan, Ficarro, and Byrne 1997) The message here is to ensure that children are learning to use their vision for the big picture and the central small details, with hands and bodies in free space, not looking at screens. These activities should be continued long past Age 3.

Children in Preschool and Early Grades

1. Get them into movement classes, children's yoga, or martial arts as early as they are available, or spend time yourself teaching them "growing up exercises" from a good book while playing music. See what your public library can lend you.

2. One thing for the older children that I think could be a very good parent/child project is doing the famous five Tibetan exercises every day with them. Start slow with few repetitions and build up your stamina. These are not easy, but not dangerous, either. I think of them as yoga calisthenics. There are a couple of books on them. One is by Christopher S. Kilham, *The Five Tibetans: Five Dynamic Exercises for Health, Energy, and Personal Power* (1994). Another book, *The Ancient Secret of the Fountain of Youth* by Peter Kelder (1998) with a preface by Andrew Weil, MD, has an imaginative and fun-to-read story to build up your motivation to do these postures. Both are available online. I have done them with great benefit.

3. Take them to a beach or a lake once a year for some extended play near water, or for shorter times during summer weekends if there are lakes or a shore near you. Use water wings to teach them to swim if they did not learn as babies.

4. Teach them to shinny up a rope, hang by their knees, go hand over hand on a horizontal ladder, walk on a balance board, and climb a gentle tree with a lot of support. Teach them to skip, jump rope, play hopscotch, and ride a bike if they are not sprinting ahead of you doing it already.

5. Have them walk with you as soon as they can, as far as they can. If they can safely walk to school, have them do that. Walk with them rather than drive them, but leave enough time so they will not be stressed, out of breath, or angry at you for rushing them.

6. Have them work in the yard or a community garden plot with you, either putting in a garden, raking leaves, or helping to shovel snow. Better still, let them plan with you their own section of the garden. Help them with weeding. Weeding kills the joy for kids.

Seven- to Eight-Year-Olds and Up

1. Consider a good outdoors summer camp for a week or two if you can afford one.

2. Get them on teams that they will enjoy. Swimming is usually fun for most kids. Soccer might or might not be, but it is good for their eyes as long as there is no "heading" of the ball.

3. If teams are not available but a basketball hoop is, shoot baskets with them, using a child-sized ball a few hours a week. Set up a badminton set or have them play croquet if you have a yard for it. All of these things used to be done before the age of electronic entertainment. They helped develop vision and the brain.

4. Make individual sports part of their life, but not the passive TV kind. Teach them to ice skate or ski, ride a bike, roller skate, play tennis, or whatever you or your babysitter can do with them. Tiny Norwegian children ski to school. There is no reason grade-schoolers in this country cannot learn these nonteam activities. Children who play sports have less chance of becoming myopic because they are more likely to have good focusing systems from movement in the light.

CHILDREN MAY NOT BE ABLE TO DO THESE THINGS WITHOUT PARENT OR TEACHER SUPPORT

This list of suggestions for parents might sound like things kids should automatically know how to do by themselves without any parental support. They don't. Believe me, they don't. I see children in my office who have never even crept. They have never helped plant a garden, or balanced on a curb, or hopped. Most of gross motor learning is from outdoor activities, which will refresh rather than tire out a parent, who is willing to go for a "roller skate walk," grow vegetables, walk up a sunny hillside, or hike through a forest path and smell the wildflowers and pines.

If parents can aim for two hours of outdoor activity a day and a lot more on the weekends, children will thrive on it and the parents will, too. That is easy for people who live in small, safe towns, suburbs, or a neighborhood in a medium-sized city like the place I grew up in south Minneapolis.

It is not easy for those in a thoroughly urban setting without parks nearby. However, an optometrist who grew up in New York City told me that he did have an outdoor life as a child. It is not the city that is the problem. It is the increasing stress, traffic, and lack of "a sense of neighborhood" that is the problem, he said. It maybe does "take a village" within a city to raise a child.

As a young boy, this optometrist had as much neighborhood play as I did in south Minneapolis. His was in the street, down the block, at the corner, across the street in an empty space with some basketball hoops, in and out of the corner stores, talking to folks on their front steps. It was a community within that huge city. It was a community that surrounded and protected those kids. We do not often have that any more.

Nevertheless, we need to get those children outdoors in the sunlight and fresh air with distance views, whatever it takes, and the greener the environment the better.

If you can get your day care center organized to handle the after-school sports, you only have to do the weekends. There is one after-school center here in Massachusetts that has kids sign up for various sports activities, one each day, and transports them to the soccer field, the ice rink, the dance and gymnastics studio, or the swimming pool. It is called the Hayden Recreation Centre in Lexington, Massachusetts. That is the wave of the future.

How could you possibly do all this and work 10- to 12-hour days? Maybe you can't. People used to have eight-hour days. Our society needs to allow for flex time and part-time work, down to five or six hour days for parents, if we want to raise children with eyes for learning. The

Harvard University Health Service has been praised by doctors and office support staff, who have raised families on what are called "mother's hours." Harvard was named one of the "100 best companies for working mothers" in 2003 by *Working Mothers Magazine*. We need many more than 100 companies trying to help families raise their children well.

The software engineers may have the worst hours, because if a problem arises, they have to service that software all through the night and often put in 12 to 16 hours or more a day. It may be okay for the kids just out of college, but this is hard on a family man or woman. Can't we all just slow down?

One woman at a prominent Boston law firm announced that she wanted to work half time after having a new baby. They said, "Okay. Halftime is nine to five, five days a week, and it is half pay." She chose to continue working full time. However, a more enlightened law firm in Minnesota has provided three short days for a niece of mine with three preschool children and a fourth on the way. She is off the partner track, but she has a nice life, extra income for the family, and something to get her out of the house a few days a week to keep her skills sharp in the law. Many more of these opportunities are needed in all jobs so that children can be raised well. This is not just for their good or for our good. It is for the good of our world.

FINE MOTOR (EYE/HAND) DEVELOPMENT

Fine motor development is essential for a child to develop not only eye/hand coordination, but also his "performance IQ." The children I see with "right brain learning problems" and "low performance, high verbal IQ scores" have not developed skills with their hands and eyes, which also means that they have not developed their brains for spatial relations, visual memory, and perception in major ways. We learn to visualize by putting things together and taking things apart. Hands-on learning for children is necessary for vision and for visualization and thought. Computer learning is not.

Here we come again to creeping and crawling, that essential part of developing a skilled human eye/hand/brain. Carla Hannaford argues that children's hand development for printing is born out of a lot of creeping (2005).

She says, "In order to print, the child must crawl for a good long time with hands forward, to develop the bones in the hand and develop upper arm strength" (Hannaford 2005, 96).

There are numbers of children who need to see occupational therapists to learn to print. Cursive handwriting is easier and takes less bone development of the hand (Hannaford 2005). However, our schools are set to teach printing first and cursive second, so we need to help our children by seeing to it that they develop their hand and arm strength before they go to school. You can help them do what Doman calls "brachiation," which is hanging by their hands to move across a high horizontal ladder (Doman 1988).

Holding their hands to help them walk before they can do it on their own is a disservice to their brain development. They need that floor time, because there are large numbers of receptors in the hands that are needed to grasp and take messages to the brain to help develop perception (Hannaford 2005, 97). Children in walkers are not developing trunk strength and upper-arm strength from extensive creeping. After creeping, they need to lift things of different shapes and weights, pull themselves up on things like furniture or large stumps or stones outdoors, and so on. Without this, they are shortchanged in the development of hand and wrist power. Printing and writing is getting even harder for children now, the occupational therapists tell me, because children are not doing the traditional home play activities that develop hands.

Since most schools will likely not change their curriculum to suit what we now know about the development of the hand, it makes sense to see to it that those children of ours have very fine hand/eye development before they enter school. Below is a list of activities that would help that process along.

Parent's Checklist for Eye/Hand Small Motor and Perception Activities

1. Eye/hand training toys. As soon as the child can sit up, purchase a hand manipulation set of activities on a crib attachment, nesting

boxes or nesting cups, and a "shape box" with basic shapes for the child to fit in through holes that match each shape but will not let others through. Get a cone-stacking toy with various sizes of plastic donuts to fit onto the cone. You will have to show them what to do with toys like this at different intervals in their development.

2. Kitchen cupboard play. Put objects like small kettles, measuring cups, measuring spoons, and plastic bowls onto the floor for the child to fit together while you are cooking. You could also stick a learn-to-dress doll in the cupboard with buttons and buckles and zippers to train small hands.

3. Sand and water. Provide sandbox experience with many types of sandbox toys. Do the same for bath time experience. Play with the child to show him what can be done with these toys that will stimulate his eyes and hands together. Beaches work for both sand and water.

4. Self care and art at two. Teach a two-year-old to clean up his toys, dress himself, help brush his teeth, and begin to draw. These activities have to do with hand movements, lifting, carrying, sorting, organizing, and finding a "home" for everything in his room. Start work with playdough-type modeling materials. Use large markers and teach circle and line drawing, and see if maybe the artist within will emerge. I know a two and a half–year-old who drew a square house with four windows and rabbit heads with ears sticking out, one in each window. Children can be amazing if we give them a chance.

5. Puzzles and beads. Three-year-olds will enjoy a number of wooden puzzles. Sometimes, two-year-olds are great at these, if they are developing rapidly. These are eye/hand activities as well as puzzles. For mature three-, four-, or five-year-olds, stringing colored plastic one-third-inch beads or picking them up with toothpicks and placing them on toothpicks stuck into a sponge are very good activities for finger skills and binocular vision at near.

6. Concepts of quantity. At three and four years, start teaching concepts of quantity, patterns, and shapes with parquetry blocks, pattern blocks, or Cuisenaire rods. Other small, colored blocks of many sizes and shapes or Legos are very good for manipulation, creative building, and thinking about quantitative topics.

7. Two and three dimensions. Later, for a five-year-old, you will want to be sure she can make a three-dimensional object from a two-di-

dimensional diagram with some form of building toy. Try Lincoln Logs, Legos, Tinker Toys, or Kinnex.

8. Cooking. Let the three- and four-year-olds help with cooking, but not the hot stove or the sharp knife parts. They can mix up anything, spread out precut fruit on a plate, wash lettuce, sprouts, and parsley for a salad, and so on. They should learn to help with dinner and set the table, and they can have a cookbook of their own for rainy weekend days when you are all housebound.

9. Building. Buy or make large building blocks for three- and four-year-olds. If you feel that your preschool is well equipped with those, you might build a simple dollhouse instead. Your child can help you build, and then you help to furnish it. It can be as simple as a fairy house with stones and small pieces of wood for chairs and beds, as well as some clothespin fairy dolls and a few nifty, store-bought furnishings. With children, it is the process, not the product that matters. The process strengthens their visualization capacities.

10. Perception activities with eyes and hands together. This includes the Brick by Brick and Shape by Shape perception games that five-year-olds can work on and older kids also love. The hard one, the brain buster for adults in my vision therapy practice, is Block by Block. Tangrams and parquetry blocks are also good for perception. Visual memory can be trained if you make a pattern with blocks (first two, then three, etc.) and give the child a one-second glimpse. Then see if he can make the same pattern. When he is older, you can speed up to half a second and then just one-fifth of a second before you cover it up again.

11. Don't forget artwork with color crayons, markers, and paints (Crayolas are nontoxic). Also keep a supply of stencils, connect-the-dots books, maze books, scissors and paste, old magazines for cutting up, and construction paper, and do not forget some old-fashioned educational coloring books that teach children to focus at near, color inside the lines (which trains their fingers), and choose attractive shades and hues. Keep these in a cupboard and dole them out one at a time when your child needs something to do. A small desk in the kitchen near you will keep him busy.

If you run out of ideas for activities for eyes and hands at your child's small desk, read *Perceptual Training Activities Handbook: 250 Games and Exercises for Helping Children Develop Sensory Skills* (Van Witsen 1979); it's out of print but still available online.

These activities are more and more important for home play, because schools are becoming more academic, earlier and earlier. Yet all these lessons need to be learned somehow.

If we ensure that eye/hand activities are part of our infant's and preschooler's *daily life* (controlling a computer mouse is not the kind of direct connection that is a truly eye/hand activity, nor does it work the fingers), their near vision skills along with perceptual skills and eye/hand coordination will develop. Their right brain learning will take place, their performance IQ will not be significantly lower than their verbal IQ, and they will have absorbed a lot of time talking and playing with a very intelligent adult for a friend.

If we cannot be there the whole time for all of the above activities, our babysitters will have to be shown what we want them to do. The main principle is that we have to be down on the floor with them from the first months, showing them by our actions and enthusiasm that the world is an interesting place yet still letting them discover and learn to entertain themselves part of that time, too.

Dr. Susan R. Johnson, a behavioral and developmental pediatrician from Fair Oaks, California, has argued in the *Journal for Waldorf Education* (2005) that early teaching of reading interferes with normal brain development if all the child's senses are not properly integrated first. It will be stressful without the underpinnings of an integrated nervous system. Her view is that reading—a left brain task—should not be forced on children who are trying to develop their right brains (a developmental task from birth to age seven) and are not yet ready neurologically for that left brain effort and the integration of left and right brain across the corpus callosum. She believes this unfortunate, too-early timing of what society is asking the child's brain to do is contributing to attention and learning problems (Johnson 2005). More work on balance and motor development is needed first. See chapters three, four, and six for discussions of how early reading is hard on vision development from behavioral optometry's view.

LIMIT TV AND COMPUTER OR VIDEO GAMES

Brain waves are harmed by too much TV. Spatial awareness, eye/hand coordination, self-soothing, and original thought and visualization are diminished by TV. Computers are a stress on the eyes, as everyone knows who has a steady computer job for any length of time.

If you can manage to limit screen time in your family's life, you might be helping those children find their true inner genius, wonder, and love of learning.

Because my children were in the care of behavioral optometrists, Dr. Amiel Francke in Washington, D.C., and Dr. James Blumenthal in Illinois (before he moved to Phoenix), we were forewarned. We prevented TV addiction problems.

Dr. Francke said to me, "It is not that TV is bad; it is what it replaces that is bad for your child's development." The more the TV is watched, the less development of the brain, eyes, and hands can happen.

Pediatricians have recommended no TV before age two (including being in the room with parents watching it), limited TV after that, and alternatives to TV in every home. The American Academy of Pediatrics also came out with a report on the importance of play, something that over-programmed and neglected TV-addicted children are not doing very much. They recommend that much of that play should be with the parents for family time (Ginsburg 2006).

PROTECTING VISION DEVELOPMENT FROM TV AND COMPUTER EXCESSES

I recommend no TV before age four. Before age four, children think what they see on TV is reality, and it also limits learning time in three dimensions and may set up a pattern of disrupted visual sequences that leads to attention problems. After four, try to limit it to one hour a day until your child's vision skills are more fully developed by age ten. After ten, one and a half hours of screen time includes computer and TV time. No computer time for children in the home before age ten is the best rule for eyes; no personal computers for kids until high school. Even then, they don't need one if there is one to share, until college. Soon enough, they will need that hour for homework on the computer, and then just a movie a week or a couple of sitcoms will use up their TV time.

There are reasons for this TV austerity, according to research in physiology. Before four, it is too stressful to the child's "heart brain," not nourishing for his "head brain," and hurtful to his "visual brain," as is discussed earlier in this chapter and other chapters. Hannaford, Pearce, and others are concerned about the fight/flight adrenalin that is pumped into a little child's muscles because of what he sees on television, when there is no reason to fight or fly to use up that adrenalin. Recall that it is the fight/flight reaction that also interferes with focusing the eyes up close. See chapters three and four for further discussion.

In addition, this hormonal reaction leaves kids hypervigilant, and after time, dulled to the constant stress they are feeling. It can aggravate or create attention deficit hyperactivity disorder (ADHD), especially in boys, because most of the violence they see on TV is acted out by men (models for them) on the screen (Hannaford 2005).

LIMITING TV AND COMPUTER USE IS DIFFICULT BUT WORTH IT

Some parents have told me that because they both work, life is pretty stressful, and they do not have time for very much. They want their children to start learning on computers at age two so they will be ready for preschool. They also have no idea what children could possibly do with themselves if they were not watching TV or playing on a computer.

The fact is those children are now in my office because they are going nearsighted or just using one eye because they still cannot converge at age five or six. They have had excessive TV and computer time that prevented normal development of vision. Some parents are trying to limit screen time for older children (Navarro 2005). A decade ago, thoughtful people worried that in the enthusiasm for computers, schools would cut out crucial items like art, physical education, and music (Oppenheimer 1997). They have.

Many children can't learn to print at age six because they did not use their hands enough as toddlers and preschoolers, and some of them are struggling with reading in spite of all the "computer learning." A mouse is not related to skilled finger coordination. Seeing something on a screen takes six repeats to learn compared to one demonstration in real space, say television researchers like Daniel R. Anderson, of the University of Massachusetts (Jackson 2005).

My young patients' vision problems occurred because their systems were not developed enough at an early age to handle the computer screen stress. Joseph Chilton Pearce, author of *Evolution's End: Claiming the Potential of Our Intelligence* (1992), bemoans the use of TV and computers for children. One reason is that both are what he calls backlit radiant light screens, which is not the way light is experienced in the visual world. Light in the visual world is reflected off of objects in space, and that is what the eyes are designed to see (Pearce 2003). Children who I see with too much screen life too early have underdeveloped "space worlds" for the mind, which affects their abilities in many categories.

Pearce calls television "play's end." What he means is that with television as the entertainer, things that were part of nurturing play for visualization, imagination, and wonder are gone. TV has replaced storytelling in most homes. It has replaced sing-a-longs in most homes. It has replaced visualization for children who used to visualize with radio or just with the stories read to them and stories they were told. It has replaced dinner conversation. It has replaced family conversation in general. It has replaced the stories that parents used to tell about their work or grandmothers used to tell about the mother's or father's childhood. It has replaced play with the children. It has replaced family Scrabble or Monopoly games. It has replaced teaching children Rummy or Rook. It has replaced reading aloud. It has replaced play.

This is not all, though, as if the above were not enough of a loss. Here is how Pearce says it:

> Perhaps most critical, television floods the infant-child brain with images at the very time his or her brain is supposed to learn to make images from within. Storytelling feeds into the infant-child as stimulus that brings

about a response of image making that involves every aspect of our triune (brain) system. Television feeds both stimulus and response into that infant-child brain, as a single paired effect, and therein lies the danger. (1992, 166)

Pearce says that by age five, the average child in the United States has watched 6,000 hours of TV. That is 6,000 hours that he was not visualizing or imagining for himself, using his hands, and building his own performance IQ.

Besides that, he might have just been in a trance the whole time. Pearce reports on research during which five- and six-year-olds saw TV shows that were selected for their age group. The sound tracks were switched and none of the children even noticed it (1992, 167).

An extremely talented, long-time fourth-grade teacher and current resource teacher in Washington, D.C., Kathryn Powers, has completed a research project to compare opportunities for learning vocabulary and structure of language from TV shows including comparing commercials and good books for kids. Here is what she learned.

KATHRYN POWERS' STUDY RESULTS

Much has been said about the benefits a child derives from listening to storytelling and reading; much has also been said about the detrimental effects of television. Because I work in an elementary school and regularly observe young children struggling to express themselves, and because I feel strongly that a child expresses himself more easily if s/he is exposed regularly to well-constructed ideas and sentences, I decided to quantify what the children hear in each case.

My study compares the language a child hears during thirty minutes of oral reading with the language he/she hears during a thirty-minute television show including the ads. Although study results will vary with different shows and books, the advantage of listening to an adult reading is sufficiently significant to make peculiar differences negligible in most cases.

For this study, I compared the text of *Midnight Is a Place* read aloud for exactly thirty minutes. I taped *The Simpsons* from the beginning of the first ad to the end of the last ad, and then I made a transcript of the tape.

In each I counted:

1. total number of words
2. total number of sentences
3. total number of nonsentences
4. total number of different words
5. total number of one-, two-, three-, four-, five-, and six-syllable words

In each I computed:

1. the number of words per punctuation mark (i.e., the number of sentences plus non-sentences)
2. the percentage of total different words that have one, two, three, four, five, or six syllables

I encountered one problem. In parts of the tape, I was unable to distinguish what was being said. I added to the TV transcript a generous two hundred words, which I distributed proportionately among the syllable groups. Much of the taped program was noisy, and there were screeches and grunts that I did not count.

Following are the results:

	Midnight Is a Place	*The Simpsons*, and Ads
Total words	5,737	3,487 (3,287 +200)
Total different words	1,673	1,110 (1,046 + 64)
One-syllable words	755 (45.13%)	539 (509 + 30; 48.6%)
Two-syllable words	626 (37.42%)	375 (353 + 22; 33.8%)
Three-syllable words	219 (13.09%)	148 (139 + 9; 13.3%)
Four-syllable words	66 (3.95%)	36 (34 + 2; 3.2%)
Five-syllable words	7 (0.42%)	10 (9 + 1; 0.9%)
Six-syllable words	0	2 (0.2%)
Total sentences	310	335
Total nonsentences	30	119
Number of words per punctuation	16.87	7.68

Clearly, the novel offers much better sentence construction and vocabulary diversity. It has over twice as many words per sentence and nonsentence as the television show. Surprisingly, there are more five- and six-syllable words in The Simpsons, although the number of one-, two-, three-, and four-syllable words is greater in the novel; and while the comparative percentages of each syllabic group of words is similar in most cases, the novel has a much higher percentage of two-syllable words.

I noticed listening to the tape [of the show] that without visual assistance, it is often difficult to discern what is happening. There are repeated disconnects every time the ads come on and whenever they change. There is a tremendous amount of confusion as the various themes from the show segue into a sequence of ads. Furthermore, there are a great many loud noises and background songs superimposed onto the text of both the show and the ads.

The other problem with television, besides the fact that it severely limits neural development and arrests visual development, is that it can breed violence. Everyone knows that violence on television can increase aggressive behavior in children. The violence in computer games is another negative influence. Pearce says that by the time our children become adults, they have seen 18,000 murders on television (1992, 170). This is not good for the brain, the eyes, or the heart brain. Children with vision cannot be grown in front of a tube.

GIVE THANKS FOR PUBLIC LIBRARIES

One thing that every parent can do easily is take their kids to the public library children's center once a week, browse for an hour, sign out books, come home, and read to them every night before bedtime. It is common knowledge that children who are read to learn to read. They also can comprehend what they read because they are practicing visualization when they listen to good books. They also enjoy reading because they know how to make pictures in their heads from hearing stories. Reading to a child is one thing that parents can easily do, even if they had a bad day at work and don't feel like playing games or shooting baskets.

If parents feel that they are not good, expressive oral readers, there are tapes in the public library of great books for children that can be listened to with the child. Some children have learned to read better by listening to Harry Potter tapes and following along in the books. This does take some parental help and input, though, in finding places and following with a finger.

WHAT CHILDREN EAT IS TREMENDOUSLY IMPORTANT FOR THEIR EYE AND BRAIN DEVELOPMENT

Many children with visual problems do not get enough protein. Children need two grams of protein for every 2.2 pounds of body weight (Kavner 1985). Adults need one gram for every two pounds. Unfortunately, most parents don't know these figures or how to count grams of protein. If their kids get the same relative amount (sized down) that the parents find adequate for themselves, the kids do not get enough. Kids need that double amount relative to their weight because they are growing brain cells and muscles at a rapid pace. Children who do not get enough protein in utero, or who fail to get enough in the first four years of life, are compromised intellectually forever afterward, nutritionists believe (Shinaur 1975; Kavner 1985).

Before a baby is born, if the mother gets at least 70 grams of protein daily, the fetus will develop a better brain. If every child got a high-protein breakfast (an egg a day is ideal, along with whole grain toast or oatmeal, fruit, and a protein drink), learning difficulties would be diminished significantly. Children also need health-promoting fats. A blender mix of three cups olive oil to one pound of organic butter will provide a safe fat that will have what they need if they have that spread on toast, vegetables, or other foods daily.

THE SUGAR PROBLEM

One thing I absolutely *know* is that cane sugar and white flour will not be good for most children over time. It is not just teeth, but also metabolism for energy that is affected negatively. Sugar also prevents them from enjoying a variety of tastes other than sweet. Without that variety, they will not be eating healthily or have high energy, and it will be difficult to maintain normal weight as all children have a right to do. Refined starches may cause myopia as well (Fox 2002).

Energy shortages affect the eyes, which are closely connected to all parts of the brain. The vision process, which is an eye/brain process, uses 25 percent of body energy. If that energy is not there, both vision and the rest of the body are compromised.

There is at least one study that suggests people who are dyslexic have better eye movements when maintaining a diet that is low in sugar and contains more complex carbohydrates (e.g., fresh fruits and vegetables and whole grains). This was a small, two-part study. In the double-blind segment, each subject served as his own control. They had to do this because of Roger Williams' research indicating that we all have our own biochemical individuality. There were provocative tests under the subjects' tongues of cane sugar, corn, and ethanol. The control chemical was saline solution (mildly salty water). The saline solution was clearly no problem. The body is filled with saline.

"The cane sugar challenge resulted in more erratic eye movements, fixations, regressions, and reduced the reading efficiency for the dyslexic subjects" (Hardman, Clary, and Leiberman 1989).

In another part of the study, all the subjects had four days of sugar and junk food, and then a return to no sugar and healthy diets with fresh fruits, whole grains, and vegetables for five days. Sure enough, the eye movements were much more erratic and the dyslexics lacked oculomotor coordination more on the sugar and refined carbohydrate diets than on the healthy diet (Hardman, Clary, and Leiberman 1989).

I hardly ever have a learning-disabled (LD) child in my office who is not hooked on sugar foods. The book *Sugars and Flours: How They Make Us Crazy, Sick, and Fat and What to Do about It*, by Joan Ifland, is in my office waiting room. A number of parents have borrowed it and several have been so enthusiastic in implementing it that the difference was visible in the children's success in the vision training and in school. One mother bought me an extra copy as a thank-you because it had given her the energy at the end of the day to stay awake and functioning until 10:00 p.m. when she had been wiped out by 6:00 prior to going on the program. The book is still in print at www.1stbooks.com I recommend it as a family nutrition manual and cook book.

There are good reasons that should motivate every parent to solve the nutrition problem based on sugar. It can lead to Type II diabetes, which is now epidemic among kids as well as adults. Laura Plunkett and Linda Weltner have written a very helpful book called *The Challenge of Childhood Diabetes: Family Strategies for Raising a Healthy Child* (2006). The big problem for these children to overcome is "poor diet and lack of exercise," says Plunkett. Both nutrition and exercise must be increased in order to cut the HBAIC blood value down to an average over three months of 6.5 to 7 to keep the pressure off the circulatory system, she explains. (Normal is between 4 and 6; diabetic children can be up to 8.5 or 9.) Otherwise, the child will not avoid long-term problems with vision and other aspects of health.

The best way to insulate your child against diabetes is to train him to eat fresh fruits and vegetables, high protein but low fat meats and fish, and other protein foods, healthy natural oils like olive oil, nuts, and a limited amount of whole grains, such as old-fashioned (not instant) oatmeal. Keep desserts for special occasions, like once a week for Friday night dinner or Sunday night supper.

Most kids in this culture get too many carbohydrates that are too often laced with sucrose (table sugar). Children with visually related learning problems often have had a lot of antibiotics for ear infections. They are having vision problems or learning problems partly because they are fostering overgrowth of candida (unhealthy yeast in the gut) because of the antibiotics that have not been compensated for by acidophilus culture. The unbalanced intestinal flora (excessive yeast) thrives on sugary foods and produces toxins for the brain, including alcohol. If children are given sugar as a bribe or a reward, sugary foods will be wanted but they will not help make the child more well. Whole grains, maybe along with eliminating wheat, are better than white flour and sugar products that cause yeast overgrowth. Alcohol, as we know, is not useful for maintaining coordinated eyes or coherent thoughts.

Ten Food Rules to Keep Children's Visual Learning on Track[2]

1. Provide a high-protein breakfast. Sometimes in the rush of a morning, children only get a little cereal and maybe milk on the cereal. Cook hard boiled eggs the night before and get them used to cold eggs with salt, which may remind them of Easter eggs and

be a pleasant substitute on mornings when no one can cook protein foods. Leftover cold chicken or other meat is also good in a rush.

2. Ensure that children get enough B vitamins. Many children are not getting them because they do not want to eat meat, those in the grains are milled out, and children won't eat greens. I see many college students who have what I call the triple stress diagnosis. They are on antidepressants; they have irritable bowel syndrome; and they have skin inflammations that are being topically medicated. It looks like subclinical B vitamin deficiency disease to me. Whatever is happening, their vision problems (and overall energy) can be improved significantly with a B complex and a multiple vitamin.

3. Provide an excellent multiple vitamin to make up for everything children won't eat and that crops grown on bad soil won't provide.

4. Never make the white flour/white sugar compromise. That means white flour bagels and toaster pastries at breakfast, and it means cupcakes, or even cookies, for snacks in their lunch boxes. It also means juice drinks that are not juice. It means candies that are sold in the produce department as well as candy bars in the drugstore.

5. If the child is on the autism spectrum, go with the gluten-free, casein-free diet, and watch to see if it helps when it is *religiously* followed. Give it several months of fanatical enforcement. Ask your Dan! Doctor about the methyl B12 treatment, also, and the vitamin creams for the soles of the feet when children cannot take pills.

6. Try to buy organic when you can. It will eliminate many toxins and hormones from your children's bodies. If not, soak the produce and wash it thoroughly.

7. Try to eliminate all bad fats. These are hydrogenated fats and transfats. That means reading labels and eliminating a lot of snack foods and packaged foods. Provide a source of good fats in fish, capsules, olive oil, and organic eggs.

8. The more raw, fresh vegetables and fruits you can get into your child, the better. If they help prepare these foods, they may be more willing to eat them. If they grow them, themselves, they will

eat them for sure. Teach them to wash and pat dry fruits and vegetables, whether organic or not, to eliminate hidden toxins or micro-organisms.

9. Limit desserts to one night a week. Try for a relatively healthy one. One patient's family who totally reversed their child's poor functional vision, LD diagnosis, and myopia decided to set up a rule that there were only desserts on Friday nights. If their child wanted any cookies or candy during the week on a particular day, that treat took the place of his Friday night dessert. Pretty soon, he was happy enough with just the Friday night dessert, and he did not even desire a candy bar thereafter. It was a radical shift in the whole dietary process in that family. The child's vision problems and the learning problems disappeared with vision therapy and the reduction of sugar.

10. Get a source of pure, lead-free, and chlorine-free water. Use water instead of sodas to quench everyone's thirst. The brain works on water. Children need a lot of it and they will drink it if it is good water.

KEEP YOUR CHILD'S BODY ALIGNED AND POSTURE BALANCED WITH PROPER DESKS FOR STUDY AND CLOSE WORK, APPROPRIATE DISTANCES FOR TV VIEWING AND COMPUTER USE, AND CAREFUL ATTENTION TO INJURIES, ESPECIALLY HEAD OR NECK TRAUMA

Much head or neck trauma results in the atlas and axis bones becoming misaligned in relation to the occipital bone. They can slide sideways a tiny bit. This reduces circulation to the brain. This is probably the most important chiropractic adjustment there is. DeJarnette and Goodheart worked out gentle ways to test for and fix these misalignments in all positions: lying down, sitting, standing, and prone (Newton 2006). Chapter five discusses in great detail the need for appropriate treatment for injuries that throw off cranial and sacral balance and consequently interfere with vision and learning.

That chapter also covers treatments that can be effective for head injuries or developmental problems. Refer to chapter five if your child has a head injury, a fall, balance problems, a high shoulder, a habitually slanted belt, excessively poor posture with back discomfort, whiplash, a chronic sore and stiff neck, or other body alignment problems.

If there are no injuries, it is important to ensure that poor posture does not develop out of the ergonomics of your home study setup because it will affect energy and vision for learning. The basic need is a desk or table that is not too high relative to the chair. If the child sits on a chair that leaves his shoulders barely above the tabletop, he needs a booster seat. Otherwise, the focusing burden will be huge, and the shoulders and arms will not work the way they should for writing.

If the child cannot reach the floor with his feet, get a footstool, because eyes do not work best if feet are dangling. Test the desk height this way: If hands are clasped in front with elbows bent, the elbows should be able to swing forward and just clear the desktop. This will allow the child to read and write at the correct distance (Francke and Kaplan 1978). The following are more of the recommendations from doctors of optometry, Francke and Kaplan.

There need to be two lights on the desk or table, one on each side, positioned so that the child's body does not cast any shadow on his work. This will give even light on both sides to avoid uneven visual adaptations.

The paper does not have to be held straight on the desk in front for writing, as some of us were taught back in first grade. If the child is left handed, paper should tilt to the right. If the child is right handed, it will slant to the left. Eye dominance is another factor for positioning work. If the child is left eyed and right handed, the paper will not tilt as far to the left as it would if he were both right handed and right eyed. If the child is right eyed and left handed, it will not be turned at as much of a slant to the right as if he were both left eyed and left handed. A slant board should be used to place a book parallel to the slightly down-turned face. The standard angle of the slant is twenty degrees from the desktop. This allows for less effort in shifting focus as the child reads down the page, as is explained in chapter six (Francke and Kaplan 1978).

After the desk and the chair are set up, distance viewing from the desk is really important. Children need to be trained to look up every couple of pages and clear the view out the window or across the room. Years ago in classrooms, teachers would tell children to stop looking out the window. What they did not know was that looking out the window was essential for kids having trouble focusing up close. I can remember personally doing it a lot in school, looking toward a hill with trees. We were resting our eyes.

Now not all schools and offices are even built to allow for windows to look out of or even rooms to look across, which is a crime against children's vision development and adult's functional vision survival in this computer age. I have people come to me with major computer eyestrain at work, because they are in a tiny cubicle with walls all around and no way to look far, no window, no high ceiling even, and no way to look out the door across a room. We have to get aerial photographs for their walls to simulate distance viewing and divergence training Magic Eye books available online to keep by the computer for relaxing their focus (N.E. Thing Enterprises 1993).

If the child's desk cannot be positioned so he can look out a window, turn it around so he can look across the room, not at a wall. Windows are best unless the late afternoon sun will blaze into them and make doing homework difficult. If the child is using an adult's computer for homework, then a booster seat will be necessary to keep him from straining his eyes by looking up at the computer.

Ergonomics of TV watching is another problem. Dr. Mary Childress, a behavioral optometrist from Longview, Texas, described in a seminar I attended how she knew from the angle of the astigmatism on a child's prescription where and how he was sitting for TV viewing. If you want to avoid functional astigmatism in your child's eyes, make sure she sits straight in front of that picture tube, but ten feet back.

Train children not to lie down on a couch to either watch a program or read a book. Astigmatism will likely be developed if body posture habitually forces the eyes into an angular position for viewing, though there are some kinds that just seem to be there at birth. Other types are obviously adaptations to help the child see better up close or at whatever angle he habitually positions himself for his near work.

MAKE FAMILY ACTIVITIES SERVE TO BUILD A SPACE WORLD FOR A CHILD'S MIND AND IMAGINATION: REMEMBER THAT A SPACE WORLD IS THE UNDERPINNING OF A GOOD VISUAL SYSTEM

This is a concept that should be in everyone's mind as we raise our children and grandchildren. It is not hard to apply because there are hundreds of family activities that qualify under this principle. TV is not one of them, unless it is one special program or movie a week that the family watches and talks about afterward. Flat screens will never build a space world for a child's mind. Children need to be outdoors, looking far, moving through space, and shifting their gaze.

The way I explain it to my vision therapy kids and their parents is this: What if you were kept in a cage all day and night and could never stretch out your legs and arms their entire length? How would your legs and arms feel? Do you think you would have strong walking and standing muscles? Would your body grow healthy and tall, or crooked and small? If they cannot visualize this, they may remember the movie or their old picture book of *Hansel and Gretel*.

I say, "Think of your eyes as a system in your body such as legs and arms. The muscles in your eyes could become weak and cramped if you only let them look up close at screens or at a wall behind the screen. They need to stretch just like your body does. They need to look out the windows, across the room, down the block, and out to the universe and beyond into your mind's eye. Eyes that are kept in the cage of a TV or computer screen won't grow up to be good eyes for everything else, because they will never have the chance to do enough moving in space, basking in the light, and looking far and away."

Below are some ideas that fulfill the goals of hands-on learning, distance sight, movement in space, visualization, and visual memory. This is just the short list, my favorite ten ideas.

1. Short trips to museums or zoos frequently to allow soaring ceilings and long views, interesting things to observe, talk about, and remember.
2. Nature walks in a woods, botanical gardens, or arboretum, looking for specific things—maybe at first, just the names of

certain trees so the child notices the shapes of leaves that distinguish oaks from maples, poplars from chestnuts, and so on. These can evolve into walks in each season to observe changes, find favorite fallen logs and see what happens to them, notice nests for birds when the leaves have fallen. As the child is older there can be a wildflower book brought along, a tree book, or a bird book with binoculars.

3. Any vacation is always a time for enormous visual learning. It will get the child outdoors, into museums, playing sight games out the car window, seeing the tall ceilings of airports or train stations, viewing out windows, walking down unfamiliar streets, and noticing changes in climate, architecture, and lifestyles.

4. Trips in the car just to karate or music lessons can be used to teach the child to look out car windows, read street signs, remember the directions, find landmarks, and know how many blocks there are on a particular street and where to turn. The children can direct you back home based on their memory of the way there.

5. Cooking or gardening together will be hands-on/eyes-on fun, as well as teaching the child to cook and garden, which will come in handy later on. One of the best things I ever did was learn to make an organic vegetable garden with my children, book in hand. It was *The Postage Stamp Garden Book* (1999) by Duane and Karen Newcomb, and it taught us how to garden the French intensive way, how to trench and deeply fertilize organically, how to put in borders that would ward off bugs, and how to companion plant to be sure that each vegetable got the best protection from possible pests.

6. Sewing, fixing, or building something together will go a long way to teach things that the schools have cut out, as well as train hands and eyes in visual spatial skills that will later help with science and geometry, mechanics, surgery, or architectural design, not to mention build that performance IQ. There are many young adults now who have no clue how to use a hammer even, not to mention fix a plug, sew and hang a curtain, build a shelf, or bake bread. If parents have projects around the house, it is good to see if a child can be included in order to learn.

7. A regular fitness activity with you or an organized lesson will program that into their lives like brushing their teeth. There is research showing that children who play sports have less nearsightedness than those who do not. It could be a team sport, walks after dinner every night, yoga with a video tape every morning in the living room, or getting to the tennis court regularly with a lesson for the child, as well as a game for the parents. There are also the activities of swimming, skiing, ping-pong, badminton, ice-skating, roller-skating, and so on. Whatever works for each of us is part of our children's heritage, and we owe it to them to pass it on and start as young as possible. Olympic skiers have started at four. The same for hockey players. Glenn Doman's students were doing "brachiation" (swinging down a horizontal ladder with help) at two.

8. Trips to the library and reading aloud every night from picture books at first, and then all the children's classics, will build visualization structures for their mind, ingrain good sentence structure and vocabulary, and help children think about all the problems dealt with in the books. Later on, reading plays as a family is also terrific fun for kids. Teaching them to videotape the play if you have or can rent that kind of equipment will be an event they will never forget.

9. Camping trips, if this is something you are up to and you can protect against ticks, will be everything you could want for development: time in nature, learning to cooperate to accomplish many hands-on tasks, enjoying the fun of a campfire, and seeing the stars that can no longer be seen in the city. Bring a tree book, a star book, and a wildflower book along. When I was eight on a beach in Florida with my Dad, he showed the family what he thought was the Southern Cross constellation. He wasn't even in the right hemisphere we learned later, but the romance of seeing stars will always be with us.

10. Rainy days are opportunities for "flow" and learning. Working with hands-on building toys, perception activities, and arts and crafts takes only a little coaching and setting up and an efficient place to store the materials. Teaching card games, dominoes, checkers, and board games on rainy weekend afternoons and one

planned evening a week is one of the best gifts you can give to your children. These activities will build intelligence, perception skills, memory, and friendship with you. Children do not learn these things early or often on their own.

We are given these eager and beautiful children as gifts and responsibilities. They do not need a roomful of commercial toys. They do not need a million lessons. They do not need fancy clothes. They do not need little league unless they love it. They must *not* have their own TV or computer. They do need us. They need us to have adventures with them as they play and explore inner and outer space, building their imaginations, building their heart brains and their head brains, building their space worlds, and building their vision.

NOTES

1. Visit HeartMath LLC, at www.heartmath.com.

2. Further information about vision and nutrition can be found in the following sources: Marc Grossman, OD, LA, and Genn Swartwout, OD, *Natural Eye Care: An Encyclopedia* (Los Angeles: Keats Publishing, 1999); Richard Kavner, *Your Child's Vision* (New York: Simon and Schuster, 1985), 148–171 (try Amazon or the library); Orfield Monograph, *Experiences with Nutrition and Vision,* available from orfieldmonograph@yahoo.com.

REFERENCES

Agarwal R. S. 1986 ed. *Yoga of perfect sight: With letters of Sri Aurobindo*, Sri Aurobindo, Pondicherry, India: Ashram Trust.

Alexander, F. Mathias. 1984. *The use of the self.* CA: Center Line Press by arrangement with Q. P. Dutton, Downey. (Originally published in 1932.)

Allen, Mary B. 1976. Lecture at the National Institutes of Health.

American Optometric Association, principal author Scheiman, Mitchell, revised, 1997, Pediatric Eye and Vision Exam (Clinical Practice Guideline 2), St. Louis, MO.

American Optometric Association, principal author Garzia, Ralph, 2000. *Optometric Clinical Practice Guidelines: Care of the patient with learning related vision problems,* St. Louis, MO.

American Optometric Association News. Feb 25, 2002. Researchers find new photoreceptor and visual system in the eye, 40, 16: 1,10.

Amillard, A., A. Berthoz, and F. Claroc, eds. 1988. *Posture and gait: Development adaptation and modulation.* New York: Elsevier Science Publishers, B.V. (Biomedical Division), 155.

Anderson, Daniel R., and Tiffany Penpek. 2005. Television and very young children. Special issue, Electronic media use in the lives of infants, *American Behavioral Scientist* 48(5): 505–522.

AOA News. 2006. "Making the grade: An analysis of state and federal children's vision care policy." August 14.

Apell, Richard, and R. C. Lowry. 1959. *Preschool vision.* St. Louis, MO: American Optometric Association.

Armstrong, Thomas. 1995. *The myth of the ADD child: 50 ways to improve your child's behavior and attention span without drugs, labels, or coercion.* New York: A Dutton Book.

Atzmon, D., P. Nemet, A. Ishay, and E. Karni. 1993. A randomized prospective masked and matched comparative study of orthoptic treatment versus conventional reading tutoring treatment for reading disabilities in 62 children. *Binocular Vision and Eye Muscle Surgery Quarterly* 8(2): 91–103.

The Autism Research Institute. 2005. Autism is treatable! Science-based effective treatments. *Dan! Conference Proceedings*, April 14–17. Boston, MA. Available at www.autismresearchinstitute.com.

Ayres, Jean. 1979. *Sensory integration and the child.* Los Angeles, CA: Western Psychological Services.

Balfanz, R., and N. Legers. 2001. How many central city high schools have a severe dropout problem? Paper presented at the *National Conference on Dropouts in America*, January. Cambridge, MA: Harvard University.

Barber, Anne, ed. 2000. *Optometry's role in juvenile delinquency remediation.* Series: Behavioral Aspects of Vision Care, vol. 41, no. 3. Santa Ana, CA: Optometric Extension Program.

Barnard, A. 2000. *Boston Globe.* Study links school breakfasts, results. Nov. 29.

Bassi, C. J., and S. Lehmkuhle. 1990. Clinical implications of parallel visual pathways. *Journal of the American Optometric Association* 61: 98–110.

Bates, William H. 1940/1981. *The Bates method for better eyesight without glasses.* New York: Owl / Henry Holt.

Beach, G., and R. S. Kavner. 1977. Conjoint therapy: A cooperative psycho-therapeutic optometric approach to therapy. *Journal of the American Optometric Association* 48, 12: 1500–07.

Beck, Joan. 1967. *How to raise a brighter child: The case for early learning.* New York: Trident Press.

Bell, Rachel, and Howard Peiper. 1997. *The ADD and ADHD diet.* East Canaan, CT: Safe Goods.

Bernard, Sally, Albert Enayati, Heidi Roger, Lynn Redwood, and Teresa Binstock. 2002. Autism: Mercury poisoning by thimerosal injections. In *Children with starving brains,* ed. Jacquelyn McCandless. Canada: Bramble Books.

Bernard, Sally, Albert Enayati, Lynn Redwood, Heidi Roger, and Teresa Binstock. April 2001. A novel form of mercury poisoning. *Medical Hypotheses* 56(4): 462–71.

Binocular Vision and Eye Muscle Surgery Quarterly, Editors' report of the annual meeting of the American Academy of Ophthalmology, December 1994.

Birch, H. G., and J. D. Gusaw. 1970. *Disadvantaged Children: Health, Nutrition, and School Failure.* New York: Harcourt, Brace, and World.

Bircher-Benner, M. 1977. *Raw fruits and vegetables book.* New Canaan, CT: Keats Publishing.

Birnbaum, Martin H. 1978. Functional relationship between myopia, accommodative stress and against-the-rule astigmia: A hypothesis. *Journal of the American Optometric Association* 49(8): 911–14.

Birnbaum, Martin H. 1984. Nearpoint visual stress: A physiological model. *Journal of the American Optometric Association* 55, 11(1/84): 825–35.

Birnbaum, Martin H. 1985. Nearpoint visual stress: Clinical implications. *Journal of the American Optometric Association* 56, 6: 480–90.

Birnbaum, Martin H. 1993. *Optometric management of nearpoint vision disorders.* Boston: Butterworth Heinemann.

Birnbaum, Martin H. 1990 . The use of stress reduction concepts and techniques in vision therapy. *Journal of Behavioral Optometry* 1, 1: 3–7.

Blakeslee, S. 1993. Seeing and imagining: Clues to the workings of the mind's eye. *Science Times* (Aug 31, 1993): C1 and C7.

Bonnett, O. T. 1994. *Confessions of A Healer.* Aspen, CO: MacMurray and Beck, 81–100.

Boston Globe. 2005. Lead levels. November 17.

Bowan, M. D. 1996. Stress and eye: New speculations on refractive error. *Journal of Behavioral Optometry* 7, 5: 115–22.

Boyce, P. R., C. Hunter, and O. Howlet. 2003. The benefits of daylight through windows. Capturing the Daylight Dividends Program, Troy, NY. Available at www.lrc.rpi .edu/programs/daylighting/pdfDaylightBenefits.pdf.

Boyce, Rensberger. 1985. *Washington Post.* Nerve cells redo wiring, report says: Neurons branch out, change contacts. June 10.

Bradley, Jeffrey. June 2006. Psychotherapist in Milton, Massachusetts, phone interview.

Brannan, Julie R., Harold Solan, Anthony Ficarra, and Editha Ong (1998), *Optometry and Vision Science,* 75 (4) April, 279–283.

Cantin, Marc and Genest, Jacques. 1986. The heart as an endocrine gland, *Scientific American* 254, 76.

Calvin, William. 1990. *The cerebral symphony: Seashore reflections on the structure of consciousness.* New York: Bantam Books.

Carr, W. K., and A. W. Francke. 1976. Culture and the development of vision. *Journal of the American Optometric Association* 47(1): 14–41.

Cassin, A., and J. A. Miller. January 2002. ESEA legislation passes, & Key provisions of the 'No Child Left Behind Act,' printed in federal Title I Report, vol. 4, no. 1.

Caunt, Jim. 2006. Personal conversations and phone interview. January and May.

CDC, 2007. Morbidity and mortality weekly report: Autism prevalence report. Available from information@autism.org.

Ciuffreda, Kenneth, D. Levi, and A. Selenow. 1991. *Amblyopia: Basic and clinical aspects.* Boston: Butterworth-Heinemann.

Ciuffreda, Kenneth. 2001. The efficacy of and scientific basis for optometric vision therapy in non-strabismic accommodative and vergence disorders. Excerpt from AOA final report. Presented at the conference *An Educational Barrier We Can Actually Eliminate: Visual Problems of Children in Poverty and Their Interference with Learning,* April 4. Harvard Graduate School of Education.

Cohen, Allen H., et al. 1986/1987. Future of vision development/performance task force special report: The efficacy of optometric vision therapy. *Journal of the American Opometric Association* 59(2): 95–105.

Cohen, Allen H. 1988. The efficacy of vision therapy, *Journal of the American Optometric Association* 59(2): 88.

Cohen, Allen H., and L. D. Rein. 1992. The effect of head trauma on the visual system: The doctor of optometry as a member of the rehabilitation team. Head trauma issue, *Journal of the American Optometric Association,* August.

Cohen, Allen H. 1992. Optometric management of binocular dysfunctions secondary to head trauma: Case reports. Head trauma issue, *Journal of the American Optometric Association,* August.

Cohen, Allen H. 1992. Optometric rehabilitation of the closed head trauma patient. Lecture at *North East Congress of Optometry*, October 25. Bedford, MA.

Cohen, A., S. Lieberman, M. Stolzberg, and J. Ritty. 1985. The NYSOA screening battery. *American Journal of Optometry and Physiological Optics* 62(3): 165–8.

Cohen, Don. 2006. The Mathman: Don's materials. Available at www.shout.net/~mathman.

Cohen, Don. 2006. Calculus by and for young people (ages 7, yes 7 and up). Available at www.shout.net/~mathman.

Cook, David L. 1992. *When your child struggles: The myths of 20/20 vision.* Atlanta, GA: Invision Press.

Cool, S. J. 1988. The roots of illiteracy in developmental neurobiology. Presentation at *COVD/OEP Conference: A Cooperative Attack on Illiteracy*, Oct. Santa Ana, CA: Optometric Extension Program.

Cool, S. J. 1993. Behavioral/functional optometry: A blending of biochemistry and psychoneuroimmunology; Mental representation and visual perception. Two lectures presented at the *23rd Annual Meeting of the College of Optometrists in Vision Development*, November. Chicago, IL.

Cool, S. J. 1993. The traditional "medical" model of practice + the "recent" psychoneuroimmunological model + behavioral/functional optometric practice. Audio tape of Skeffington memorial lecture presented in August in Keystone, CO.

Cool, S., and E. L. Smith, eds. 1977. Gesell Institute paper. In *Frontiers in Visual Science: Proceedings of the University of Houston College of Optometry Dedication Symposium*, March. Houston, TX.

Cooper, S., D. P. Yolton, M. Kaminiski, A. McClain, and R. Yolton R. 1993. Effects of vitamin and mineral nutriture on systemic and visual function: A review. *Journal of Behavioral Optometry* 4(1): 3–14.

Costanza, M. A. 1994. Visual and ocular symptoms related to the use of visual display terminals. *Journal of Behavioral Optometry* 5(2): 31–6.

Coulter, Catherine. 2001. *Homeopathic sketches of children's types.* Bethesda, MD: Ninth House Publishing.

Cousens, Gabriel, with Tree of Life Chefs. 2003. *Rainbow green live food cuisine.* Berkley, CA: North Atlantic Books.

COVD, OEP, and PAVE. 2002. Learning disabilities: The visual connection, January 31.

Crewther, J., S. G. Nathan, D. P. Crewther, and P. M. Kiely. 1984. Effects of retinal image degradation on ocular growth in cats. *Investigative Ophthalmology and Vision Science* 25(11): 1300–6.

Cromie, William J. 1996. Mind's eye is discovered. *Harvard University Gazette* 91, 15: 1, 8.

Cromie, William J. 2006. When the blues keep you awake, blue light can set your biological rhythms. *Harvard University Gazette* 101, 15: 1, 8.

Csikszentimihalyi, Mihaly. 1990. *Flow: The psychology of optimal experience.* New York: Harper & Row.

Csikszentimihalyi, Mihaly. 1994. Flow: The psychology of optimal experience. Audio cassettes. A Nightengale Conant Production, New York: Simon & Schuster.

Damari, D. A., J. Liu, and K. B. Smith. 2000. Visual disorders misdiagnosed as ADHD: Case studies and literature review. *Journal of Behavioral Optometry* 11(4): 87–91.

Darwin, K. 1982. The cause and effect of visual training on the vergence system. *American Journal of Optometry and Physiological Optics* 59(3): 223–7.

Davis, Adelle. 1959/1981/2001. *Let's Have Healthy Children*. New York: Harcourt, Brace & World.

Davis and McCall 1990 study; Applebee et al. 1987 study. Cited in Center for the Study of Reading, Children's Research Center. 1993. *The at risk dilemma: A synthesis of reading research*. Champaign, IL.

Dawkins, Hazel Richmond, Ellis Edelman, and Constantine Forkiotis. 1990. *Suddenly successful student*. Santa Ana, CA: Optometric Extension Program.

Dawkins, Hazel Richmond, Ellis Edelman, and Constantine Forkiotis. 1991. *Suddenly successful student*. Santa Ana, CA: Optometric Extension Program.

Delacato, Carl H. 1961. *The treatment and prevention of reading problems: The neuropsychological approach*. Springfield, IL: Charles C. Thomas.

Delacato, Carl. 1970. *A new start for a child with reading problems: manual for parents*, David McKay.

DeMille, Richard. 1967. *Put your mother on the ceiling: Children's imagination games*. New York: Walker Company.

Dennison, Paul. 2004. *The Dynamic Brain*. Private circulation.

Dennison, Paul, and Gail Dennison. 1989. *Brain gym teachers' edition*. Ventura, CA: Edu-Kinesthetics, Inc.

Developmental Delay Resources. 2006. *New Developments* 2(3).

Doman, Glenn, 1964. *How to teach your baby to read*. New York: Random House.

Doman, Glenn. 1993. *How to teach your baby*. Philadelphia: Gentle Revolution Books.

Doman, Glenn, 1998. *What to do about your brain injured child*. Philadelphia: Better Baby Press.

Doman, Glenn, Douglas Doman, and Bruce Hagy. 1988. *How to teach your baby to be physically superb: Birth to six*. Philadelphia: Better Baby Press.

Doman, Glenn, and Janet Doman. 2006. *How smart is your baby? Develop and nurture your newborn's full potential*. Philadelphia: Gentle Revolution Books.

Duckman, R., and T. Festinger. 2000. Seeing and hearing: Vision and audiology status of foster children in New York City. *Journal of Behavioral Optometry* 11: 59–67.

Duckman, R., and T. Festinger. 2001. Delivery of vision care to children in foster care placements in New York City. Paper presented at the Harvard Graduate School of Education conference, *An Educational Barrier We Can Actually Eliminate: Visual Problems of Children in Poverty and Their Interference with Learning*, April 4. Printed in the *Journal of Optometric Vision Development* 33(2).

Duke-Elder, S. W. 1942. *The textbook of ophthalmology*. Vol. 2. St. Louis: C. V. Mosby.

Dwyer, P. 1992. The prevalence of vergence and accommodation disorders in a school-age population. *Clinical and Experimental Optometry* 75(1): 10–7.

Dzik, D. 1996. Vision and the juvenile delinquent. *Journal of the American Optometric Association*, 461–8.

Edwards, M. H., S. S. F. Leung, and W. T. K. Lee. 1996. Do variations in normal nutrition play a role in the development of myopia? *Optometry and Vision Science* 73(10): 638–42.

Eklind, David. 2006. *Boston Globe*. The hidden power of play. October 9.

Eklund, N. H., P. R. Boyce, and S. N. Simpson. 2000. *Lighting and sustained performance: Sustained performance under three lighting installations*. Palo Alto, CA: EPRI.

Engelmann, Siegfried, and Therese Engelmann. 1966. *Give your child a superior mind: A program for the preschool child.* New York: Simon and Schuster.

Environmental Health Coalition of Western Massachusetts, (n.d.) *The hidden dangers of fragrances,* a pamphlet.

Farrar, R., M. Call, and W. C. Maples. 2001. A comparison of the visual symptoms between ADD/ADHD and normal children. *Optometry* 72: 441–51.

Fischbach, G. D. 1992. Mind and brain. Special issue on the brain, *Scientific American,* September.

Fischbach, L., D. Lee, R. F. Englehardt, and N. Wheeler. 1993. The prevalence of ocular disorders among Hispanic and Caucasian children screened by the UCLA Mobile Eye Clinic. *Journal of Community Health* 18(4): 201–211.

Fisher, Barbara Loe. 2004. In the wake of vaccines. *Mothering,* November: 38–45.

Forkiotas, C. 1989. Focus on vision. Video tapes from *Annual Gesell Seminar,* New Haven: Frydenborg Productions.

Forrest, Elliot. 1981. *Visual imagery: An optometric approach.* Santa Ana, CA: Optometric Extension Program.

Forrest, Elliot. 1988. *Stress and vision.* Santa Ana, CA: Optometric Extension Program.

Fox, Douglas, April 2, 2002, *New Scientist Print Edition,* Shortsightedness may be tied to refined diet, from Acta Ophthalmologica Scandinavica (vol. 80, p. 125), retrieved from NewSientist.com

Francke, Amiel W. 1975. An autistic, schizophrenic retardate? *Journal of the American Optometric Association* 46, 6: 601–6.

Francke, Amiel W. 1977. Lecture to the Schizophrenia Association of Greater Washington.

Francke, Amiel W., and Walter J. Kaplan. 1978. Easier and more productive study and desk work. *Journal of the American Optometric Association* 49, 8.

Francke, Amiel W. 1988–1989. *Introduction to optometric visual therapy,* Curriculum II. Vol. 60 and 61. Santa Ana, CA: Optometric Extension Program.

Francke, Amiel W. 2003. Syntonic home therapy. Videotaped lecture at the *2003 Syntonic Optometry Conference.* Longmont, CO: Backcountry Productions.

Friedhoffer, A., and M. Warren. 1988. The effect of nearpoint visual demands upon the central visual fields and the effects of nearpoint low plus spheres upon these changes. In *Introduction to optometric visual training,* ed. Amiel Francke. Santa Ana, CA: Optometric Extension Program.

Friedman, N. E., Robert I. Sholtz, and Anthony J. Adams. 1993. Report presented at the American Academy of Optometry meeting, December. Boston, MA.

Fulk, G. W., L. A. Cyert, and D. E. Parker. 2000. A randomized trial of the effect of single vision vs. bifocal lenses on myopia progression in children with esophoria. *Optometry and Vision Science* 71: 579–84.

Furth, Hans. 1986. *Piaget for Teachers,* 2nd ed. Washington, D.C.: C.A.E. Inc.

Furth, Hans, and Harry Wachs. 1974. *Thinking goes to school: Piaget's theory in practice.* New York: Oxford University Press.

Gallop, Steven J. 1994. Myopia reduction: A view from the inside. *Journal of Behavioral Optometry* 5(5): 123–31.

Gallop, Steven J. 1996. Peripheral visual awareness: The central issue. *Journal of Behavioral Optometry,* 7(6): 151–5.

Gallop, Steven J. 2002. *Looking differently at nearsightedness and myopia: The visual process and the myth of 20/20.* Broomall, PA. Published by author.

Gardner, Howard. 1983. *Frames of mind: the theory of multiple intelligences.* New York: Basic Books.

Garzia, Ralph, principal author. 2000. *Care of the patient with learning related vision problems*, AOA booklet.

Garzia, Ralph, ed. 1996. *Vision and reading.* Mosby's optometric problem-solving series. St. Louis, MO: Mosby.

Garzia, R., J. Richman, S. B. Nicholson, and C. S. Games. 1990. A new visual verbal saccade test: The developmental eye movement test (DEM). *Journal of the American Optometric Association*, 62: 124–5.

Garzia R., et al. 2000. Care of the patient with learning related vision problems. *American Optometric Association manual*, June 20.

Gelb, Michael. 1981. *Body learning: An introduction to the Alexander technique.* New York: Delilah, released by Aurum Press, London.

Gesell, Arnold, Frances Ilg, Janet Learned, and Louise Ames. 1943. *Infant and child in the culture of today.* New York: Harper & Row.

Gesell, Arnold. 1949. *Vision: Its development in infant and child.* New York: Paul B. Holber Inc. (Medical Department of Harper & Brothers).

Gesell, Arnold. 1952. *Infant development: The embryology of early human behavior.* New York: Harper & Brothers.

Getman, Gerald. N. 1962. *How to develop your child's intelligence.* A Research Publication. Luverne, MN: The Announcer Press.

Getman, Gerald N., and Streff, John. 1992. *Mommy and Daddy, you can help me learn to see: Help me understand the language of light.* St. Louis: American Foundation for Vision Awareness.

Getzell, Jeffrey. 1995. The eyes have it: A look at behavioral optometry. *TBI Challenge*, Spring: 21–2.

Getzell, Jeffrey. 2006. Telephone interviews, January and May.

Gilman, G, and J. Bergstrand. 1990. Visual recovery following chiropractic intervention. *Journal of Behavioral Optometry* 1(3): 73–4.

Ginsberg, Kenneth R. 2006. The importance of play in promoting healthy child development and maintaining strong parent-child bonds. *American Academy of Pediatrics Annual Report*, October 9, 2006.

Goddard, Sally. 2002. *Reflexes, learning, and behavior: A window into the child's mind.* Eugene, OR: Fern Ridge Press.

Goddard, Sally. 1995. The role of primitive survival reflexes in the development of the visual system. *Journal of Behavioral Optometry* 6(2): 31–5.

Goleman, Daniel. 1985. *New York Times.* New evidence points to growth of the brain even late in life. July 30.

Goss, David A. and Winkler, R. 1983. Progression of myopia in youth; age of cessation. *American Journal of Optometry and Physiological Optics* 60(8): 651–58.

Goss, David A., Michael J. Hampton, and Gary M. Wickham. 1988. Selected review on genetic factors in myopia. *Journal of the American Optometric Association* 59(11): 875–82.

Goss, David A., and T. Grosvenor. 1990. Rates of childhood myopia progression with bifocals as a function of nearpoint phoria: Consistency of three studies. *Optometry and Vision Science* 67: 637–40.

Goss, David A., and Tonya Jackson. 1993. Optometric findings prior to onset of myopia in youth: Zone of clear single binocular vision. Research report presented at the *American Academy of Optometry Meeting*, December. Boston, MA.

Goss, David A., and. E. F. Uyesugi. 1995. Effectiveness of bifocal control of childhood myopia progression as a function of near point phoria and binocular cross cylinder. *Journal of Optometry and Vision Development* 26, 1.

Gottlieb, Ray. n.d. Neuropsychology of myopia. Excerpted from doctoral dissertation, Humanistic Psychology Institute.

Gottlieb, Ray. 2005. *Attention and memory training: Stress point learning on the trampoline: Based on the work of Robert Pepper, OD.* Santa Ana, CA: Optometric Extension Program.

Gottlieb, Ray, and Larry Wallace. 2001. Syntonic phototherapy. *Journal of Behavioral Optometry* 12, 2: 31–8.

Green, P. R. n.d. Axial myopia: Plastic deformation of the sclera? *Proceedings of the Second International Conference on Myopia*, BioMechanics Group, Division of Applied Sciences. Cambridge, MA: Harvard University, 115–24.

Green, P. R. 1980. Mechanical considerations in myopia: Relative effects of accommodation, convergence, and the extraocular muscles. *American Journal Optometry and Physiological Optics* 57(12): 902–4.

Green, P. R. 1981. *Myopia and the extraocular muscles.* Documenta Ophthalmologica Proceedings Series, Vol. 28, ed. H. C. Fledelius, P. H. Alsbirk, and E. Goldschmidt. The Hague: Dr. W. Junk Publishers.

Greenspan, S. A. 1975. A study of near point lenses: Effects on body posture and performance. *An Optometric Extension Program Monograph.* Santa Ana, CA: Optometric Extension Program, 1–17.

Grisham, J. D., and H. D. Simons. 1986. Refractive error and the reading process: A literature analysis. *Journal of the American Optometric Association* 57(1): 44–55.

Groffman, Sidney, and Solan, Harold. 1994. *Developmental and perceptual assessment of learning-disabled children: Theoretical concepts and diagnostic testing.* Santa Ana, CA: Optometric Extension Program.

Grossman, Marc S., and Glenn Swartwout. 1999. *Natural eye care: An encyclopedia.* Los Angeles, CA: Keats Publishing.

Grossman, Marc S., and Vinton McCabe. 2001. *Vision is learned: Research on eye/brain connection.* Los Angeles, CA: Keats Publishing.

Grosvenor, Theodore, David M. Perrigin, Judith Perrigin, and Bernard Maslovitz. 1987. Houston myopia control study: A randomized clinical trial; Part II, final report by the patient care team. *American Journal of Optometry and Physiological Optics* 64(7): 482–496.69b.

Grosvenor, Theodore. 1989. Myopia: What can we do about it clinically? *Optometry and Vision Science* 66(7): 415–9.

Gwiazda, Jane, Frank Thorn, Joseph Bauer, and Richard Held. 1993. Emmetropization and the progression of manifest refraction in children followed from infancy to puberty: MIT study. *Clinical Vision Science* 8(4): 337–44.

Gwiazda, Jane, Frank Thorn, Joseph Bauer, and Richard Held. 1993. Myopic children show insufficient accommodative response to blur. *Investigative Ophthalmology and Vision Science* 34, 3.

Gwiazda, Jane, Joseph Bauer, Frank Thorn, and Richard Held. 1993. Shifts in tonic accommodation after near work are related to refractive errors in children. Paper on the MIT Infant Vision Lab study. Cambridge, MA.

Gwiazda, Jane, Leslie Hyman, Mohamed Hussein, Donald Everett, Thomas Norton, Daniel Kurtz, Cristina M. Leske, Ruth Manny, Wendy Marsh-Tootle, Mitch Scheiman, and the COMET Group. 2003. A randomized clinical trial of progressive addition lenses versus single vision lenses on the progression of myopia in children. *Investigative Ophthalmology and Visual Science* 44(4): 1492–500.

Hainstock, Elizabeth. 1968. *Teaching Montessori in the home.* 5th printing. New York: Random House.

Hannaford, Carla. 1995. *Smart moves: Why learning is not all in your head.* Arlington, VA: Great Ocean Publishers, 147–150.

Hannaford, Carla. 1997. *The dominance factor: How knowing your dominant eye, ear, brain, hand and foot can improve your learning.* Arlington, VA: Great Ocean Publishers.

Hannaford, Carla. 2002. *Awakening the child heart: Handbook for global parenting.* Captain Cook, HI: Jamilla Nur Publishing.

Hannaford, Carla. 2005. *Smart moves: Why learning is not all in your head,* 2nd ed., Salt Lake City, UT: Great River Books.

Hardman, Patricia K., Judith Clary, and Allan Lieberman. 1989. *Journal of the American Optometric Association* 60, 1.

Harmon, D. B. 1957/1958. *Notes on a dynamic theory of vision,* 3rd Rev. Austin, TX. Published by author.

Harp, L. 1995. Study links school productivity to governance: A review of the recommendations of the Consortium on Productivity in the Schools (including more homework). *Education Week,* September 6: 3.

Harris, Gardnerk, and Anahad O'Conner. 2005. *New York Times.* "On autism's cause: It's parents vs. research." June 25.

Harris, Paul. 1989. The prevalence of visual conditions in a population of juvenile delinquents. *Journal of Behavioral Optometry* 61(4): 1–24.

Harris, Paul. 1995. Current thoughts on the neurology of vision. *Journal of Optometry and Vision Development* 26(1), Spring 1995.

Harris, Paul. 2000. The Baltimore inner city in-school vision treatment project: Preliminary results for learning. Presented at the conference *An Educational Barrier We Can Actually Eliminate: Visual Problems of Children in Poverty and Their Interference with Learning,* April 4. Harvard Graduate School of Education.

Harris, Paul. 2002. Learning related vision problems in Baltimore City: A long-term program, *Journal of Optometry and Vision Development* 33(2): 75–115.

Harvey, Erin, Velma Dobson, and Joseph Miller. 2006. Prevalence of high astigmatism, eye glass wear, and poor visual acuity among Native American grade school children. *Optometry and Vision Science* 83(4): 206–12.

Healy, J. 1990. *Endangered minds: Why children don't think and what we can do about it.* New York: Simon & Schuster.

Heggie, Jack. 1985. The use of the eyes in movement. Dallas, TX: Woodstone Books.

Heggie, Jack. 1993. Some thoughts on the relationship between: Vision-proprioception-kinesthetics. *Journal of Behavioral Optometry* 4, 4.

Hein, A. 1972. Visually coordinated behavior. *Physical Therapy* 52 (September): 926–34.

Hellerstein, L. F., W. C. Maples, S. Miller, and L. Press. 2001. Optometric guidelines for school consulting. *Journal of Optometry and Vision Development* 32(2): 56–75.

Helmholz, H. 1867. *Handbuch der physiologischen optik*, Vol. 3. Leipzig: Leopold Voss.

Herscu, Paul. 1991. *Homeopathic sketches of children's types*. Berkeley, CA: North Atlantic Books.

Heschong, L., R. W. Wright, and S. Okura. 2002. Daylighting impacts on human performance in school. *Journal of Illuminating Engineering Society* 31: 101–14.

Hirshberg, Laurence, Sufen Chiu, and J. A. Frazier. 2005. Emerging brain-based interventions for children and adolescents: Overview and clinical perspective. *Child and Adolescent Psychiatry Clinics of North America*, 14: 1–19. Reviewed in *The Brown University Child and Adolescent Psychopharmacology Update*. February 2005. Providence, RI: Manisses Communications Group, Inc.

Hoffman, Lou G. 1982. The effect of accommodative deficiencies on the development level of perceptual skills. *American Journal of Optometry and Physiological Optics* 59(552): 4–9.

Hoffman, Lou G. 1985. Incidence of vision difficulties in children with learning disabilities. *Journal of the American Optometric Association* 56: 560–2.

Hoffman, Lou G., and Michael Rouse. 1980. Referral recommendations for binocular functions and/or developmental perceptual deficiencies. *Journal of the American Optometric Association* 51(2): 119–26.

Hokoda, S. C. 1985. General binocular dysfunctions in an urban optometry clinic. *Journal of the American Optometry Association* 56: 560–2.

Hoopes, Ann, and Townsend Hoopes. 1979. *Eye power: The first report on visual training*. New York: Alfred Knopf.

Hubel, David H. and Wiesel Torsten N., 2005, *Brain and visual perception*, New York: Oxford University Press.

Hung, L., and E. Smith. 1996. Extended-wear, soft, contact lenses produce hyperopia in young monkeys. *Optometry and Vision Science* 73(9): 579–84.

Hung, L., Crawford M. L. J., and Smith, E. 1995. Spectacle lenses alter eye growth and the refractive status of young monkeys. *Nature Medicine* 1(8): 761–5.

Huxley, Aldous. 1982. *The art of seeing*. Berkeley, CA: Creative Arts Book Company. Originally published by Harper & Row in 1942.

Ifland, Joan. 1999/2000. *Sugars and flours: How they make us crazy, sick and fat and what to do about it*. 1st Books Library at www1stbooks.com.

Ingersoll, Steve. 2005. Smart Schools: A visually based education model; Critical role of oculomotor function on cognitive style; Hyperactivity and attention deficits as anomalies of visual development; Reading failure and visual development; Writing, math, and vision; Smart School's approach to reading instruction and various education problems. Lectures given at the 65th Annual Northeast Congress of Optometry, September 18 and 19. Worcester. MA. Optometric Extension Program.

Jackson, Maggie. 2005. *Boston Sunday Globe*. Don't let TV be the baby sitter. July 17, Boston Works.

Jacobs, J., L. M. Jimenez, S. Gloyd, J. Gale, and D. Crothers. 1994. Treatment of acute childhood diarrhea with homeopathic medicine. *Pediatrics* 93: 719–25.

Johnson, C. A., R. E. Post, L. M. Chalupa, and T. J. Lee. 1982. Monocular deprivation in humans: A study of identical twins. *Investigative Ophthalmology and Visual Science* 23, l.

Johnson, R. A., R. J. Blair, and J. Zaba. 2000. The visual screening of Title I reading students. *Journal of Behavioral Optometry* 11(1): 3–6.

Johnson, R., and J. N. Zaba. 1999. The visual screening of adjudicated adolescents. *Journal of Behavioral Optometry* 10(1): 12–7.

Johnson, Susan R. 2005. Does early reading contribute to attention and learning difficulties in our children? *Renewal: A Journal of Waldorf Education* (spring–summer): 22–4.

Johnson-Brown, Stephanie, Ronald E. Kimmons, Robert Cienkus, and Sharon Daluga. 2001. Review of an eight-year program to incorporate vision therapy in a remedial reading program in a school setting. *Journal of Optometric Vision Development*, 32(Fall): 142–52. Presented at the conference *An Educational Barrier We Can Actually Eliminate: Visual Problems of Children in Poverty and Their Interference with Learning*, April 4, 2001. Harvard Graduate School of Education.

Kandel, E., and R. Hawkins. 1992. The biological basis of learning and individuality. *Scientific American* (September): 79–86.45.

Kaplan M. 1979. *Vertical yoked prisms*. Duncan, Oklahoma: Optometric Extension Program, Inc.

Kaplan, Melvin. 2006. *Seeing through new eyes: Changing the lives of children with autism, Asperger's syndrome, and other developmental disabilities through vision therapy*. London and Philadelphia: Jessica Kingsley Publishers.

Kaplan, Robert Michael. 1987. *Seeing beyond 20/20*. Hillsboro, OR: Beyond Words.

Kaplan, Robert Michael. 1995. *The power behind your eyes*. Rochester, VT: Inner Traditions.

Kasamatsu, T. 1982. Enhancement of neuronal plasticity by activating the norepinephrine system in the brain: a remedy for amblyopia. *Human Neurobiology* 1: 49–54.

Kasamatsu, T. 1987. Norepinephrine hypothesis for visual cortical plasticity: Thesis, antithesis, and recent development. *Current Topics in Devlopmental Biology* 21: 367–89.

Kaseno, S. L. 1985. The visual anatomy of the juvenile delinquent. *Academic Therapy* 21(1): 99–105.

Kattouf and Steele. n.d. Visual perceptual skills in low income and rural children. *Journal of Optometry and Vision Development* 31, 2: 71–5.

Kavner, Richard S. 1985. *Your Child's Vision*. New York: Simon and Schuster, 148–171.

Kavner, Richard S., and Lorraine Dusky. 1978. *Total Vision*. New York: A&W Publishers.

Kelder, Peter. 1998. *Ancient Secret of the Fountain of Youth*. New York: Bantam Books.

Kennedy, Robert F., Jr. 2005. Deadly immunity. *Rolling Stone*, June 30–July 14, 57–66.

Kilham, Christopher S. 1998. *The Five Tibetans: Five dynamic exercises for health, energy, and personal power*. Book 1. New York: Doubleday Dell.

Kirby, David. 2005. *Evidence of Harm*. New York: St. Martin's Press, 173.

Kohler, Amy Orfield. 1999. *Dance movement therapy with applied behavior analysis for children with autism: A valuable combination.* Available from wdainc1@yahoo.com.

Kosslyn, S., et al. 1993. Visual mental imagery activates topographically organized visual cortex: PET Investigations. *Journal of Cognitive Neuroscience* 5(3): 236–87.

Krumholz, I. 2000. Results from a pediatric vision screening and its ability to predict academic performance. *Optometry* 71(7): 426–30.

Kuller, R., and C. Lindstren. 1992. Health and behavior of children in classrooms with and without windows. *Journal of Environmental Psychology* 12: 305–17.

Kulp, M. 1999. Relationship between visual motor integration skills and academic performance in kindergarten through third grade. *Optometry and Vision Science* 76: 159–63.

Landrigan, Philip J., Herbert L. Needleman, and Mary Landrigan. 2001. *Raising healthy children in a toxic world: 101 smart solutions for every family.* Emmaus, PA: Rodale.

Lane, Ben. 1981. Calcium, chromium, protein, sugar, and accommodation in myopia. In H. C. Fledelius, P. H. Alsbirk, and E. Goldschmidt (eds.). Documents Opthalmoligica Proc. Series (Vol. 28, Third International Conerence on Mypia), Copenhagen, The Hague: Dr. W. Junk Publishers, pp. 141–148.

Lane, Ben. 1982. Myopia prevention and reversal: New data confirming the interaction of accommodative stress and deficit-inducing nutrition. *Journal of the International Academy of Preventive Medicine* 7, 10: 17–30.

Lane, Ben. 1994. Nutrition, the glaucomas, and myopia development and reversal. Lectures given at the *Northeast Congress of Optometry*, Oct. 2 and 3. Bedford, MA. Optometric Extension Program.

Langer, Ellen J. 1997. *The power of mindful learning.* New York: Addison Wesley.

Lansky, Amy L. 2003. *Impossible cure: The promise of homeopathy.* California: RL Ranch Press.

Lansky, Amy L. 2006. The hope of homeopathy. Special autism edition, *Mothering*, January–February.

Larson, Gena. 1972. *Better food for better babies.* New Canaan, CT: Keats Publishing, Inc.

Leber, L., and T. A. Wilson. 1993. Myopia reduction training with a computer-based behavioral technique: A preliminary report. *Journal of Behavioral Optometry* 4(4): 87–92.

Leeds, Joshua. 2001. *The power of sound.* Rochester, VT: Healing Arts Press.

Lerner, Patricia S. 2006. How recent changes have contributed to an epidemic of autism spectrum disorders. *Journal of Behavioral Optometry* 17(3): 72–7.

Lenn, N. 1993. Psychoneuroimmunology lectures at the Western States Congress.

Levin, Myron. 2005. *Los Angeles Times.* Memo warned of mercury in shots, retrieved from the Freedom of Information Center. Feb. 8.

Leventhal, T., and J. Brooks-Gunn. 2000. The neighborhoods they live in: The effects of neighborhood residence on child and adolescent outcomes. *Psychological Bulletin* 26(2): 3090–337.

Liberman, Jacob. 1991. *Light: Medicine of the future.* Santa Fe, NM: Bear & Company.

Liberman, Jacob. 1992/1993. Lectures given at the *Conference on Light and Vision.* College of Syntonic Optometry.

Liberman, Jacob. 1995. *Take off your glasses and see*. New York: Three Rivers Press (Crown).

Linde, K., N. Clausius, G. Ramirez, D. Melchart, F. Eitel, L. Hedges, and W. Jonas. 1997. Are clinical effects of homeopathy placebo effects? A meta-analysis of placebo-controlled trials. *The Lancet* 250: 834–43.

Logan, L., B. Gauer, and R. L. Yolton. 1993. Learning problems and juvenile delinquency: A review. *Canadian Journal of Optometry* 55(2): 101–5.

Louv, Richard. 2005. *Last child in the woods: Saving our children from nature deficit disorder*. Chapel Hill, N.C., Algonquin Books of Chapel Hill.

Louv, Richard. 2006. The nature child reunion, *National Wildlife*, special issue: Why nature is good for your mind and body, June/July, National Wildlife Federation. 22–30.

Lovegrove, W., F. Martin, and W. Slahius. 1986. A theoretical and experimental case for a visual deficit in specific reading disability. *Cognitive Neuropsychology* 3: 225–67.

MacDonald, Lawrence W. 1993. *The collected works*, Vol. 2 (1968–1979), ed. Ira Schwartz and Abraham Shapiro. Santa Ana, CA: Optometric Extension Program.

Magaziner, Allan, Linda Bovie, and Anthony Zolezzi. 2003. Chemical free kids: How to safeguard your child's diet and environment, New York City: Twin Streams.

Maino, Dominic. 2005. Editorial. *Optometry and Vision Development* 36, 2.

Manzo, K. K. 2002. Some educators see reading rules as too restrictive. *Education Week*, February 20, 1: 22.

Maples, W. C. 1996. Visual profile of the Navajos. *Journal of Behavioral Optometry* 7: 59–64.

Maples, W. C. 2000. Test retest reliability of the College of Optometrists in vision development quality of life outcomes assessment. *Optometry* 71: 579–84.

Maples, W. C. 2001. A comparison of visual abilities, race, and socio-economic factors as predictors of academic achievement. *Journal of Behavioral Optometry* 12(3): 60–5.

Maples, W. C. 2001. Optometry's paradigm shift. *Journal of the American Optometric Association* 72(9): 567–9.

Maples, W. C. 2001. Visual factors more significant than socio-economic and cultural factors as a predictor of school success in Northeastern, Oklahoma rural, Native American and Caucasian population. Presented at the conference *An Educational Barrier We Can Actually Eliminate: Visual Problems of Children in Poverty and Their Interference with Learning*, April 4. Harvard Graduate School of Education.

Maples, W. C. 2002. Test-retest reliability of the College of Optometrists in vision development quality of life outcomes assessment short form. *Journal of Optometry and Vision Development* 33: 126–34.

March of Dimes. Five tips for a healthier baby. Printed reminder card distributed by the March of Dimes.

Mark, Vernon H., with Jeffrey P. Mark. 1989. *Brain power: A neurosurgeon's complete program to maintain and enhance brain fitness throughout your life*. Boston: Houghton Mifflin Company.

Marrone, A. 1991. Peripheral awareness. *Journal of Behavioral Optometry* 2(1): 7–11.

Marusich, Carol. 2002. Integration of primitive reflexes: Why should I care? A CD from a lecture at the *COVD Conference* in Fort Lauderdale. Santa Ana, CA: Optometric Extension Program.

Masgutova, Svetlana, Nelly Akhmatova, and Svetlana Goncharova. 1998/2003. *Integration of dynamic and postural reflexes into whole body movement system: Educational kinesiology approach.* Moscow and Warsaw.

Masgutova, Svetlana. 2003. *Integration of dynamic and postural reflexes.* Warsaw, Poland: International Neurokinesiology Institute of Movement Development and Reflexes Integration.

Masgutova, Svetlana. 2004. Integration of dynamic and postural reflexes into whole body movement system. Course on the neurokinesiology of reflexes, Level 1, February 5–8.

Mayor, Tracy. 2005. Autism in America. *Child,* November, 171–80.

McCandless, Jaquelyn. 2002. *Children with starving brains: A medical treatment guide for autism spectrum disorder.* Canada: Bramble Books.

Mitchell Scheiman, Lynn Mitchell, Susan Cotter, Jeffrey Cooper, Marjean Kulp, Michael Rouse, Eric Borsting, Richard London, Janice Wensveen (2005)for the Convergence Insufficiency Treatment Trial (CITT) Study Group, "A Randomized Clinical Trial of Treatments for Convergence Insufficieny in Children," *Archives of Ophthalmology,* January; 123 (1):14–24.

Moore, B. 2001. Reforming vision screening and treatment of preschool children in America. Presented at the conference *An Educational Barrier We Can Actually Eliminate: Visual Problems of Children in Poverty and Their Interference with Learning,* April 4. Harvard Graduate School of Education.

Minneapolis Star Tribune. 2001. Tests show fourth grade kids don't read well: Good readers are doing even better, but poor readers are losing ground. April 7.

Moore, Bruce, Stacey A. Lyons, and J. Walline. 1999. A clinical review of hyperopia in young children. *Journal of the American Optometric Association* 70(4): 215–24.

Montessori, Maria. 1967. *The Discovery of the Child.* New York: Ballentine Books.

Moroz, J. M. 2001. A chance to grow optometric services: Summary of results for New Visions School, Available from Bob DeBoer at actg@mail.actg.org.

Mozlin, Rochelle. 2001. Editorial: Baby steps. *Journal of Behavioral Optometry* 12(3): 59.

Mozlin, Rochelle. 2001. Poverty, neurodevelopment, and vision: A demonstration project with an adolescent population. *Journal of Behavioral Optometry* 12(3): 71–4. Presented at the conference *An Educational Barrier We Can Actually Eliminate: Visual Problems of Children in Poverty and Their Interference with Learning,* April 4. Harvard Graduate School of Education.

Mozlin, Rochelle. 2001. The epidemiology of school vision screenings. *Journal of Behavioral Optometry* 13(3): 59–64.

Napear, Peggy. 1974. *Brain child: A mother's diary.* New York: Harper & Row.

National Center for Education Statistics. 1999. *The NAEP 1998 Reading Report Card: National and State Highlights.* Brochure. U.S. Department of Education.

National Center for Educational Statistics. 2001. *Dropout rates in the United States: 2000.* U.S. Department of Education.

National Center for Education Statistics. *Digest of Education Statistics 2000.* U.S. Department of Education, table 158.

National Center for Education Statistics. 2001. *The nation's report card: Fourth grade reading 2000.* U.S. Department of Education.

National PTA Resolution. 1999. Learning related vision problems, education and evaluation. *Journal of Behavioral Optometry* 10: 111.

Navarro, Mireya (October 23, 2005). Parents fret that dialing up interferes with growing up, *New York Times*, Sunday Styles Section 9, 1, 10

Newcomb, Duane G., and Karen Newcomb. 1999. *The postage stamp garden book*. Rev. ed. Holbrook, MA: Adams Media Corp.

Newton, David, interview, June 2006.

Nielson, A. C., Co. 1990. *Nielson report on television, 1990*. Northbrook, IL: Nielsen Media Research. Cited in Hannaford, 1995, *Smart moves*.

Nicholson, S. B., and R. P. Garzia. 1988. Astigmatism at nearpoint: Adventitious, purposeful and environmental influences. *Journal of the American Optometric Association* 59(12): 936–41.

Northrup, Christiane. 2005. *Mother daughter wisdom: Creating a legacy of physical and emotional health*. New York: Bantam Books.

Norton, Thomas, and J. T. Siegwart Jr. 1995. Animal models of emmetropization: Matching axial length to the focal plane. *Journal of the American Optometric Association* 66: 405–14.

Norton, Thomas. 1999. Animal models of myopia: Learning how vision controls the size of the eye. *Institute for Laboratory Animal Research Journal* 40: 59–97.

NOVA. 2005. *Einstein's Big Idea / Ancestors of E= Mc²*, aired on October 11. PBS. Available at www.pbs.org/wgbh/3213_einstein.html.

Ong, E., and K. J. Ciuffreda. 1997. *Accommodation, nearwork, and myopia*. Santa Ana, CA: Optometric Extension Program.

Oppenheimer, Todd. 1997. The computer delusion, *Atlantic Monthly*, July, 45–62.

Optometric Clinical Practice. 1998. *Care of the patient with accommodative and vergence dysfunction*. St. Louis, MO: American Optometric Association.

Optometric Clinical Practice. 2000. *Care of the patient with learning related vision problems*. St. Louis, MO: American Optometric Association.

Optometric Extension Program. *Visual hygiene*. Pamphlet. Santa Ana, CA: Optometric Extension Program Foundation, Inc.

Orfield, Antonia. 1994. Seeing space: Undergoing brain reprogramming to reduce myopia. *Journal of Behavioral Optometry* 5(5): 123–131. Available at www.optometrists.org/Boston.

Orfield, Antonia. 2001. Unpublished study of the Reading Recovery kids at Mather School in fall 2001.

Orfield, Antonia, Basa Frank, and Yun John. 2001. Vision problems of children in poverty in an urban school clinic: Their epidemic numbers, impact on learning, and approaches to remediation. *Journal of Optometry and Vision Development* 32: 114–41. Presented at the conference *An Educational Barrier We Can Actually Eliminate: Visual Problems of Children in Poverty and Their Interference with Learning*, April 4. Harvard Graduate School of Education.

Ornish, Dean. 1990. *Program for reversing heart disease*. New York: Ballantine Books.

Ott, John. 1973. *Health and light*. Old Greenwich, CT: Devin-Adair.

Ott, John. 1982. *Light, radiation, and you: How to stay healthy*. Old Greenwich, CT: Devin.

Padula, William. 1988. *A behavioral approach for persons with physical disabilities*. Santa Ana, CA: Optometric Extension Program.

Painter, Genevieve. 1971. *Teach your baby.* New York: Simon and Schuster.

Pangborn, Jon, and Baker, Sidney MacDonald. 2005. *Autism: Effective biomedical treatments; Individuality in an epidemic.* Boston: DAN!, 10.

Pearce, Joseph Chilton. 1981. *The bond of power.* New York: E. P. Dutton, 6.

Pearce, Joseph Chilton. 1992. *Evolution's end.* San Francisco: Harper San Francisco.

Pearce, Joseph Chilton. 2003. Nurturing the growth stages in pregnancy and beyond. Videotaped lecture to midwives at the *Choices for Children Conference.*

Pearce, Joseph Chilton. 2003. Awakening intelligence: How the brain develops, Parts I and II. Lecture DVDs from *Choices for Children Conference,* February 15.

Pearce, Joseph Chilton. 2003. The optimum learning between children and adults, Parts I and II. Lecture DVDs from *Choices for Children Conference,* February 15. Carbondale, IL: Dayemi Tariqat.

Perricone, Nicholas. 2001. *The wrinkle cure.* New York: Warner Books.

Pert, Candace. 1997. *Molecules of Emotion.* New York: Scribner.

Peters, H. B. 1984. The Orinda study. *American Journal of Optometry and Physiological Optics* 61, 6.

Pines, Maya. 1966/1967. *Revolution in learning: The years from birth to six.* New York: Harper & Row.

Plunkett, Laura, and Linda Weltner. 2006. *The challenge of childhood diabetes.* Available at challengeofdiabetes.com.

Pollen, Michael. 2003. *New York Times Magazine.* The way we live now. October 12, 41–8.

Prevention Magazine Editors. 1984. *Understanding vitamins and minerals.* Emmaus, PA: Rodale.

Ratey, John. 2001. *A user's guide to the brain.* New York: Pantheon Books.

Raviola, E. and Wiesel, Torsten N. 1979. Increase in axial length of the macaque monkey eye after corneal opacification. *Investigative Ophthalmology and Visual Science* 18(12): 1232–1236.

Reichenberg-Ullman, Judyth, and Robert Ullman. 1996. *Ritalin free kids: Safe effective homeopathic medicine for ADD and other behavioral and learning problems.* Rocklin, CA: Prima Publishing.

Reichenberg-Ullman, Judyth, and Robert Ullman. 1999. *Rage-free kids: Homeopathic medicine for defiant, aggressive and violent children.* Rocklin, CA: Prima Publishing.

Reichenberg-Ullman, Judyth, Robert Ullman, and Ian Luepker. 2005. *A drug-free approach to Asperger syndrome and autism: Homeopatic care for exceptional kids.* Edmonds, WA: Picnic Point Press.

Reisan, Austen. 1961. Stimulation as a requirement for growth and function in behavioral development. In *Function of Varied Experiences,* ed. D. W. Fiske and S. R. Maddi. Homewood, IL: Dorsey.

Reynolds, Gretchen. 2006. *New York Times.* A little flabby around the eyeballs: Why some are claiming your vision is the next thing that could use a good workout. February 5, Play section.

Robbins, Jim. 1996. Wired for miracles? *Psychology Today,* March/April.

Robbins, Jim. 1998. Wired for miracles? Neurofeedback therapy, *Psychology Today,* May/June, l998

Roca, P. D. 1971. Ocular manifestations of whiplash injuries. Paper presented at the *Fifteenth Annual Conference of the American Association of Auto Medicine*, October 20–24. Colorado Springs, CO.

Roll, J. P., and R. Roll. 1988. From eye to foot: A proprioceptive chain involved in postural control. In *Posture and gait: development adaptation and modulation*, ed. A. Amillard, A. Berthoz, and F. Claroc. New York: Elsevier Science Publishers, B.V. (Biomedical Division), 155.

Rosborough, Pearl M. 1963. *Physical fitness and the child's reading problems: A report on a technical study of twenty "problem readers," their physical handicaps, and therapy*. An Exposition University Book. New York: Exposition Press.

Rosenfield, M. 1994. Accommodation and myopia: Are they really related? *Journal of Behavioral Optometry* 5(1): 3–11.

Rosenfield, M., K. Ciuffreda, and L. Novogrodsky. 1992. Contribution of accommodation and disparity-vergence to transient nearwork-induced myopic shifts. *Ophthalmology and Physiological Optics* 12(October): 433–6.

Rosner, J., and J. Rosner. 1986. Some observations of the relationship between the visual perceptual skills development of young hyperopes and age of first lens correction. *Clinical Experimental Optometry* 69: 166–8.

Rosner, J., and J. Rosner. 1987. Comparison of visual characteristics of children with and without learning difficulties. *American Journal of Optometry and Physiological Optics*, 64: 531–3.

Ross, Jolene. 2005–2006. Interviews during neurotherapy treatments. October through January.

Rousse, M. W., et al. 1999. Frequency of convergence insufficiency among fifth and sixth graders. *Optometry and Vision Science*, 76, 9: 643–9.

Russek, L. B., and G. E. Schwartz. 1994. Interpersonal heart-brain registration and the perception of parental love: A 52 year follow-up of the Harvard mastery of stress study. *Subtle Energies* 5(3): 195–208. Reviewed in Hannaford, 2002, *Awakening the Child heart*, 40–1.

Sacks, Oliver. 2006. A neurologist's notebook: Stereo Sue. *The New Yorker*, June 19, 64–73.

Santacreu, J. 1995, A health psychology-based rationale for the prevention of myopia. *Journal of Behavioral Optometry* 96(6): 147–150.

Scharre J. E., Creedon M. P. 2002. Assessment of visual function in autistic children, *Optometry and Vision Science* 69: 433–9.

Scheiman, Mitchell, et al. 1990. Vision characteristics of individuals identified as Irlen Filter candidates. *Journal of the American Optometric Association* 61: 600–4.

Scheiman, Mitchell M., and Michael W. Rouse, eds. 1994. *Optometric Management of Learning-Related Vision Problems*. St. Louis: Mosby.

Scheiman, Mitchell, Susan Cotter, et al., 2005. A randomized clinical trial for treatments of convergence insufficiency in children. *Archives of Ophthalmology*, January.

Scheiman, Mitchell, M. Gallway, and R. Coulter. 1996. Prevalence of vision and ocular disorders in a clinical pediatric population. *Journal of the American Optometric Association* 67: 193–202

Schmitt, Walter H. 2005. *The uplink: Merging contemporary chiropractic neurology and nutritional biochemistry in the tradition of applied kinesiology*, 35, summer.

Schore, Allan N. 1994. *Affect regulation and the origin of self: The neurobiology of emotional development*. Hillsdale, NJ: Lawrence Erlbaum.

Schulman, Randy. 1994. Optometry's role in the treatment of autism. *Journal of Optometric Vision Development*, winter.

Science Daily. 2000. Press release: Ophthalmologist discovers relationship between eye condition and attention deficit hyperactivity disorder.

Seiderman, Arthur S. 1980. Optometric vision therapy: Results of a demonstration project with a learning disabled population. *Journal of the American Optometric Association* 5(5): 80.

Seiderman, Arthur S., and Steven E. Marcus. 1989. *20/20 is not enough: The new world of vision*. New York: Alfred A. Knopf.

Selye, H. 1976. *The stress of life*. Rev. ed. New York: McGraw-Hill.

Shankman, Al. 1988. *Vision enhancement training*. Santa Ana, CA: Optometric Extension Program.

Sharp, Evelyn. 1969. *Thinking is child's play*. New York: Avon Books.

Shatz, Carla J. 1992. The developing brain. *Scientific American*, September, 61–7.

Sherman, A. 1993. Clinical management of the myopic patient. *Journal of Behavioral Optometry* 4, 1.

Shinaur, E. 1975. *The malnourished mind*. Garden City, NY: Anchor Books.

Shipman, Virginia I., 1954, The Restriction of the perceptual field under stress, thesis summary, presented to the Eastern Psychological Association, January, reprinted in Francke, Amiel, Introduction to Optometric Visual Therapy, OEP, 1988–89, Curriculum II, Vol. 60–61, bound.

Sicile-Kira, Chantal. 2004. *Autism spectrum disorders: The complete guide to understanding autism, Asperger's syndrome, pervasive developmental disorder, and other ASDs*. New York: Perigree,

Singer, W. 1982. The role of attention in developmental plasticity. *Human Neurobiology* 1: 41–3.

Small, Roxanne. 2005. *Building babies better*. Canada: Trafford Publishing.

Smith, Earl L. 1994. Lectures at the *1994 COVD Meeting*.

Solan, Harold A., and A. P. Ficarra. 1990. A study of perceptual and verbal skills of disabled readers in grades 4, 5, and 6. *Journal of the American Optometric Association* 61(8): 628–34.

Solan, Harold, John Shelley-Trembay, Anthony Ficara, Michael Silverman, and Steven Larson (2003), Effect of attention therapy on reading comprehension, *Journal of Learning Disabilities*, Vol. 36 (6) November, 556–62.

Solan, Harold, Julie R. Brannan, Anthony Ficara, and Robert Byrne (1997) Transient and sustained processing: effects of varying luminance and wavelength on reading comprehension, *Journal of the American Optometric Association*, August, reprint.

Solan, Harold A., and Rochelle Mozlin. 1997. Biosocial consequences of poverty: Associated visual problems. *Optometry & Vision Science* 74(4): 185–9.

Solan, Harold A., and Rochelle Mozlin. 1997. Children in poverty: Impact on health, visual development and school failure. *Journal of Optometry and Vision Development* 1(28): 7–25.

Sperduto, R. D., D. Seigel, J. Roberts, and M. Rowland. 1983. Prevalence of myopia in the United States. *Archives of Ophthalmology*, March (101): 405–07.

Spitler, Harry Riley. 1941. *The Syntonic Principle: Its relation to health and other prob-lems*. Eaton, Ohio: College of Syntonic Optometry.

Spurlock, Morgan, prod. and dir.; J. R. Morley and Heather Winters, exec. prods. 2004. *Supersize Me: A Film of Epic Proportions*. Kathbur Pictures. Distributed by Hartsharp Video.

Stahl, Leslie. 2006. Lethal and Leaky. Interview on *60 Minutes*, April 20.

Streff, John W. 1975. Optometric care for a child manifesting qualities of autism. *Jour-nal of the American Optometric Association* 46, 6.

Streff, John W. 1977. The Cheshire study: Changes in incidence of myopia following program of intervention. A Gesell Institute paper. In *Frontiers in Visual Science: Pro-ceedings of the University of Houston College of Optometry Dedication Symposium*, ed. Steven Cool and Earl L. Smith. Houston, Texas: Springer-Verlag.

Streff, John W. 2006. Phone interview regarding the Cheshire, Connecticut Schools study. October 19, 2006.

Streff, John W., and Ellen Gunderson. 2004. *Childhood Learning: Journey or Race? A Parents and Teachers Guide*. Santa Ana, CA: The Optometric Extension Program Foundation, Inc.

Stumbo, Janet. 2006. *Endless journey: A head-trauma victim's remarkable rehabilita-tion*. Rev. ed. Santa Ana, CA: Optometric Extension Program Foundation, Inc.

Suchoff, Irwin B. 2006. An optometric overview of acquired brain injury. Lectures at the New England College of Optometry, April 30. Boston, MA.

Suchoff, Irwin B., and Rochelle Mozlin. 1991. Vision screening of an adolescent inner-city population: A high failure rate and low compliance on follow-up care. *Journal of the American Optometric Association* 62(8): 598–603.

Sullivan, Joseph. 2001. The Kansas project of state funding for optometric vision ther-apy for third graders with convergence insufficiency of the eyes for near tasks: A dra-matic success story. Presented at the conference *An Educational Barrier We Can Ac-tually Eliminate: Visual Problems of Children in Poverty and Their Interference with Learning*, April 4. Harvard Graduate School of Education. Cited in Groffman, Syd-ney. 2001. Editorial. *Journal of Optometric Vision Development*, Fall, 32: 112.

Super, Silwyn. 1995. Prism use in vision therapy. In *Clinical uses of prism*, ed. Susan Cotter, 259–278. New York: Mosby Yearbook, Inc.

Sussman, Martin, Ernest Loewenstein, and H. Sann. 1993. *Total health at the computer*. Barrytown, NY: Station Hill Press.

Swartwout, Glen. 1991. *Electromagnetic pollution solutions: What you can do to keep your home and workplace safe*. Hawaii: Aerai.

Tassinari, J. D. 1995. Excessively close working distance. *Journal of Behavioral Optom-etry* 6(4): 87–9.

Thau, A. P. 1991. Vision and literacy: *Journal of Reading* 35: 196–9.

The Orinda Vision Study. 1959. *American Journal of Optometry and Archives of Amer-ican Academy of Optometry* 36, September.

The Environmental Health Coalition of Western Massachusetts. *The Hidden Dangers of Fragrance*. Pamphlet.

Thing, N. E. 1993. *A new way of looking at the world*. Provincetown, MA: N. E. Thing Enterprises, Inc. and Magic Eye, Inc.

Thomas, J. 1992. Myopia control. Presented at *22nd Annual Meeting, College of Op-tometrists in Vision Development*, October. Newport Beach, CA.

Todd, G. P. 1985. *Nutrition, health, and disease*. West Chester, PA: Whitford Press.

Torgeson, N., and L. Frost. 1998. "Autism: the experiential jigsaw puzzle," *Patients with special needs*. Series: Behavioral aspects of vision care. 39(1). Santa Ana, CA: Optometric Extension Program.

Toxics Action Center. 2005. Toxics Action Center says, "Refuse to use ChemLawn." *Member Update Newsletter* L9(1), winter.

Trachtman, Joseph N. 1990. *The etiology of vision disorders: A neuroscience model*. Santa Ana, CA: Optometric Extension Program.

Tracy, Jan. 2006. *Boston Globe*. Public school students take up a tougher course: At Beacon Academy, hope for academic success tested. June 3.

Trevarthen, Colwyn. 1968. Two mechanisms of vision in primates. Offprint from *Psychologische Forschung* 31, nos. 1 and 4.

Trevarthen, Colwyn, and Roger W. Sperry. 1973. Perceptual unity of the ambient visual field in human commisurotomy patients. *Brain* 96: 547–70.

Ullman, Dana. 2002. Homeopathic family medicine: Integrating the science and art of natural health care. E-book available at www.homeopathic.com.

Van Witsen, Betty. 1979. *Perceptual training activities handbook: 250 games and exercises for helping children develop sensory skills*, 2nd ed. New York: Teacher's College Press.

Vaughn, Wanda, W. C. Maples, and Richard Hoenes. 2006. The association between vision quality of life and academics as measured by the College of Optometrists in Vision Development Quality of Life Questionnaire. *Optometry: Journal of the American Optometric Association* 77(3): 116–23.

Vernon, Mark. 1999. *Brain power: A neurosurgeon's complete program to maintain and enhance brain fitness throughout your life*. Boston: Houghton Mifflin.

Ward. Betty J. (May 1989). Maximum available desk-to-eye distance for students in grades one and two: regional norms and statistical comparison to distance used for near point screening, PhD dissertation,Texas Woman's University, Denton Campus.

Ward, Betty J., personal conversations and e-mails April and June 2006.

Waterkeeper Alliance. 2006. Available at www.waterkeeper.org.

Weil, Andrew. 1995. *Dr. Weil's 8 week plan for optimal healing power*. Pamphlet reprinted from the book, Weil, Andrew. *Spontaneous healing*. New York: Alfred A Knopf.

Weiskrantz, L. 1992. Unconscious vision: The strange phenomenon of blindsight. *The Sciences*, September/October.

Wick, Bruce, M. Wingard, Susan Cotter, and Mitchell Sheiman. 1992. Anisometropic amblyopia: Is the patient ever too old to treat? *Optometry and Vision Science* 69, 11: 866–78.

Weisel, T. N. and Raviola, E. 1977. Myopia and eye elongation after neonatal lid fusion in monkeys, *Nature*, 266: 66-68.

Wiesel, Torsten N., and E. Raviola, 1979. Increase in axial length of the macaque monkey eye after corneal opacification. *Association for Research in Vision and Ophthalmology* 18, 12: 1232–6.

Willett, Walter C. 2001. *Eat, drink, and be healthy*. New York: Simon and Schuster.

Williams, L. J. 1985. Tunnel vision induced by a foveal load manipulation. *Human Factors*, 27(2): 221–40.

Williams, Roger J. 1956. *Biochemical individuality*. New York: John Wiley & Son, Inc.

Williams, Roger J. 1967. *You are extraordinary*. New York: Random House.

Williams, Roger J. 1977. *The wonderful world within you*. New York: Bantam Books.

Wolff, Bruce R. 1987. From sight to vision. Text of a speech to the *Ohio Valley Congress*, 1987. Reprinted in Jones, Beverly. 1990. *Visual behavior*. Cincinnati: Lockwood Press.

Wunderlich, Ray C., Jr. 1976. *Improving Your Diet*. St. Petersburg, FL: Johny Reader, Inc.

Wunderlich, Ray C., Jr. 1991. *Pediatric optometry: A pediatrician's perspective*. Rev. ed. Santa Ana, CA: Optometric Extension Program.

Wunderlich, Ray C., Jr. 1998. *Candida-yeast syndrome: The spreading epidemic of yeast-connected diseases*, New Canaan, CT: Keats Publishing, Inc.

Wunderlich, Ray C., Jr., and Dwight K. Kalita. 1984. *Nourishing your child: A bioecologic approach*. New Canaan, CT: Keat Publishing, Inc.

Yoo, R., et al. 1999. Vision screening of abused and neglected children by the UCLA Mobile Eye Clinic. *Journal of the American Optometric Association* 70, 7: 461–46.

Young, F. A. 1961. The effect of restricted visual space on the primate eye, American Journal of Ophthalmology, 32: 799–806.

Young, F. A., et al. 1969. The transmission of refractive errors within Eskimo families. *American Journal of Optometry* 46, 9: 676–685.

Zaba, Joel. 2001. Social, emotional, and educational consequences of undetected children's vision problems. *Journal of Behavioral Optometry* 12, 3: 66–70.

Zaba, Joel, and R. Johnson. 1994. The link: Vision and illiteracy. *Journal of Behavioral Optometry* 5, 2: 41–3.

Zadnik, Karla, William A. Satariano, Donald O. Mutti, Nina E. Friedman, Robert I. Sholtz, and Anthony J. Adams. 1993. The effect of parental history of myopia and near work on children's ocular components. A Berkeley study presented at the *American Academy of Optometry meeting*, December. Boston, MA.

Zeki, J. 1993. *A vision of the brain*. Oxford: Blackwell Scientific Publications.

Zill, N., and J. West. 2000. Entering kindergarten: a portrait of American children when they begin school. In *The Condition of Education 2000*, xvi–xlvi. National Center for Education Statistics 2000–062. Washington, D.C.: National Center for Education Statistics.

INDEX